P9-BZV-833

"The words and works of Luis Palau have touched millions. May this book do the same."

Max Lucado, senior pastor, Oak Hills Church of Christ

"This is an articulate book by one of the great Christian leaders of our day. I heartily recommend Luis Palau's work."

Charles W. Colson, Prison Fellowship Ministries, Washington DC

"In this book Luis Palau points those searching for enduring truth, hope, and love to the only One who can give it, the Lord Jesus Christ. Filled with biblical insight and practical suggestions, *High Definition Life* will help readers experience God's best for their lives. Read it, then pass it on to somebody who needs it."

Franklin Graham, president and CEO, Billy Graham Evangelistic Association
and Samaritan's Purse

"Luis Palau's heart for people is matched by his mind's capacities to speak with penetrating insight and practical relevance to honest souls who seek satisfying answers to today's questions, doubts, or personal needs."

Jack W. Hayford, founding pastor, The Church on the Way;
chancellor, The King's College & Seminary

"*High Definition Life* is a powerful reminder that the abundant life is freely offered by Jesus. In the pages of this book, so full of material relevant to all, Luis Palau separates out the chaff and leaves the reader with the pure seed of Jesus, which always grows into the abundant life promised by him."

Millard Fuller, president, Habitat for Humanity International

"Imagine the possibilities of a life lived to the full! That's Jesus's amazing promise to each one of us. In this book, my friend Luis Palau shows how the Lord's power can positively change each area of your life. Don't settle for less!"

Robert H. Schuller, founding pastor, Crystal Cathedral Ministries

"Love, joy, peace, hope—these are qualities that most of us desire to experience in our lives. For many, these wonderful qualities have become an illusion or even an impossibility. In this remarkable book, Luis Palau shares the profound, yet simple, steps that can lead you to enjoy life at its best!"

Paul Cedar, chairman, Mission America Coalition

"With captivating simplicity and gripping personal illustrations, Luis Palau in this book lifts up the Good News of Jesus Christ. Exciting reading for anyone who wants to know how to experience life at its best."

Robert E. Coleman, distinguished professor of evangelism and discipleship,
Gordon-Conwell Theological Seminary

"Luis Palau speaks knowingly and with keen compassion to those who seek an end to their private wars."

Howard G. Hendricks, distinguished professor, Dallas Theological Seminary; chairman, Center for Christian Leadership

"Here is a thrilling and delightful book. Luis Palau tells you not only about true joy, but guides you step-by-step into the realization of the most satisfying life this side of heaven."

D. James Kennedy, senior minister, Coral Ridge Presbyterian Church

"If you want to move from simply 'existing' in the Christian life to enjoying the magnitude of abundant life in Christ, this book should be added to your 'must read' list."

Joseph M. Stowell, president, Moody Bible Institute

"If you can read this book without becoming more whole, more healthy, more holy, you're not human. A masterpiece."

Leonard Sweet, Drew Theological School, George Fox University, preachingplus.com

"This book brings me great pleasure. It reminds me how to strengthen weaknesses in my own life, and it is a book I can give to Christian friends to strengthen them. And for men and women who are not particularly interested in religion, it will be an enjoyable read and may turn out to be a godsend that will change their lives."

Kenneth Taylor, chairman, Tyndale House Publishers; translator of *The Living Bible*

"When you read *High Definition Life*, you feel like Luis is having a warm and friendly conversation with you. His message is clear as he encourages the reader to look to Jesus for the longings of the heart. Reading this book is spiritually refreshing. It's a book you will want to recommend or give to a friend."

Harry L. Thomas, cofounder of Creation Festivals; director, Come Alive Ministries, Inc.

"Drawing on a wealth of personal experience and the life stories of others, Luis Palau in an engaging style explains the only answer to our quest for true happiness, meaning, and forgiveness."

John D. Woodbridge, research professor of church history and Christian thought, Trinity Evangelical Divinity School

High Definition Life

Other books by Luis Palau

God Is Relevant
Where Is God When Bad Things Happen?
It's a God Thing

High Definition Life

Trading Life's Good for God's Best

Luis Palau

with Steve Halliday

Revell
Grand Rapids, Michigan

Published by Fleming H. Revell
a division of Baker Publishing Group
P.O. Box 6287, Grand Rapids, MI 49516-6287

Printed in the United States of America

Library of Congress Cataloging-in-Publication Data
Palau, Luis, 1934–
    High definition life : trading life's good for God's best / Luis Palau and Steve Halliday.
       p.   cm.
    Includes bibliographical references (p.   ).
    ISBN 0-8007-1865-8 (cloth)
    1. Christian life. I. Halliday, Steve, 1957– II. Title.
BV4501.3.P355 2005
248.4—dc22   2004021711

Published in association with the literary agency of Alive Communications, Inc., 7680 Goddard Street, Suite 200, Colorado Springs, CO 80920.

Contents

Foreword

As I read *High Definition Life*, the following incident came to mind.

It was the spring of 1995, and I had just arrived in San Juan, Puerto Rico. I would be participating in the Global Mission Christian Workers Conference that was held in conjunction with Global Mission, an evangelistic outreach that went live by satellite to the entire world from a San Juan soccer stadium. My mother, who was with my father for the Global Mission, met me at the international airport, which was teeming with incoming and outgoing tourists, as well as locals eager for a little extra business.

As Mother and I waited in the car for my bags to arrive, I noticed in the rearview mirror a policeman who was staring intently our way. He began to walk slowly toward us with a scowl on his face. I was sure he was going to say we would have to move the vehicle. I knew it would be very difficult for me to comply with his command because the driver, along with the car keys, was in baggage claim!

I was bracing myself for a confrontation when out of the terminal bounced Luis Palau, who had just arrived for the Christian Workers Conference also. Whether or not he understood our predicament, he strode right for the policeman, engaged him in friendly conversation punctuated with laughter, then escorted the officer to our car, where he proceeded to introduce him to us! The policeman graciously allowed us to stay for the additional moments necessary before my bags and driver reappeared—and in the meantime, Luis shared the gospel with him!

My heart is still warmed as I reflect on that incident. I have been privileged to share many platforms with Luis and am always blessed by his presentation of the gospel. But his credibility in my eyes comes not just from what he says, but also from who he is. His entire demeanor exudes an enthusiastic zest for life, a zealous commitment to the gospel, and a keen, compassionate interest in people.

These characteristics shine through in this volume you now hold in your hands. *High Definition Life* not only vividly describes the abundant Christian life, it also clearly reflects the heart of the author. To be in Luis Palau's presence for even a few moments is to know that he himself has said good-bye to life's good and has embraced—with abandonment—God's best! My heart resonates with his thoughts expressed on these pages, because I long to embrace those things, too!

This longing has caused my heart to cry out for *more than just enough* . . .

> to escape a fiery hell,
> > to be saved from God's wrath,
> > > to manage my guilt,
> > > > to get a ticket to heaven,
> > > > > to squeak through heaven's gate.

I long for more than just the bare minimum God has to offer.
I long for more than what the average Christian seems to settle for.
I long for *everything* God wants to give me.[1]

My heart grieves for the average church member who seems to settle for so much less than what God wants to give. And my heart breaks for those who turn away from Jesus Christ because they think the Christian life will cheat them out of all they are looking for, when the exact opposite is true!

So . . .

If you are saved, but not satisfied . . .

If you are on your way to heaven but not enjoying the journey . . .

If you are a member of a church but derive more pleasure from being a member of a club . . .

If you are restless with what you have . . .

Then it's time for a change!

It's time to move beyond the things of the moment and embrace the things that last!

It's time for you to receive and experience the High Definition Life!

Introduction

I Never Knew It Was Like That

Every fall it was the same. An excited Angie would plop down in front of the family's television set, bowl of buttered popcorn in hand, and sit enthralled for the next two hours as the classic film *The Wizard of Oz* filled her living room with magical visions of witches and munchkins, wizards and cowardly lions. Long before the advent of VCRs or DVD players, Angie had but one chance a year to catch the broadcast of her favorite movie. She planned her whole schedule around its annual appearance.

One year a friend invited Angie over to her house to see the beloved 1939 film. She eagerly accepted. The pair giggled their way through the first few minutes of the show, softly sang along with Dorothy as she dreamed about a place somewhere over the rainbow, and clutched their pillows when Miss Gulch transformed herself into the broomstick-riding Wicked Witch of the West. Angie grabbed a handful of popcorn as the twister dropped Dorothy's house into a land far distant from Kansas. She was about to take a mouthful when Dorothy opened the door to Munchkin Land . . . but the warm kernels fell back, uneaten, into the bowl. Angie stared at the screen in disbelief. She'd seen the movie dozens of times. But she'd never seen this.

Color! Brilliant, astonishing, impossible color! Munchkin Land blazed before her in bright reds, vibrant greens, breathtaking blues, and eye-popping yellows. The fantastic city seemed more alive, more real, more wonderful than anything she'd ever imagined. Until then, she had no idea that her favorite film had been one of the first to use color. She'd simply assumed that the whole thing played out in monochrome. But now—*look at it!* At that moment she vowed never again to watch the wizard and his friends on a black-and-white television set.

Even today when Angie talks about her celluloid epiphany so many years ago, she exclaims, "It was so vivid! I never knew it could be like that."

I think Angie's reaction to the film's unforeseen color and her pledge never to go back to black and white provides a good model for life in general. That is, I think too many of us settle for a life in sepia tones when we could be enjoying it in all the brilliant hues of God's pallet. We opt for "good enough" when God offers us "excellent." We pull in to Slim's Greasy Spoon for a hamburger and fries when we've been invited to Paris for a six-course meal prepared by Europe's finest chefs—all expenses paid.

That's not to say hamburgers or black-and-white televisions are bad; I'd still rather have a hot sandwich (or *The Wizard of Oz* in monochrome) than nothing at all. But why choose a slab of fried ground beef when you can have succulent tenderloin steak? Why continue to watch in black and white when you can enjoy the movie as the producer intended, in color?

Why take an amethyst when you could have a diamond?

Why shoot for a consolation prize when you could win the jackpot?

Why spend a weekend in Amarillo when you could enjoy a fourteen-day cruise to Tahiti?

This book is not about deciding between "bad" and "good," but about choosing "best" over "good enough." It's about getting everything out of life that your Creator intended for you to have. It's about trading life's good for God's best. It's about trading in a low resolution experience for a high definition life.

I want to paint a picture of the great possibilities offered to you by God when you choose the dynamic Christian life. If I could, I would like to get you drooling at the possibilities that are yours in Jesus Christ.

Perhaps I could borrow as my "theme statement" a line written two thousand years ago by a celebrated man who knew all about choosing "best" over "good enough." In a letter to some friends in which he laid out a template for successful living, he wrote, "And now I will show you the most excellent way"; or as another translation has it, "First, however, let me tell you about something else that is better than any of them!"[1]

That's what I want to do in this book—tell you about "the most excellent way," or "something else that is better than any of them." I'd like to take a look at ten "good" areas of life and show how something even better and more excellent awaits every one of us.

Along the way we'll keep in mind a memorable statement made by the late Lillian Dickson, who told a young American visiting her in Taiwan, "Young man, remember that your life is like a coin. You can spend it any way you want, but you can spend it only once."

My question is, how are you going to spend it? You can settle for "good enough," or you can opt for the "best." The choice is yours.

One day an Anglican bishop sat down to tea. As he held his cup just so, sipping in the very proper British fashion, he said, "I wonder why it is that everywhere Saint Paul went they had a revolution, while wherever I go they serve a cup of tea?"

It's a good question. What happens when you and I show up in town? Do little cups of tea get served—clink, clink—or do we cause a spiritual revolution?

Again, there's nothing wrong with tea. I like it. But in addition to stirring sugar into my tea, I'd like to partner with God in stirring up spiritual revolutions around the world. I'd like to help feed the hungry hearts of men and women in every part of the globe.

Once you exchange the run-of-the-mill perspective of black and white for the wonder of brilliant color, you'll never want to go back. And you'll be saying, along with Angie, "I never knew it could be like that."

Don't settle for less than the abundant life Jesus offers you. Move beyond the feeble comforts of a "good enough" life and choose instead the robust delights of living at its best—a high definition life.

1

A Festival in Your Heart

Pleasure or Happiness?

[O God,] You have made known to me the path of life;
you will fill me with joy in your presence,
with eternal pleasures at your right hand.

King David of Israel, in Psalm 16:11

Can a simple definition set you on a disastrous life course?

It can, if you're reading from the wrong dictionary.

Look up the word "happiness" in the quirky lexicon written by re-nowned curmudgeon Ambrose Bierce, for example, and here's what you find:

Happiness, *n.* An agreeable sensation arising from contemplating the misery of another.[1]

A vastly greater literary light, William Shakespeare, turned the tables on Bierce's definition, yet still came up with a depressing outlook on the topic. In his play *As You Like It*, he writes, "O, how bitter a thing it is to look into happiness through another man's eyes!"[2]

How is it, I wonder, that something so appealing and desirable as happiness could generate such bad press? How could a commodity so universally coveted generate such dismal reviews? I'd be willing to bet that notions as jaundiced as these fester into existence when a man or woman desperately pursuing happiness fails to find it.

All of us want to be happy. All of us want to enjoy life, have fun, and experience the delicious pleasures this world offers. I think psychologist Dr. Joyce Brothers is right on target when she writes, "True happiness is what makes life worthwhile. Yet happiness can be elusive—despite the fact that we seem to be wired for it."[3]

And why does happiness so often elude us? Anna Quindlen, a Pulitzer Prize–winning columnist and author of the book *A Short Guide to a Happy Life*, suggests that some of us miss out on happiness because we're just not looking. "I think a lot of us sleepwalk our way through our lives," she writes, "when, if we really opened our eyes, we would realize how much we were missing."[4]

The moment of clarity hit for Quindlen at age nineteen when her mother died. She refers to those years as "before" and "after," and says her mother's death "was the dividing line between seeing the world in black and white and in Technicolor. The lights came on, for the darkest possible reason."[5]

The real question for us is, how can we open our eyes (and hearts) to genuine happiness? How can we step from a black-and-white world to one bursting with all the colors of the rainbow? If Robert Louis Stevenson was right when he declared, "There is no duty we so much underestimate as the duty of being happy,"[6] then just how can we become truly happy?

Beware of Detours

The road to happiness, alas, teems with detours. Sometimes we miss out on true happiness because we get confused about what it really is and so choose the wrong route. At other times we refuse to accept happiness when it pulls up alongside us. Sad to say, I think many Christians have rumbled down both of these bumpy highways.

One day my British friend Nigel Gordon and I stopped by an English pub for lunch. Over the fireplace in front of the bar hung a sign that read: "Good ale, good food, good times."

Man, I thought, *that sounds almost like Christians were meant to be.*

But never say any such thing to some Christians! Too often we give the impression that to follow Jesus Christ is a grim experience; that only the most somber, frowning, Secret Service–looking types qualify for Christianity. Some of us almost refuse to have a good time.

How terrible that God offers us a unique way of life—beautiful, victorious, triumphant over sin, a life filled with the Holy Spirit and with the assurance of eternal life—and yet many of us don't really enjoy it.

Some time ago my wife was reading *The God of All Comfort* by Hannah Whitall Smith, author of *The Christian's Secret of a Happy Life*. In chapter 1 Smith says she wrote the book because an agnostic fiercely challenged her faith. In essence he said, "Do you know why I will never consider God? It's because Christians, according to their religion, should have absolute joy and peace, happiness and victory. And yet they often look like the most miserable people in the whole world."[7]

Sadly, he hit too close to home.

Years ago we held a rally in a Western European city and suffered through one of the most miserable meetings ever. The music was funereal and a spirit of gloom filled the auditorium, yet the rally was led by some of the most distinguished evangelical leaders of that nation. I could not get out of there fast enough. When we drove away, we didn't even want to down a Coke in that town.

When thirst got the better of us, however, we started looking for a place to stop. The only open establishment in the countryside appeared to be a pub, so we parked our car behind the building and went in. As soon as we walked through the doors, the patrons recognized our nationality and bellowed, "Welcome, Americans!" Someone was playing an accordion, others were banging and scratching on other instruments, the people laughed and clapped and sang while smoke filled the place and everything reeked of alcohol, but they even offered us a free drink as honored foreigners. We accepted—a Coca-Cola.

What a contrast! I felt far happier in that bar than in the Christian meeting.

Who sold us a bill of goods that dark dress, somber faces, and worried expressions somehow qualify as more spiritual than being joyful and happy and free and delighting in abundance? I cannot for the life of me figure it out. But perhaps it explains why a lot of people turn down Christianity—it seems to go against human nature's desire for happiness, and against what I believe God desires for us.

The Joyful Heart of God

"Can you imagine what it would be like if the God who ruled the world were not happy?" asks author John Piper.

What if God were given to grumbling and pouting and depression like some Jack-and-the-beanstalk giant in the sky? What if God were frustrated and despondent and gloomy and dismal and discontented and dejected? Could we join David and say, "O God, you are my God, earnestly I seek you; my soul thirsts for you, my body longs for you, in a dry and weary land where there is no water" (Ps. 63:1)? I don't think so. We would all relate to God like little children who have a frustrated, gloomy, dismal, discontented father. They can't enjoy him. They can only try not to bother him, and maybe try to work for him to earn some little favor.[8]

But that is not the God of the Bible! The God who reveals himself in the Scriptures overflows with joy. God is a good God. God is a loving God. God is an eternally happy God, the fountain of all delight—and he wants the faces of his children to reflect his own boundless joy. It is no accident that Jesus Christ, who perfectly mirrors the very nature of God, loved to proclaim what he called "the Good News"—and the secret of the Good News is that life is meant to be good. Jesus Christ offers us a joy-filled life, not a somber one.

C. S. Lewis once remarked, "Joy is the serious business of heaven." If I interpret him correctly, he meant that God passionately desires his people to enjoy life, to be happy and contented.

Lewis learned this from Jesus Christ, for in Matthew 7:11 the Savior says, "If you, then, though you are evil, know how to give good gifts to your children, how much more will your Father in heaven give good gifts to those who ask him!" We want our kids to be happy. We want them to rejoice and laugh and settle into a contented life. And according to Jesus, God wants this more than we do.

Rejoice and Be Glad

It is not God's will that we trudge grimly through life, that we squeak by with gritted teeth, that we sweat profusely just to barely make it to the golden shores. It *is* God's purpose that, within the limitations of an imperfect world, his people rejoice. Consider a few of the dozens of verses in the Bible that make this point:

> But may the righteous be glad
> and rejoice before God;
> may they be happy and joyful.

> Psalm 68:3

I know that there is nothing better for men than to be happy and do good while they live. That every man may eat and drink, and find satisfaction in all his toil—this is the gift of God.

Ecclesiastes 3:12–13

So I commend the enjoyment of life, because nothing is better for a man under the sun than to eat and drink and be glad. Then joy will accompany him in his work all the days of the life God has given him.

Ecclesiases 8:15

Ask and you will receive, and your joy will be complete.

John 16:24

May the God of hope fill you with all joy.

Romans 15:13

Be joyful always.

1 Thessalonians 5:16

There's no way around it; the spiritual life was meant to exude joy. The famous "fruit of the Spirit" passage in the fifth chapter of Galatians makes this abundantly clear. Most interpreters suggest two main ways of looking at this text. (Theologians must have their fun, and I think the Lord left a few things hanging so there could be seminaries.) Some Bible scholars teach there are nine fruits of the Spirit: love, joy, peace, patience, kindness, goodness, faithfulness, gentleness, self-control. Others insist the Spirit produces only one fruit, love, which blossoms in eight aromatic ways—the first being joy. Either way you take it, joy takes a lead role.

Years ago on the radio I heard a woman read the Galatians passage, along with the final line: "Against such things there is no law." She then said something that encourages me to this day: "There is no law against too much love. There is no law against too much joy."

Such a simple thought, but it assures me that the serious business of heaven really is joy. Much of the Bible was written to convey this joyful element of the Good News. John says, for example, that he writes his first letter "to make our joy complete" (1 John 1:4). If we live by the principles God reveals in his Word, we will be filled with happiness and joy. And when a person overflows with joy—whether he or she is the bouncy type or a good deal more reserved—it shows everywhere, and not by the noise or the style.

I wonder, when was the last time you cracked open a Bible to look for all the goodness God offers you? What the Bible calls the "new covenant" (briefly described in Heb. 8:7–12) really is an excellent covenant. It's new because it's for today, not for some ancient time.

In the new covenant you'll discover that God really does love you. He really does have a wonderful plan for your life. God presents himself as your almighty Father who has everything you need. And he promises to meet all your needs according to his glorious riches in Christ Jesus (Phil. 4:19).

So if that's all true, then why *can't* you have a great time? The logic of it seems inescapable to me.

If all your sins are forgiven; if your body is the temple of the Holy Spirit; if you have unlimited access to all of heaven's resources; if you have God's Word to guide you; if God promises never to leave you nor forsake you; if you're going to heaven when you die; if you'll live forever with a God who loves you—then shouldn't you be ecstatically happy?

The Holy Spirit calls upon believers to rejoice. When the Spirit of God comes to live within us, we gain the potential to enjoy life even in bad times. Make no mistake, troubles will come. "In this world you will have trouble," Jesus told those who followed him (John 16:33). "In fact, everyone who wants to live a godly life in Christ Jesus will be persecuted," the apostle Paul said (2 Tim. 3:12). But we can remain happy in the Lord even in the midst of adverse circumstances. After all, what is the worst thing that could happen? Death? For a Christian, death is not the end of life, but the beginning of life in heaven in God's presence.

Choosing Joy

In every situation, therefore, we have the *potential* for joy. Joy is a choice. You can choose to rejoice today, or you can choose to depress yourself and every unfortunate soul near you. It's a choice made possible because the blessed Holy Spirit, the source of all joy, lives within every believer.[9]

Of course, you can choose to remain behind iron bars of discouragement, cynicism, and joylessness. You don't have to choose freedom. If you want, you can decide to remain inside a prison of your own making. Perhaps it won't be so bad. Even in jail you do enjoy a certain amount of freedom. You can move around—but only within the 10x10 dimensions of your little cell. You're not dead, only a prisoner.

When Jesus Christ comes, he opens the doors of the prison created by your own mind, your own fears, your own habits. Christ turns the key in the lock and swings the doors open wide. It's up to you to walk out.

The Biggest Detour of All

Prison cells and open doors are one thing; detours are another. Sometimes, even when we make it out of jail and onto the open road, we still take a wrong turn and miss the destination so beautifully portrayed in the travel brochure.

I have a friend who has zero sense of direction. A few years ago while on a business trip, he planned to drive from Danville, California, to Fresno, a trip that generally takes about three hours. Almost six hours into his drive, my friend still had not come close to his planned destination. Just then a carload of teens pulled up alongside his vehicle at a stoplight and asked, "Hey, man, do you know how to get to the J.C. Penney's store?" My frustrated friend popped his head outside the driver's side window and said flatly, "Gentlemen—I can't even find *Fresno*." To which one of the teens replied, "Oh, wow, man, you're even more lost than we are!" and away they zoomed.

I believe pleasure can become one of the biggest detours to true happiness. While we all want to be happy—truly happy—too often we settle for mere pleasure. We enjoy moments of delight, but satisfying and lasting happiness (what the Bible calls joy) eludes us.

And just how can pleasure get in the way of joy? It's not that pleasure is bad and joy is good. Don't think for a moment that I'm belittling pleasure! But while pleasure titillates the senses, joy satisfies the soul. Pleasure comes from the outside; joy erupts from within. Pleasure vanishes in the presence of pain; joy can sustain a person even in the midst of great sorrow.

Simply put, pleasure feels good, but joy feels better. True happiness surpasses mere pleasure in at least five important ways:

Pleasure	Happiness
• External	• Internal
• Sensory	• Wholistic
• Fleeting	• Enduring
• Solitary	• Shared
• Limited Capacity	• Boundless Capacity

Let's take a look at each of these five comparisons and see how it's possible to make the jump from pleasure to lasting happiness, contentment, and peace.

External vs. Internal

We feel pleasure when some outside source gratifies one or more of our five senses. We delight in the purr of a kitten, the fragrance of a rose, the fur of a puppy, the visual feast of a Rembrandt, the succulence of a cherry pie. God has designed our bodies to enjoy the pleasures of his creation.

"Dying people don't cling to life for something transitory or illusory," says Anna Quindlen. "And they sure don't cling to life to make another million or get on Leno. They cling to life because, all of a sudden, on the water slide into the great unknown beyond, they understand with blinding clarity that it doesn't get a whole lot better than a lilac bush with a butterfly on it."[10]

While I like Quindlen's basic take on happiness, I can't agree that we don't know what lies beyond this life. Nor can I nod my head at the idea that life "doesn't get a whole lot better than a lilac bush with a butterfly on it." Happiness needn't depend on outside sources to thrive—as beautiful as a butterfly-crowned lilac bush can be. Even when the plant dries up and the insect flutters away, we can experience a deep kind of joy that bubbles up from the inside. Genuine happiness comes from within, not without.

How is this possible? Jesus explained that "Whoever believes in me, as the Scripture has said, streams of living water will flow from within him" (John 7:38). Notice: not from without, but from within! The Gospel writer leaves us no doubt about what Jesus intended by his metaphor, for he adds, "By this he meant the Spirit, whom those who believed in him were later to receive" (v. 39).

The Bible continually connects joy with the Spirit of God. Jesus was "full of joy through the Holy Spirit" (Luke 10:21). The disciples were "filled with joy and with the Holy Spirit" (Acts 13:52). The kingdom of God is a matter of "joy in the Holy Spirit" (Rom. 14:17). And even despite "severe suffering," it is possible to overflow "with the joy given by the Holy Spirit" (1 Thess. 1:6).

I saw this happy truth in action a few years ago on a trip to the former Soviet Union. Viktor Hamm, my excellent interpreter, described how Josef Stalin had sentenced Viktor's father to a Siberian prison camp as punishment for expressing his faith. Viktor himself was born in Siberia but eventually escaped to Europe, married a German, and moved to Canada.

The elder Mr. Hamm and the other prisoners in the gulag worked every day in a mine. Each morning they'd stand in line to receive their picks and shovels, and every evening they'd return to hand in their equipment. Soon Mr. Hamm began to pray, "Lord, there has to be a Christian somewhere in this camp. Help me to find him, someone with whom I can pray."

One day, as he was praying, he thought he recognized a certain look about the fellow who doled out the mining equipment. "I think he's a Christian," he said to himself. But he thought, *How shall I approach him without giving myself away? If he's KGB, I'm finished. But let's see who he is.*

With joy and fear rising simultaneously in his heart, he said to the man, "You know, they expect us to achieve our goals, but they don't give us the bricks and the water and the straw to get the job done."

Any old-time Bible reader would recognize the allusion to Moses and the days of Hebrew slavery in Egypt. The fellow looked at Mr. Hamm for a moment and then said slowly, "Wait a minute. Stand here." When all the other men left he asked, "Why did you mention the straw and the water? Where did you get that?"

"Oh, I read about it in a pretty good Book," replied Mr. Hamm, trying hard to keep from trembling.

"Yes, I think I read that Book too," said the man. Then he paused. "I notice that you don't swear like the other men. They are always fighting, but you don't get into that sort of thing. Why is that?"

"My Father won't let me."

The conversation paused again. As the man carefully looked Mr. Hamm up and down, he finally asked, "Your Father wouldn't be my Father, would he?"

"My Father has only one Son," said Mr. Hamm, getting excited.

"My Father has only one Son, too," replied the man.

"Believer?"

"Believer!"

And with great joy despite their miserable surroundings, they discovered each other. Immediately they began to pray in secret. But their prayer times didn't stay secret for long; their joy just wouldn't allow it. Joy insists on multiplying itself in others. By the time the pair gained their release, *three hundred* prisoners had come to follow Jesus Christ.

Josef Stalin might have been able to deprive millions of prisoners every pleasure in the Soviet empire, but he had no power to shut out joy. When a river of joy flows from deep within, nothing can dam the torrent. Joy continues to sprout and bloom even when evil men try to blot out the sun.

The Old Testament compares joy with an overflowing cup. The psalmist said to God, "You anoint my head with oil; my cup overflows" (Ps.

23:5). Which prompts an important question: Is your cup overflowing? Is it running over? Or do you say, "Ugh, don't bug me. Wait till after I get a hamburger, then maybe it will start overflowing."

Is my cup running over? It's a great question to ask yourself. Not when you have a vacation next week, and not on Sunday morning when you have nothing to worry about. But is your cup running over *now*? Are you fueled with the Holy Spirit *now*? One of the great realities of the Christian life is the staggering inner treasure we have through the fullness of the Holy Spirit.[11]

Sensory vs. Wholistic

The body, and particularly the five senses, provides the main channel to human pleasure. When our nerve endings sense certain kinds of stimuli, they send electrical pulses to the brain, which interprets them as pleasurable. Pleasure is chiefly a sensory experience.

Joy, on the other hand, involves far more than the body. This kind of rich happiness reaches down into the soul and extends up to the spirit. Happiness and joy can thrive even when there exist few or no physical stimuli to nourish them. "Studies show that people with strong religious faith and affiliations are happier than those without such faith, and they also regain happiness more quickly after experiencing a crisis," reports Dr. Joyce Brothers.[12]

Anna Quindlen agrees that those seeking happiness need something deeper than mere sensory excitation. She calls this deeper something a sense of "mission" and warns that a "sense of floating aimlessly through your own days is terrifying and debilitating. . . . One of the questions I ask people sometimes is, if you were told tomorrow that you had only a year to live, would you live it differently than you're living today? If so, doesn't that mean you need to reassess how you're living today?"[13]

It was exactly this sense of missing a greater mission that led one woman to discover the source of all joy. She owned all the pleasures of wealth and power, but still felt as if she were floating aimlessly through her days.

But all that changed through a single, memorable encounter.

I met this remarkable woman when she was about forty-five years old. As soon as she entered the room, I felt as though the Queen of England had appeared—only more so. She spoke with authority, exuded class, and carried herself with regal bearing. She spoke French, English, and Arabic, and had memorized most of the Koran. Her father held the second highest position of power in her country.

Despite her privileged station in life, however, she had been searching, desperately looking for spiritual reality. She felt no joy, no peace. Despite all the pleasures lavished on royalty, she felt empty. Then one evening Jesus appeared to her in a dream, just as he did to Abraham, to Moses, to David and Daniel and all the prophets, and to the apostle Paul.

I've since learned this happens frequently in the Islamic world. Jesus often breaks through in the Muslim community today through dreams and visions. Muslims who have come to Jesus Christ through these unusual visitations tell me, "The Lord said to me, 'I am Jesus, of whom you read in the Koran. You don't know much about me yet, but I'm real. And I'm alive. I'm your Savior. Trust me! Obey me. And I will be speaking more to you soon.'"

While many Muslims believe in curses and evil spirits, they also trust in the supernatural power of God. So when God reveals himself in a dream, they don't search for a naturalistic explanation (Too much pizza last night?). No, when they have a dream or a vision, they say, "God spoke to me."

Jesus spoke to this woman, and she listened.

The dream revolutionized her. She knew it had to be the Lord, even though she knew almost nothing about him. She had never seen a Bible. And in her country not a single church facility had ever been built. She told her father about the vision, and perhaps because he dabbled heavily in occultism—he had even cast out demons—he listened.

Five years went by. In that time her mother came to Jesus Christ, then her father (who gave up all his occult practices). Her children accepted the Lord, then several friends—all without knowing much more about Jesus than what the Koran says of him.

One day a foreigner entered her country with the *Jesus* video—the Gospel of Luke put to film—and a pile of Bibles hidden in his suitcase. Somehow the two bumped into each other. He gave her a Bible and the video, the first time she'd touched God's Word since she trusted Jesus Christ through the dream. Just moments after she began reading, this intelligent, powerful, articulate, highly educated woman was filled with deep joy.

She cried without shame while watching the video, sobs of joy mixed with deep sadness. Again, that seems to be a common reaction in the Islamic world. I've been told that among the Kurds in Yemen, the audience begins to weep as scenes of the crucifixion draw near. The rumbling begins quietly at first, but as the Roman soldiers push the crown of thorns into Jesus's scalp and lift him up on the cross, grown men begin to sob and moan, sometimes so loudly that you can't hear the film.

These new believers make the same discovery made years ago by this elegant lady: Jesus offers true and lasting joy, with spiritual pleasures far beyond any physical delights.

Fleeting vs. Enduring

Pleasure lasts just so long as the brain continues to receive neural signals that the mind interprets as pleasurable. Shortly after the signals terminate, so does the sensation of pleasure. That's why you can eat a double scoop of triple chocolate ice cream one moment, and crave another double scoop thirty seconds later. Pleasure delights only so long as it lasts. It's great, but fleeting.

Authentic joy, on the other hand, endures. While it varies in intensity and changes shape and color depending on many factors, true happiness radiates from the core of one's being. Joy can sustain a person even in the midst of great sorrow, which helps to explain why one biblical writer listed only one motivation for how Jesus "endured the cross, scorning its shame": It was "for the joy set before him" (Heb. 12:2).

Dr. Brothers comes close to the biblical idea here when she writes, "Happiness comes down to being quietly content most of the time."[14] We might well describe joy as an inner, lasting contentment. As one scholar notes, the Bible portrays joy not merely as an emotion, but as "a characteristic of the Christian."[15]

It is God's delight that his children live out their days in joy and contentment. If our consciences remain clear, the Lord wills that we feel happy, even if by temperament we're not the giddy type. By spiritual nature, believers ought to rejoice in the Lord over the good things he brings their way. "The LORD has done great things for us, and we are filled with joy," said the psalmist (Ps. 126:3).

Unfortunately, some of us have a tendency to lose our joy. Sometimes we lose it by focusing on unpleasant events. Sometimes we lose it by forgetting the riches we have in Jesus Christ. And sometimes we lose it because we confuse pleasure with joy.

Those who make this mistake believe happiness comes only rarely, and passes with the speed of light. To look at their faces, you'd swear God never sent his Son into the world. They remind me a whole lot more of Jana than of Jesus.

I met Jana, a Russian news reporter, just before the dismantling of the Soviet Union. She scheduled an interview with me as we prepared for a crusade in Leningrad. Over lunch she looked at me and muttered, "You seem so peaceful and happy."

"Oh?" I replied, "Does it show? Well, I *am* peaceful and I *am* happy."

We dropped the subject almost immediately and continued the interview, but by the end of our time together she looked so *un*happy that I said, "You know, Jana, you look so unpeaceful and unhappy."

"Of course I'm unhappy," she snapped. "We atheists, we're never happy."

I've never been able to forget her words. A few days later, at a crusade in Riga, I quoted Jana and said to the crowd, "You atheists, you're so unhappy."

To my surprise the Russians enthusiastically responded in chorus, "Da, da!" "Yes, yes!"

Their response amazed me. When I gave the invitation a few minutes later, it seemed as though half the crowd surged forward, hoping to find joy in Jesus Christ. I could hardly believe it.

Still, I have a harder time believing that many of those who have already found Jesus Christ still search for joy. Somehow they never learned to tap the infinite resources to which they're entitled in Christ. They feel miserable, not because Jesus Christ has proven deficient, but because they mistake conversion for a vital, dynamic relationship with Jesus. The two are not the same. You can't have the latter without the former, but you certainly can have the former and still not have the latter. Conversion to Christ does not guarantee a life of joy, but it does open the door to it. As I said, you must choose to enter.

I wonder if some believers fail to enter into joy because they've fallen for one of Satan's clever lies. In his classic book *The Screwtape Letters*, C. S. Lewis exposes this diabolical deception through the correspondence of two fictional demons. Screwtape, an Undersecretary of Temptation, slanders the happy Christian life by calling it "the Same Old Thing." He advises his nephew, Wormwood, to encourage his human "patient" to reject it simply because of its antiquity. God, says Wormwood, "wants men, so far as I can see, to ask very simple questions: Is it righteous? Is it prudent? Is it possible? Now, if we can keep men asking: 'Is it in accordance with the general movement of our time? Is it progressive or reactionary? Is this the way that History is going?' they will neglect the relevant questions."[16]

This tactic has proven to be exceptionally effective. In America, especially, we despise the Same Old Thing. We want everything new. But in the spiritual life, the Same Old Thing is what Satan fears most. It's the gospel, the Same Old Thing, that wields the only power able to transform lives and defeat the power of hell. The gospel message doesn't change; it remains settled forever. Jesus Christ lives in me! Jesus is a risen Savior! I am saved by grace through faith! Joy is mine through the indwelling Spirit!

Satan never trembles at fresh novelties. But he desperately fears the Same Old Thing. He frets that we will return to the basics . . . and discover lasting joy.

If you've lost the thrill and freshness of the gospel, you need to do a personal checkup. If you're bored, you're bored with Jesus Christ. The solution? Share Jesus Christ with others. "I pray that you may be active in sharing your faith," the apostle Paul wrote, "so that you will have a full understanding of every good thing we have in Christ" (Philem. 6). Give the Good News and you'll appreciate it anew yourself.

Solitary vs. Shared

Pleasure is intensely personal. No one can taste that Swiss chocolate sliding down my throat but me. Nobody but me can feel the masseuse's strong fingers working out the tension in my neck.

We could, of course, organize a party where dozens of us get physically stimulated at the same time—the Romans called them orgies—but even then, it would take multiple expressions of individual acts to create a faux sort of communal pleasure. (And ironically, loneliness, they tell us, can strike hardest in the middle of orgiastic excess.)

But because joy cannot be restricted to the physical plane, it can be shared in ways that transcend sensual pleasure. True happiness finds its fullest expression not in isolation, but in community. If we liken pleasure to a case of measles, then happiness is a worldwide epidemic.

I believe this is a major reason Jesus Christ founded and blessed the institution of the church. He knew that "in this world" we would "have trouble" (John 16:33). So he commanded his followers to love one another, going so far as to say, "All men will know that you are my disciples if you love one another" (John 13:35). He created the church as a harbor from the storm, an oasis in the wilderness, a refuge for the wayfarer, a hospital for the injured. He intended it to be a place of healing, rest, strength, and joy. In the church he wants us to "consider how we may spur one another on toward love and good deeds," and he advises us to "not give up meeting together, as some are in the habit of doing, but let us encourage one another" (Heb. 10:24–25).

Who can doubt that the church Jesus envisioned is a cheerful place? It ought to make people feel at home. It should proclaim that the Creator meant life to be enjoyed.

At a recent international conference in Amsterdam I met with Rick Warren, senior pastor of Saddleback Church in Lake Forest, California. My wife and I and a few members of my team ate dinner with him at a little café and discussed the festival concept we're developing in communities across the nation. I marveled at this busy pastor's friendly spirit, his genuine enthusiasm, and his joy in Jesus Christ. He lit up as we explained what we were trying to accomplish and said it sounded like something that could excite both him and his church.

Man, I thought, *this pastor is enjoying the Christian life to the full. Why can't all Christians follow his lead?* His daughter and her fiancé accompanied him, along with a few other members of his staff. All of them exuded the same kind of positive spirit. I couldn't help but think, *This is the way it was meant to be. You're contented and at peace and happy to meet somebody. You chat together and you eat and you laugh. And God is at the center of everything.*

How can a person who is not happy in the Lord be a blessing to other people? Sure, God can use anyone who communicates his truth, but if you want your *life* to bring happiness to others, you had better be a person who is filled with the Holy Spirit, whose fruit is joy. Christianity is a contented religion. It's a happy faith, the most wonderful life there is.

I believe I have only fifteen years of very active life left, should God allow me to keep my full health. I want to use those years to help this generation see Christianity as the best ride in town. It *is,* for goodness' sake, so let's say it. And let's use every possible vehicle to share the Good News.

Some years ago our team felt the Lord calling us to Denmark. Like many Protestant countries, Denmark seems hardened to the gospel message. We held a press conference at a hotel in Copenhagen. Now, the press from Protestant countries employs some of the most cynical individuals on the planet. In my experience, Western reporters treat religious types far worse than communists do.

I had barely settled into my chair when members of the press sneered, "You are from South America; what are you doing here in Denmark? We're a Christian nation. Everybody is baptized here."

First of all, they are not all baptized, even if they all talk as if they were. I ignored the insult and said, "Well, I'll tell you. My objective in coming—at the invitation of many of your ministers—is that all of Denmark will hear the voice of God."

"And how many days are you going to be here?" they asked.

"Six," I replied.

"And in six days, all of Denmark is going to hear the voice of God?"

"That's right."

"How are you going to do it?"

"That's why I called this press conference," I admitted. "I need your help. Without your help, I cannot get all of Denmark to hear the voice of God in six days. So I want you television people to please help me. I want you newspaper men and women, please help me. You fellows and women who are in radio, please help me. I need your help so that all of Denmark can hear the voice of God."

Suddenly these most secular of news people started looking at each other, unsure how to respond. It appeared as if they couldn't believe their ears.

But you know what? We got on television, in prime time. The national newspaper, what some call the *New York Times* of Denmark, dedicated all of Page 1, Section 2, to coverage of my opening message. The editors printed a big, red heart spanning the page, and in a banner headline over the graphic wrote the title of my talk: "Jesus wants you happy." Imagine! My secular friends had dedicated an entire page of their newspaper to the gospel of Jesus Christ—and then delivered it to every home in Denmark, absolutely free of charge.

The unadulterated message of Jesus Christ deserves to be declared to everyone with ears to hear. The happiness it brings cannot be contained, locked up in solitary confinement, but insists on breaking out to bless ever-growing multitudes. The church, at its best, brings believers together for encouragement, instruction, worship, and service. And the result, by God's grace, is overflowing joy.[17]

Limited Capacity vs. Boundless Capacity

Limits exist to most physical pleasure. Pass beyond certain boundaries, and you'll perceive further stimulation as pain. With pleasure, there really is such a thing as too much of a good thing. Eat too much pastry, you get sick. Stay in the sun too long, you get burned. Listen too long to loud music, you go deaf. Overindulge in any normally pleasurable activity, from sex to sailing, and at some point you'll cross the line into pain.

If there exists a similar "threshold of pain" for joy, however, I have yet to find it. So far as I can tell, nothing limits the amount of joy one person can experience. When you're younger, you think you could not be happier than the day you talk for hours to that cute boy or girl you've had your eye on . . . and then you get engaged. As you plan the ceremony you find yourself thinking, *Nothing can compare to how I feel at this moment!* . . . and then comes the wedding. During those few seconds it takes to say "I do," you doubt whether you could possibly find more love in your heart . . . and then your first child is born. And so it goes.

"Limits" and "joy" simply do not go together. They live in entirely different neighborhoods, speak entirely different languages.

I've noticed, though, that while most people recognize the limits to pleasure, they assign boundlessness not to joy, but to unhappiness. Writer

Carolyn Kizer spoke for this pessimistic crowd when she said, "Happiness is a Chinese meal; sorrow is a nourishment forever."[18]

Because so many smash into the limits to pleasure but doubt the potential for unlimited happiness, they give up on life, sentence themselves to prison, then slam and lock the cell door. Perhaps that is why, not so many years ago, a book with the title *Good Morning, Unhappiness* rocketed to the top of best-seller lists in France.

Thousands of men and women get up every morning and wish they could fall asleep again. Millions take Valium or Prozac just to keep from having to deal with a disappointing life. They're convinced they must keep floating one foot off the ground just to survive.

A friend of mine, an elder in our church, went to visit a woman whom he knew as a teenager. He made the trip at the urging of the woman's sister, who warned him, "She's in really bad shape."

The woman recognized her old friend immediately when he knocked at her door.

"Barry, what are you doing here?" she gasped.

"Your sister said you might like a visit, so I decided to stop by," he replied.

"Well, come on in."

Barry said that his old friend looked unbelievably miserable, sad, and discouraged. "Where's the young girl I used to know twenty years ago?" he asked. "You were so happy, so free. What's happened to you?"

"Forget it," she said. "I'm like a zombie now. I sit here smoking my cigarettes, watching my television."

Soon they began talking about the woman's sister, who at that moment lay dying of cancer. "You could be happy," Barry said. "Look at your sister. She's going to be gone in a few months, yet she cheers up those who come to visit her. Why are you so sad?"

"I wish *I* were my sister," she replied, "because I'd love to die."

Humanly speaking, the woman had ample reason for her despair. Her alcoholic husband kept a steady job, but never showed her the tiniest ounce of love. All she knew of marriage was that it hurt, and kept on hurting. She felt lonely and empty and worthless. With her youth gone and no spiritual resources to draw on, any happiness she ever knew had dwindled to a memory. The limits to pleasure, she knew. But an inexhaustible capacity for joy? That she could not even imagine.

Maybe you find yourself in the same boat. As a teenager, you felt happy. But now you feel no joy, no happiness, no delight in God. Where has all the happiness gone? *Something* happened. Maybe you married badly. Maybe you lost your health. Maybe you got hooked on drugs or alcohol. Or maybe it was something else. But something has gone wrong, and today the Lord has brought you to this book to speak directly to your heart.

The Lord Jesus says to you, "I want your joy to be complete. I want to give you the full measure of my joy. I want you to experience the kind of contentment that can flood your soul regardless of your circumstances. I want you to enjoy the deep happiness that comes from knowing you're divinely loved."

If you feel alone, empty, and confused, if happiness has fled your soul—then open your heart to the Lord Jesus. Say, "Lord Jesus, if you really love me, come into my heart. Despite my problems, be real to me. Lord, be my Savior, my Friend, my God." Discover for yourself the limitlessness of his joy.

Can Unbelievers Feel Happy?

But perhaps you have a question. "Do you mean to say that men and women can never experience true happiness apart from Jesus Christ?" you ask. "Because if that's your message, I don't buy it. I know plenty of non-Christians who seem pretty happy to me."

Actually, so do I. The Bible declares that even those with no relationship to Jesus can still enjoy a certain type of happiness. On one of his missionary journeys, the apostle Paul, accompanied by his friend Barnabas, told the citizens in the ancient city of Lystra that God had shown them kindness by filling their "hearts with joy" (Acts 14:17). That wasn't a sham joy, or a counterfeit joy. But they didn't know the joy available only to those indwelt by the Spirit of the Living God.

I tried to make this clear to two English callers who were listening to a radio interview I did in 1998 on the BBC's "Five Live" program, but I'm not sure I succeeded. The show's host, Nicki, asked me if people could be "truly happy if Jesus is not in their lives." I suggested they could not. I said someone might have "money in your pocket, and your body's in shape this week, but the inner core—the spirit, the inner person—is never fulfilled without Jesus Christ. . . , If you don't know God, a third of your personality remains empty, dead."

Nicki then invited non-Christian listeners to phone in if they considered themselves truly happy. Andy, a self-avowed atheist from Leeds, soon took to the airwaves, blasting Christians and claiming to be extremely happy. "I have set my own moral laws and live by them," Andy insisted. "If something goes wrong in my life, it's me to blame or somebody else to blame. I do not blame this blasted God thing."

The next caller, Norman, took even greater exception to my comments. "I was slightly appalled by his statement that nobody can be truly happy if you do not believe or have Jesus in your life," he said. "I think that's the biggest lot of nonsense I've heard in my life."

"Why do you say that?" I asked.

"Well, I believe that Jesus existed in history, although I'm not a Christian. I'm not a particularly religious person, but in my life I am truly happy. I'm married, I have two children, I'm healthy, my wife's healthy, my children are healthy, we have no financial problems. We are truly happy in every sense."

"That's great," I said.

"We do not have Jesus in our lives, so your statement, in my opinion, is incorrect," Norman reiterated.

"Norman, look," I replied, "you are missing out on one-third of your life. You are happy on the physical dimension. You are happy on the soul dimension—intellect, emotions, and will. But what about your spirit,

Norman? You're missing out there. I'm glad you're happy and I never claim that non-Christians can't experience some measure of true happiness—but you cannot be *fully* happy till your spirit lives."

We exchanged a few more comments, then I said, "Norman, one question. A serious question. I was in Bristol last year and an attorney, a solicitor just your age, had two little kids. His little girl died. He did not go to church, didn't believe in Jesus. He was absolutely devastated because he had no idea: *Where did she go? Where am I going? Will I ever see her again?* That's the spiritual, eternal dimension. Norman, you've got to give it time. Right now, you're happy, your body's in shape, your kids are great. But what about eternity, buddy?"

My radio friend had an answer for that, but not an entirely satisfactory one. "I believe that when we die, we do not die," Norman said. "I believe we go somewhere else. I have relatives and close family members who have died, and I take solace in the fact that I don't believe that this is the only place where we exist. But that doesn't mean I believe in Jesus. I believe that this isn't the only planet we go to. We will all go somewhere, eventually."

On what Norman based his hope, he didn't say. Of what his hope consisted, he didn't clarify. In blind faith he simply declared that somewhere in this vast universe there exists a planet (apparently) to which the dead somehow transport themselves. What sort of conditions there prevail, what occupies the inhabitants, what they know of their past life, where they are headed—and a thousand other questions—he left hanging.

I admire Norman for his ability to find hope and "solace" in such an apparently rootless belief, but I confess I find no hope in it. And certainly no joy. His comments convinced me more than ever that while God makes limitless joy available to us, we will never experience it apart from what the Bible calls the "new birth." We may feel happy on the dimensions of the physical and the soul, but until we ask God to breathe life into our spirits, we can never know happiness in the largest of the three dimensions. And therefore we will never enjoy the promise of Jesus: "that my joy may be in you and that your joy may be complete" (John 15:10).

What does it mean to experience "complete joy," joy that knows no limits? To be overwhelmed with God's presence—"filled to the measure of all the fullness of God" (Eph. 3:19)—so that the limitless joy of heaven becomes our experience on earth? I don't know, but I'm eager to find out.

God Wants You Happy

Jeremy Taylor, a seventeenth-century Anglican bishop, once said, "God threatens terrible things if we will not be happy." Sounds like quite a contradiction, doesn't it? But the more I think about his statement, the more I think the old preacher may have been on the right track.

Perhaps Taylor had in mind a text like Deuteronomy 28:47–48:

> Because you did not serve the LORD your God joyfully and gladly in the time of prosperity, therefore in hunger and thirst, in nakedness and dire poverty, you will serve the enemies the LORD sends against you. He will put an iron yoke on your neck until he has destroyed you.

Joy is the serious business of heaven, and God takes it so seriously that he "threatens terrible things if we will not be happy." Why such threats? Because, I think, the stakes are so high. The Lord created us to be happy, to enjoy a festival in our hearts, and through Jesus Christ he has offered to give us an inexhaustible capacity for joy. He speaks promise after promise of blessing, assuring us of joy in his presence and eternal pleasures at his right hand.

If any divine threat exists, it exists purely for our own good. The truth is that God does not want anyone to miss out on the party he plans to throw for us in heaven.

So why miss it?

How to Be Happy According to the Bible

1. *Believe in God.*
   "The jailer . . . was filled with joy, because [he] had come to believe in God" (Acts 16:34).

2. *Trust in God.*
   "May the God of hope fill you with all joy and peace as you trust in him" (Rom. 15:13).

3. *Embrace the salvation God offers.*
   "Even though you do not see him [Jesus] now, you believe in him and are filled with an inexpressible and glorious joy, for you are receiving the goal of your faith, the salvation of your souls" (1 Peter 1:8–9).

4. *Don't be passive about your happiness, but work toward it.*
   "We work with you for your joy, because it is by faith you stand firm" (2 Cor. 1:24).

5. *Ask Jesus to meet your needs.*
   "Until now you have not asked for anything in my name. Ask and you will receive, and your joy will be complete" (John 16:24).

6. *Become familiar with Jesus's promises.*
   "I say these things while I am still in the world, so that they [Christians] may have the full measure of my joy within them" (John 17:13).

7. *Express your love for Jesus Christ by obeying him.*
   "If you obey my commands, you will remain in my love, just as I have obeyed my Father's commands and remain in his love. I have told you this so that my joy may be in you and that your joy may be complete" (John 15:10–11).

8. *Don't be a loner, but spend time with other believers.*
   "I will continue with all of you for your progress and joy in the faith, so that through my being with you again your joy in Christ Jesus will overflow on account of me" (Phil. 1:25–26).

9. *When life gets hard, remember the rewards God has in store for you.*

"You sympathized with those in prison and joyfully accepted the confiscation of your property, because you knew that you yourselves had better and lasting possessions" (Heb. 10:34).

"Though outwardly we are wasting away, yet inwardly we are being renewed day by day. For our light and momentary troubles are achieving for us an eternal glory that far outweighs them all" (2 Cor. 4:16–17).

10. *Remember that happiness is a choice made possible by God.*

"But may the righteous be glad and rejoice before God; may they be happy and joyful" (Ps. 68:3).

2

An Oasis of Delight

Sex or Love?

Dear friends, let us love one another, for love comes from God. Everyone who loves has been born of God and knows God. Whoever does not love does not know God, because God is love.

The apostle John, in 1 John 4:7–8

Several years ago, during a visit to the United States, Mother Teresa stunned reporters by declaring that a terrible famine was sweeping America, a shortage every bit as ferocious as anything to plague impoverished India.

"There is a famine in America," she proclaimed. "Not a famine for food, but a famine for love."

Tragically, the same famine rages on today.

Josh McDowell often tells collegiate audiences, "Men and women, each one of you has two fears. One is the fear that you will never be loved. Second is the fear that you will never be able to love someone else."

45

College students, of course, aren't the only ones haunted by these twin fears. Factory workers, teachers, politicians, soldiers, artists, gas station attendants, stockbrokers, homemakers—at times we all tremble before these awful fears. Maybe your own heart feels the terror right now. Perhaps at this very moment you're one of the millions desperately searching for love. You want it, you crave it, you need it—but somehow it continues to escape your grasp. Be honest, do you ever find yourself asking:

Will *I* ever be loved?

Will *I* ever be able to love someone else?

Do *I* suffer from a famine of love?

Driving from my neighborhood in Portland, Oregon, I used to see an advertisement painted on a bus stop bench. "Call for love," it urged, followed by a phone number. "Only $3.75 a minute." Some folks feel so desperate for love that they'll pony up $3.75 a minute to talk to a stranger.

The Bible gives you far better news than a 1-900 phone number. Scripture declares that God created you for love. To love and be loved was God's original purpose for us all. When you and I give and receive love, every area of our lives becomes a marvelous experience. We enjoy the world in new, unexpected ways.

When we love and receive love in return, even the difficult roads of life grow smoother and less steep. When we come to understand what the Creator says about love, we discover for ourselves how to find it and enjoy it to the maximum.

The Gift of Sex

We all want to be loved. We long for someone to care for us from the heart, to cherish us and delight in our company.

But many of us struggle to find true love because we confuse it with something else. When a television or movie hunk turns to his gorgeous girlfriend and says, with leering eyes, "Give me some love, baby," we all know they're headed off to the bedroom. Our culture has conditioned us to equate sex with love—but they're not the same thing at all.

While God designed sex as a means for married partners to express their love to one another, we shouldn't confuse the two. Sexual intercourse within marriage is but one way God has invented for love to be shown.

The Bible teaches that God created human sexual impulses for our benefit. Our heavenly Father gives us all things richly to enjoy, including sex. Sex is not sinful or dirty, contrary to what some may think. It's clean and pure, wonderful and fun, even marvelous.

So what has happened? We have so corrupted the sexual relationship that many of us feel embarrassed to talk about it. I've talked about God's view of sex for years during our campaigns and festivals; I usually get a few letters of criticism. "You mustn't talk about those evil things," they scold.

Evil? Who said sex is evil? The Bible says sex is a gift of God. In the beginning he made man and woman and gave them the physical equipment necessary for enjoying one another sexually. Sex is not some odd invention that happened accidentally along the way.

Think of sex like an automobile (and I'm not talking about the backseat). You can use it as a useful means of transportation, or you can use it to run over little old ladies. The problem is not with the car, but with the operator.

In the same way, sex is great within the boundaries God set for it—but ignore those limits, and you become a danger to yourself and others. I enjoy reading, but I'd be a fool to peruse a new book while driving in rush-hour traffic. Likewise, in the Bible God sets an appropriate time and place for sex. Violate his directions, and you'll find yourself hailing a tow truck very soon.

Could that be why we see dented fenders, broken glass, and flashing yellow lights everywhere we go in America?

We in the church are partly to blame for this mess. We have not accurately taught what the Bible says about sex. My dad died when I was ten, and nobody volunteered to talk to me about this crucial subject. I felt no differently from any other kid; I wanted to know the scoop on sex.

But no one in my church ever discussed it, except when some preacher got really hot under the collar, pointed with his bony finger, and decried "Adulterers!" I used to think: *I wonder what that is?* It sounded naughty and apparently you went to hell if you practiced it, but I wondered why no one ever told me about the positive side of sex.

And what a positive side it is! Scripture declares that a husband and wife become "one flesh." The sexual relationship of a married couple, united in Jesus Christ, reflects something both marvelous and sacred: the unity of the soul with God. Sexual enjoyment in marriage is a gift of God to be enjoyed all through life. It's not love itself, but God invented it as a way to express love.

The tremendous force we call sex is powerful—it can make or break you. If you handle it right with the power of God, you can enjoy great success and feel happy and free. You will be able to look at yourself in the mirror without shame or embarrassment, with no haunting memories. But sex can also destroy you. One of the most common ways it does so is by masquerading as love.

Choose the Best

Because sexual activity binds people together in powerful and mysterious ways, God directed that it be reserved for a man and woman joined in holy matrimony. Of course, sex can *feel* good even outside of those boundaries. But extramarital sex is something like arsenic-laced Kool-Aid: sweet-tasting poison, deadly to the last drop. Nevertheless, because we all crave love—both to receive it and to give it—we grasp for any glimmer of *amor* we can find. And let's be honest: love is a much rarer commodity than sex (even within marriage). Some of us have never experienced true love in our entire lives. So why not at least enjoy sex?

My answer: No one who wants true love has to settle for mere sex. Sex is fun and enticing, but it can't substitute for love. Why not go after the real thing?

Don't be content with less than what God wants to give you! True love, the kind Jesus Christ offers to help you find, surpasses the sensual delights of sex in at least five ways:

Sex	Love
• Goal Is Orgasm	• Goal Is Intimacy
• Values Performance	• Values Person
• Emphasizes Looks	• Emphasizes Character
• Desires to Get	• Desires to Give
• Means to an End	• The End Itself

Goal Is Orgasm vs. Goal Is Intimacy

Those who seek sex and those who seek love generally pursue different goals. While sex treasures orgasm, love craves intimacy. The first concentrates on the body, while the second focuses on the soul. The first desires to grow close physically and erotically; the second wants to draw near emotionally and spiritually.

This distinction came alive for me while watching reports on the trial of Rae Carruth, a former professional football player accused of murder. Cherica Adams died December 14, 1999, from wounds suffered in a car shooting allegedly planned by Carruth. In the weeks leading up to the trial, the press consistently identified Adams as Carruth's "girlfriend," a description Carruth vehemently protested. "I didn't even know her full name," he insisted, maintaining she amounted to nothing more than a sex partner. Eventually a jury found Carruth guilty of conspiracy to commit murder, shooting into an occupied vehicle, and using an instrument to destroy an unborn child—his own (a son, born ten weeks premature).

Orgasm may be good, friends, but it's a poor substitute for love.

Sex outside of marriage is ugly—it causes division, cruelty, perversion, guilt, and a tremendous sense of emptiness. I have never had sex outside of marriage, but I have spoken with hundreds who have, and almost to a person they describe an aching void inside. Illicit sex might feel exciting for a moment, but when it ends, many individuals hate and blame their "partner."

And some even pull a trigger.

A world of difference exists between developing an intimate relationship with someone you love and spending a hot session with an available body. Love "is not self-seeking," the apostle Paul says; in fact, "it always protects" (1 Cor. 13:5, 7). Protection like this can't be found in a condom, but thrives only within relationships where both individuals seek the other's best interests.

And how does one develop deep, other-centered concern? To my way of thinking, only one route works—a road the Bible calls "the way of holiness." The Bible says, "Make every effort to live in peace with all men and to be holy; without holiness no one will see the Lord" (Heb. 12:14). God himself says, "Be holy, because I am holy" (1 Peter 1:16).

To be "holy" doesn't mean you become a phony, superficial, judgmental nut. Holy means you have nothing to cover up. Holy means you can look God in the face with a clear conscience and say, "Thank you, Lord, that I have nothing to be ashamed of, nothing to hide, no skeletons in the dark corners of my mind."

Did you know the Bible says your body can be both sacred and eternal? As the apostle Paul told his fellow Christians in 1 Corinthians 6:19: "Your body is a temple of the Holy Spirit." Therefore we can't behave like cats and dogs or cows and horses. That's why the Bible urges each of us to "honor God with your body" (1 Cor. 6:20).

God wants the best for us, and that means purity, happiness, and satisfaction. The Bible says, "Blessed are the pure in heart, for they will see God" (Matt. 5:8). Don't fall into the trap that destroys so many today. Don't buy the lie of the media. It isn't great "fun" to have sex outside of marriage. Oh, I'm sure there's a certain kick, but it goes away very quickly, leaving behind guilt and emptiness and a deep sense of despair. Don't fall for it. The way of God is the best.

You may say, "Luis, I can't do it. I don't have the power." None of us has the power! But the Bible says, "You will receive power when the Holy Spirit comes on you" (Acts 1:8). Power is the gift of God, too. God gives us the gift of sex to enjoy and he gives us the power of the Holy Spirit to keep it under control. The Lord says to you, "I can keep you. I'll guard your heart. I'll protect you. I'll fulfill you and fill you with the Holy Spirit."

That doesn't mean, of course, that all your struggles immediately cease. Mine didn't! Many years ago a doctor asked a conference audience, "Have you ever thanked God for your body?" As I sat in the crowd I thought, *No, I haven't. All these temptations, all these thoughts cross my mind, and I know some aren't right.* I wondered what to do.

First, I discovered that while temptation comes to all of us, temptation isn't sin. Temptation is merely the inclination, the desire to sin. But in the power of Jesus, you and I can overcome temptation. The Bible says, "I can do everything through [Jesus Christ] who gives me strength" (Phil. 4:13).

"But Luis," you reply, "what about me? I've already messed up."

I once spoke on this topic in Medellin, Colombia. After I finished, a sixteen-year-old girl ran up to the platform, weeping. "Mr. Palau," she cried, "does this mean there's no hope for me? Two years ago I did it." She told me her father sexually abused her, and she felt so dirty that she turned promiscuous. "Can God ever forgive me?" she wanted to know. "Will God never give me a decent husband?"

I told that brokenhearted young woman that God is good and compassionate. I assured her that the blood of Jesus Christ, which he shed on the cross when he died for our sins, would purify her conscience from evil works so she could serve the living and true God (Heb. 9:14). I admitted that some things might never be quite the same, but insisted she could start over. If she came to God's Son and surrendered her past, her memories, her failures, and her immorality, Jesus would forgive her. Furthermore, I said, Jesus promised to make the power of the Holy Spirit available to her.

I tell you the same thing. Holiness *is* an option for you, no matter who you are or what you may have done. You, too, can join millions of others in choosing intimacy over mere sex.

I believe the best gift you can give your betrothed is purity—to be able to look deep into his or her eyes on your wedding day and have nothing to hide. Holiness means reserving something beautiful and precious for one person, until you say, "I do."

I have four sons, all married. How thrilling it was to see each of my daughters-in-law walking up the aisle at her father's arm, and to see each of my sons standing at the front, knees shaking! I'll never forget each father holding his daughter's arm and looking at the bridegroom, as if to say, "You hurt my girl and I'll deal with you personally, boy."

At each service I saw a pair of young people who love God, who love the Bible, and who remained pure by the power of God. I wanted to weep as I watched them get on their knees and look each other in the eye, with no secrets to keep hidden, no dirt, no guilt. They could gaze at each other on that happy day with bright smiles and say, "I belong to you and nobody else. I have nothing to cover up before the Lord."

I tell you, it's beautiful. And it can be yours.

Values Performance vs. Values Person

Walk into any major bookstore and you'll have no trouble finding several shelves of books and manuals on how to improve your sexual technique. Techniques from the East, techniques from sex therapists, techniques from ancient religions, techniques from modern scientific studies. Nearly all of them assume that if you become a more proficient lover, you will at last find the love you've always desired.

Sorry, but I don't think you will.

Better technique may increase one's sensual pleasure, but in place of genuine love, it may actually increase the emotional distance between partners. Those who focus on performance rather than on the person inevitably devalue the sexual partner, who becomes little more than a handy receptacle for bodily fluids—and who dreams of becoming *that*?

Great lovers are not those who know how to push all the right erotic buttons, but those who treat a loved one as an individual, not merely as a nicely assembled body. The main trouble with technique divorced from love is that it almost always fuels the kind of pride and self-centered smugness that values conquests and trophies more than it does men and women made in God's image.

The story of Joseph in Genesis, chapter thirty-nine, illustrates my point. Joseph, a handsome teenager, worked for a wealthy Egyptian named Potiphar. Potiphar's wife made it clear (in her husband's absence) that she had noticed Joseph's handsome face and rippling muscles. "Come to bed with me!" she told him. But Joseph refused. "How then could I do such a wicked thing and sin against God?" he asked (v. 9).

Not easily dissuaded, the woman kept up her assault, approaching Joseph day after day with the same proposition. She appeared so enamored with Joseph, so much in love. What a tremendous temptation for a healthy teenager living so far away from home! She had both riches and influence—and who would find out?

One day while Joseph attended to his duties inside the otherwise unoccupied house, this lustful wife approached Joseph again with the same demand: "Come to bed with me!" The godly young man once more refused, this time running out of the house.

No sooner had Joseph's feet flown out the front door than the woman turned against him. Five seconds earlier she supposedly loved him: "Sleep with me, sleep with me!" But when he adamantly refused, she did a sudden about-face and tried to destroy him. She falsely accused Joseph of attempted rape and had him thrown in prison.

What a switch, from the desire for sex to the lust for punishment! What explains such a fast change? I think the answer is simple: Wounded pride. The Bible says love "does not boast, it is not proud" (1 Cor. 13:4). The woman didn't love Joseph; she saw him merely as a pretty trophy. When it became clear she couldn't obtain that trophy, she set out to smash it. It's a pattern often repeated when sex-as-performance gets confused with love-for-the-person.

Pride, not love, has led many a Joe to say to many a Sarah, "Do you love me?"

"Yes," answers Sarah.

"Are you willing to show me that you love me?" asks Joe.

"Yes," says Sarah.

"Well, if you *really* love me, Sarah, you will do this and this and this."

"Uh . . . *that* too, Joe?"

"Well, if you *really* love me . . ."

Just as soon as Joe gets what he wants, he says, "Bye-bye." And then he goes to Jenny and pulls the same trick.

Why does the cycle continue? Because Joe values the performance over the person. He boasts of his conquests and thinks nothing of using and then discarding one "lover" after another. Somehow, neither Joe nor Sarah stopped to ask themselves a couple of pertinent questions:

- Does anyone *really* find contentment by pairing up with dozens of sexual partners?
- Do such brief liaisons *really* produce lasting happiness?

I'm not asking, "Does it feel good?" God created sex to provide intense sensations of physical pleasure, and that doesn't change just because the intercourse occurs outside of marriage. The Bible teaches that sin can indeed deliver pleasure—but only "for a short time" (Heb. 11:25). In the end, illicit passions and pleasures always lead to enslavement and deception (Titus 3:3).

If you talk with as many people as I do, you're bound to find men and women whose arguments for unfaithfulness sound persuasive. Some time ago on a flight, I began talking to a Nike executive in his mid-thirties. Let's call him Tim. "What do you do?" Tim asked.

"I'm a minister," I replied.

"You're a minister—you have a church?" he wondered.

"No, I don't have a church. I just travel around, talk to people."

"What kind of traveling around? Is it a good life?"

"Yes, it's a pretty good life; better than you think, actually. I often talk about the family."

That's when Tim's face grew sour and his tone flattened.

"Oh, the family," he sneered. "I suppose you're against adultery, fornication, and the whole bit."

"You might say so," I responded.

"I'll tell you something about marriage," Tim declared. "You guys with your Bibles, you want everybody to be married for fifty, sixty years. But when you get to be fifty-five, if you stay with the same old lady, you're going to be so bored."

"Well, I'm past fifty-five and I'm still with the woman I married forty years ago," I admitted. "And yes, I suppose it could get a little boring sometimes. But it doesn't have to be."

"Listen, in the old days women would have two or three kids, then die off," Tim continued, "so the guy married another woman. Back then it was easy to say, 'One wife until death do us part.' But it doesn't make any sense today. She lives too long."

I suppose Tim's arguments could be persuasive (even if he didn't get his facts right)—so long as one forgets the central truth: love is really about the person, not the performance. Love concerns much more than sexual technique and erotic novelty. It's about getting to know a person deeply, about caring for that person from the heart and developing a bond far stronger than anything raging hormones can produce.

I fear that unless Tim changes his mind, he will continue to chase one sexual experience after another. And he will never discover the deeper, richer joy he could have by getting to know a person intimately.

Emphasizes Looks vs. Emphasizes Character

When someone confuses sex with love, he or she usually emphasizes good looks over good character. I can't help but wonder if this confusion partially explains why so many Hollywood marriages go belly-up.

One of the most publicized Hollywood breakups of the past few years has to be that of Tom Cruise and Nicole Kidman. "Say it isn't so!" lamented one news flash. "Hollywood's golden couple are separating after 11 years of marriage."[1]

A spokesperson for the pair said the decision was made "regretfully," but that divergent careers had made it impossible for the couple to spend enough time together. Ironically, less than three years before, Kidman had said about her marriage, "It's been nine years and I'm past the seven-year itch. When you're loved for your flaws, that's when you really feel safe."[2]

If nothing else, the breakup of Tom Cruise and Nicole Kidman demonstrates that great looks alone are not enough to keep a love affair going. Physical appearance can legitimately draw two people to one another, but it's never enough to keep them together. Richard Burton and Elizabeth Taylor proved that truth spectacularly.

Taylor married Burton twice (somewhere among her other six marriages). On her fiftieth birthday, Hollywood's elite gathered to celebrate at a London club and a reporter asked Burton if the pair would ever marry again. No, Burton replied, explaining, "We love each other with a passion so furious that we burn one another out."

Wow! Many men and women read "hot" comments like this and say to each other, "I've never had a passion with my spouse that burns *me* out. What am I missing?"

You know what you're missing? Nothing. Don't believe the hype. We're all tempted to think that because we feel physically attracted to someone, we've found real love . . . but probably we haven't. Very likely it's just passion—very exciting, very real, but miles from real love.

Love involves body, soul, spirit, devotion, will, and emotions. Passion is purely sexual, often aroused by physical appearance. When someone says to a new boyfriend or girlfriend, "I love you so much I can't wait any longer to have sex with you," what that person really means is, "I am sexually stirred by the way you look. My passion has been kindled, and I have to find physical release. I think you'll do."

"But Luis," you say, "I really *am* looking for love. I want to find someone. I want to have a boyfriend or girlfriend. I'm actively looking—and isn't sex part of it?"[3]

Believe me, if you want real love that will last forever, the physical side will come in due time. You needn't jump the gun just because his or her looks drive you wild. The Old Testament hunk Samson chose looks over character, and it brought him no joy. When he saw a pretty face in a neighboring town he told his parents, "Get her for me, for she looks good to me" (Judg. 14:3 NASB). Over their objections, Samson married the girl. The marriage lasted only a few days and resulted in bitterness, hurt, and multiple deaths. In the end, Samson lost his wife and eventually his life.

So do looks mean nothing? I'd never say that. I think physical attraction should enter into the romantic mix, but it's not the only part and *certainly* isn't the most important part. Every study I know affirms that character counts for far more in a fulfilling relationship than does physical appearance. You can hardly go wrong by focusing on character, but an unbalanced concern for looks often leads to heartache.

One day, at age twelve, I was riding in a truck with a worker in my late father's company. Suddenly the driver stopped his vehicle and pulled out a pornographic book featuring all sorts of pictures of men and women in weird sexual positions. "I will make a man out of you, boy," he said, and told me a bunch of garbage. He filled my mind with perverse images, and not until after my twenty-third birthday did a missionary take me aside and tell me the truth. All my teenage years I struggled with the lies I heard and saw when I was twelve.

Too many contemporary magazines, books, television shows, and movies paint a totally unrealistic picture of sexuality. Our ministry counsels men all over the world who have been deceived and enslaved by pornography: They were gravely injured by a picture of sex that never has been, and never will be, true.

Be very careful how you deal with visual stimuli! If you toy with pornography, if you sit in front of a television and watch a "dirty movie," you contaminate your soul. You also run a high risk of addiction—and a downward spiral from there. You'll want more and more, but will never find satisfaction. Jesus said, "I tell you that anyone who looks at a woman lustfully has already committed adultery with her in his heart" (Matt. 5:28).

On the other hand, the Bible gives the following counsel to men looking for a godly partner: "A wife of noble character who can find? She is worth far more than rubies" (Prov. 31:10). Looks count, but character counts for much more. And when we energize our search for character by tapping into the power of God, we can make possible a quality of life unattainable in any other way.

Best-selling author Zig Ziglar once told an audience: "On a very personal note, let me say I've always loved my family. I've always particularly loved my wife; the children have always called us 'the love birds.' But I'm here to tell you that I had no idea what it meant to love until I learned to love through Jesus Christ. When you love your family, when you love your fellow human beings through Christ, there's a power and a love and a depth and a strength which is absolutely unimaginable to the non-believer."

He's right. The Bible says you can know *real* love, *pure* love, when you know God in your heart through Jesus Christ.[4]

Desires to Get vs. Desires to Give

We've all met individuals with a far greater interest in receiving than in giving. Most of us dislike spending much time with such ravenous, self-centered men and women.

And yet a craving for sex apart from a commitment to love leads almost inescapably to a nasty form of greedy narcissism. Without love, sex becomes increasingly self-absorbed and selfish. Experiencing new pleasures becomes everything; the other person seems entirely irrelevant, apart from his or her sexual equipment.

True love doesn't act that way at all. When you genuinely love another, you feel exhilarated to give him or her something precious. "It is more blessed to give than to receive" (Acts 20:35) is more than a biblical dictum; it's a real-world fact. Nothing can compare to giving a well-chosen present to a loved one, especially a surprise gift. His or her look of delight cannot be bought at any price.

Giving lies at the heart of the Christian faith. The desire to give from a heart of love prompted Jesus to say, "Even I, the Son of Man, came here not to be served but to serve others, and to give my life as a ransom for many" (Mark 10:45 NLT).

The longing to give ought to characterize every Christian marriage. So the Bible says, "Husbands, love your wives, just as Christ loved the church and gave himself up for her" (Eph. 5:25). Scripture teaches that marriage partners should satisfy each other's needs, and to please one another, not to deny each other (1 Cor. 7:5). In other words, it's mutual.

There's nothing like sex within marriage in a solid Christian home; It promises genuine pleasure, joy, and satisfaction. God encourages both the man and the woman to initiate lovemaking. In the Song of Solomon—the Bible's preeminent love poem—the wife pursues her husband just as much as her husband goes after her. Both partners are to show sexual interest in the other. But when this instruction gets overlooked, trouble results.

Years ago I met a sad couple in the British Isles who believed that sexual relations were to be reserved for conceiving children. They had only one child (no surprise there). The husband was a bitter, discouraged man, despite his role as a local Bible teacher. And his wife looked miserable.

God never intended marriage to be like that! Love wants the best for the other person and delights in giving. A man is most fully a man and a woman most fully a woman when they love each other with the sacrificial love of Jesus Christ.

I remember one unhappy young woman who came to me for counsel. Her husband roamed the world, never staying home. One day, one of her children said to her, "Momma, why don't you laugh anymore? You never say anything happy."

This poor woman confessed to me, "Luis, you know what my husband has done to me? I have lost the capacity to laugh."

I wept inside when I heard her terrible words. She had lost her joy, her happiness, her womanhood. This couple had married because they loved each other, but somehow the husband stopped following the biblical rule. He became harsh. And so his wife lost her spirit and forgot how to laugh.

How many men have killed their wife's spirit? If you are one of those men, repent! Say before the Lord, "O God, what have I done to my wife? I promised to love her. I promised to take care of her. I promised to make her happy. What have I done? Forgive me, Lord, and help me change. Let me see my wife laugh again." It's never too late to come back to God.

"But Luis," you say to me, "I've lost my love for her."

Then you need the love of God in your heart. What you thought was love in your youth may only have been physical attraction; what you need is supernatural love. The Bible says, "God has poured out his love into our hearts by the Holy Spirit, whom he has given us" (Rom. 5:5).

You *can* love her again, because love is more than an emotion. Emotion should follow love, but love involves more than feelings. You decide to love by the power of the Holy Spirit. Ask your heavenly Father to fill you with his supernatural love, then go back to your wife and ask her to forgive you. Then pray together.

Have you ever prayed with your wife in your arms? I know it may sound crazy, but when I hug my wife in bed and pray with her, I choke up every time—and I've been married for more than forty years. No love can compare to the love that grows between a man and a woman hugging each other in the presence of God! I challenge you to do it tonight. It has nothing to do with sex (sometimes before and after, but that's another story).

During our festivals we often broadcast a television program that offers biblical counsel, live on the air. Viewers telephone us at the station and ask questions, many related to the home.

One night after praying with a man I said to him, "Now that you have repented and opened your heart to Jesus Christ, go to your wife and say, 'Come and kneel with me by our bedside.' Then put your arm around her and read a chapter from the Bible together; I suggest John 1. When you finish reading with her at your side, remain on your knees with your arm around her and discuss what you read. Then pray with your wife."

A medical doctor, fifty-two years old, was listening to the program. A few days later he wrote me a long typewritten letter. "Palau," he said, "when I went to medical college, I was married. I took a post-graduate course and was gone for nine months. I did not know anything about Jesus Christ. During that time, I was unfaithful to my wife. Just once, but it broke me. I came home and told my wife, and that was the practical end of our marriage. We have continued to live together for the last twenty-five years, but we haven't been happy. We've had an empty relationship. We hardly talk to each other. My boy is now in medical college; he is an alcoholic. My eighteen-year-old daughter is rebellious. My youngest boy is uncontrollable.

"Palau, nobody ever suggested to me that I should talk tenderly to my wife, open up the Bible, kneel with her, embrace her, ask forgiveness, and pray together. I never even thought of such a thing. When I saw you on television, I decided to receive Jesus Christ and ask for my wife's forgiveness. She came into the bedroom after I prayed, not knowing what was going on. She knelt down beside me, I put my arm around her, we read a chapter of the Bible, and we prayed together. I want to tell you that love is coming back into our home."

God doesn't reserve miracles like these for listeners of religious television broadcasts. They can happen in *your* life, too, when you agree with

God that it really is better to give than to receive—and then you start giving.[5]

Means to an End vs. the End Itself

God designed sex as a means within marriage to express genuine love. He never intended sex to be an end in itself.

When we treat food as an end in itself, rather than as a means to sustain life, we become gluttons. When we treat a prescription drug as an end in itself, rather than as a means to promote health, we become addicts. When we treat our job as an end in itself, rather than as a means to provide for our family, we become workaholics. In the same way, when we treat sex as an end in itself, rather than as a means to express love to our spouse, we open ourselves to a vicious array of dysfunctional and destructive behaviors.

Don't buy the lie of "recreational sex." Sex is far more than a form of fun physical exertion, an end in itself no different from a game of basketball or a leisurely bicycle ride. Sex is different because God *made* it different. Those who champion "recreational sex" usually claim that it sets people free from the chains of restrictive, puritanical mores—but the truth lies elsewhere. According to God's Word: "They mouth empty, boastful words and, by appealing to the lustful desires of sinful human nature, they entice people who are just escaping from those who live in error. They promise them freedom, while they themselves are slaves of depravity—for a man is a slave to whatever has mastered him" (2 Peter 2:18–19).

Sex outside of God's plan always results in slavery and emotional imprisonment, while its expression within the Lord's boundaries produces joy, peace, and freedom.

Jesus said, "So if the Son sets you free, you will be free indeed" (John 8:36). Free! Free to serve the Lord. Free to pray. Free to worship—and not with a guilty conscience or with a hypocritical smile. You live free when you open your heart to Jesus Christ: "You will know the truth, and the truth will set you free" (John 8:32). The Bible also says, "It is for freedom that Christ has set us free" (Gal. 5:1). Sexual satisfaction and freedom come when you know the truth that sets you free. Jesus Christ is *for* sexual satisfaction and freedom!

Someone may object, "But isn't God oppressive? Isn't he a joy-killer? He's always saying, 'Don't do this, don't do that.'"

No, just the opposite. It is as if the Lord put up some fences and said, "Within this fence, you are free to do whatever you want. You can enjoy my gift. I installed the fences so you won't wreck your life. These are my rules to play and live by."

I believe many today are saying, "I want to know the rules." But you won't find the rules in the newspaper advice columns. You won't find them in a horoscope. You won't find them in most universities or schools.

The only place to find the rules is in the Bible because God created sexuality. The Designer who made us wrote the manual we call the Bible. If you play by his rules, you'll find success in the area of sexuality.

Decades ago a young man bought a Model A Ford. As he drove on an Indiana road, his car suddenly sputtered and died and rolled to a stop. The young man jumped out and opened the hood. He cranked the engine countless times, but the car refused to budge.

After several minutes, a big, black, elegant automobile pulled off the road and parked about thirty yards behind the Model A. An older gentleman, dressed to kill, got out of the car and walked over to the stranded young man.

"What's the matter with your car?" he asked.

"It won't work," said the young man, anger rising in his face. "Can't you *see*?"

"Let me help you fix it," the old man volunteered.

The boy looked at him: coat, tie, tails, manicured fingernails. He looked as if he were going to some high-society party. *What does this old man know?* he thought.

"No thanks," the young man declared, "I'll fix it myself."

He fiddled with some wires, cranked the engine again, but still the car wouldn't start. So the old man offered again: "Hey, let me give you a hand."

"No, sir," the young man insisted. "I'll do it myself."

But after twenty more minutes of futility, he realized his car just wasn't going to start. So he turned to the man, resignation in his voice, and said, "Okay, do what you can."

"Get in the car," the old man commanded.

He slumped down in his car while the man went to work under the hood. A few moments later the man said, "Turn the key."

The young man did so—and the car coughed to life.

The young man leaped out of his car, stared at the man in wonder, and asked, "Who *are* you?"

"I'm Henry Ford," the man said. "I invented that car. The moment I saw it, I knew exactly what was wrong."

You know something? God is our Henry Ford. He made us. He knows what makes us work. He says to you, "Give me your heart! I know your problems; I know what wires are crossed. I know what is going on in your life. I invented men and women and I invented sex. I made you the way you are. Let me be your heavenly mechanic."

If you live by the rules of God—not hiding behind masks, not putting on a facade, not settling for a show-business Christianity, but choosing the real thing—I tell you, you'll be a happy man or a happy woman. You'll be free! And you'll enjoy true love.

A Many-Splendored Thing

When the love of God invades the human heart, everything changes. Whites look whiter, reds seem redder, blues look bluer. Love changes *everything*.

A friend of mine visited the Cook Islands in the South Pacific. On a boat trip around the turquoise-blue lagoon of Aitutake, a guide named

Ke talked with a wide smile on his face and laughter in his voice. "Before the missionaries came, we were headhunters," Ke said. "You may have heard these islands were named after Captain Cook, but that's not true. They got their name because we would cook you and eat you. But now we don't want to cook you; we want to love you."

I heard a similar story while I was in the Fiji Islands. Christian missionaries brought the gospel message to Fiji almost two centuries ago.

A European count visited the islands after hearing of its beautiful girls, wild dances, pristine beaches, and great weather. But when he arrived, he saw the Fijians all dressed up and not cutting loose, as he had been prepared to expect. He felt great disappointment.

He complained to a tribal chief, "What a pity that you people listened to those missionaries and followed what they said about the Bible. I come from Europe, and in Europe we discarded the Bible long ago. You have to realize that it is outdated, that it has no meaning, that it has no power. It's just a pity that you Fijians, who used to live such a free and happy life on your beaches, now behave like any other dull Christian."

"Sir," the chief replied, "do you see that rock over there?"

"Yes."

"You should thank the missionaries that they came and taught us the way of love."

"Why should I thank them?" asked the count. "It's all a bunch of myths, anyway."

"Do you know what we used to do on that rock before the missionaries came?" the chief continued. "We would take people like you and cut off their heads. And do you see that great oven with the big pot? We used to take the people whose heads we cut off, boil them, and eat them. So, you'd better thank the missionaries that they came and that we believed their message of love. Because if it wasn't for them, we'd have your head off right now and you'd be boiling for dinner tonight."

Love makes all the difference!

God made you to be loved and to love, to enjoy love's delicious fruit. But you can never experience real love, no matter who you are, unless you first know Jesus Christ. If you want genuine love, you must have the love of God in your heart—not just a few Bible verses tucked away in your brain, but God himself alive in your innermost soul.

Love truly is a many-splendored thing. And true love is God in action in the human heart.

How to Find Love According to the Bible

1. *Recognize that all true love comes from God.*
   "Dear friends, let us love one another, for love comes from God. Everyone who loves has been born of God and knows God. Whoever does not love does not know God, because God is love" (1 John 4:7–8).
2. *Put your hope in God.*
   "May your unfailing love rest upon us, O LORD, even as we put our hope in you" (Ps. 33:22).
3. *Call out to God.*
   "You are forgiving and good, O LORD, abounding in love to all who call to you" (Ps. 86:5).
4. *Love God's Son, Jesus Christ.*
   "Jesus said, 'He who loves me will be loved by my Father, and I too will love him and show myself to him'" (John 14:21).
5. *If you want to be loved, start by loving others.*
   "He who refreshes others will himself be refreshed. . . . He who seeks good finds good will" (Prov. 11:25, 27).
6. *Make specific plans to bless others.*
   "Those who plan what is good find love and faithfulness" (Prov. 14:22).
7. *Don't look for sexual love outside of marriage.*
   "A man who commits adultery lacks judgment; whoever does so destroys himself" (Prov. 6:32).
8. *If you are married, look for ways to love your spouse.*
   "He who loves his wife loves himself" (Eph. 5:28).
9. *Don't harbor grudges, but be quick to forgive.*
   "He who covers over an offense promotes love" (Prov. 17:9).
10. *Realize that love is more than an emotion; it must take action.*
    "Dear children, let us not love with words or tongue but with actions and in truth" (1 John 3:18).

3

A Friend Who Sticks Closer Than a Brother

Popularity or Connectedness?

A man of many companions may come to ruin,
  but there is a friend who sticks closer than a brother.

King Solomon of Israel, in Proverbs 18:24

A few years ago in Spokane, Washington, a group of college students noted their empty bank accounts and decided they needed some money. After considering their options, they rented an empty storefront building downtown and put up a big, handwritten sign: "We listen, $15 an hour."

They gave no counsel. Suggested no direction. Offered no prayer. They simply offered to listen for $15 an hour.

And people lined up by the hundreds to talk. The students made thousands of dollars just by listening.

You know the most surprising thing about this story? Apart from its entrepreneurial slant, the Spokane experience could be multiplied the world over. Men and women so yearn for human connection that they will share their most private thoughts with total strangers.

A cover story in *USA Today* headlined "Deep Secrets Told among Passengers on Airlines"[1] reported how a thirty-one-year-old man suddenly started revealing his darkest secret to the stranger sitting next to him. The man confessed how his fiancée had spent the past year cheating on him. He revealed everything—how he discovered the guy's car outside his house, how she admitted she'd begun to shop around because he wasn't good enough, how he felt alone and betrayed. The article told several other comparable stories; I trust the reporter's accuracy, because eerily similar things happen to me.

Once my son Andrew and I were seated in the front row of a flight to North Carolina. Two flight attendants started arguing, and one of them sat in a seat facing us, right in front of me.

"You don't look happy," I said to her.

"You'd better believe I'm not happy," she retorted. "I tried to speak with my boyfriend from the San Francisco airport, but he wouldn't talk to me. And just now I spilled something on a passenger."

I'm a priest receiving confession on the airplane, I thought.

"I saw you reading the Bible," she continued. "Are you a pastor?"

"Well, sort of. What's the matter with your boyfriend?"

"Oh, he's in New York. I called him but he hung up on me in forty-five seconds."

"Where did you meet him?"

"On an airplane."

Before I knew it, this young woman was telling me her whole life story. She said she wanted to get married, but couldn't find a decent guy. I suggested she needed God to help her. Andrew just sat there, mouth open. A total stranger! On an airplane!

Why do individuals seek out heart-to-heart talks with strangers? According to *USA Today*, they do it because it's safe. Second, strangers don't pass judgment, like family members often do. Third, strangers don't tattle, because they don't know the individual who's "confessing." All three factors create what psychiatrists call "instant intimacy."

Instant intimacy suffers from a big problem, however; it's more instant than intimate. We pour out our hearts to strangers because we lack close, trusted friends with whom we can safely reveal the secret fears and hidden longings we keep locked away.

God built us for friendships, for rich, vital connections with others. Our hearts crave the kind of spiritual kinship that transcends the miles and years. After smashing victories or terrible defeats, we long to get on the phone with a friend whom we know will genuinely care. When we need a concerned ear, we spend whatever it takes to get in touch with a trusted friend.

So long as we have one.

Popular, but Lonely

Unfortunately, close friendships don't easily develop in a fast-paced, transient society like ours. We often don't remain long enough in one spot to discover who might become a great friend. And when we do stick around, we get so busy that we might as well live on the moon.

While all of us instinctively recognize the need for trusted friends, we don't feel at all sure how to find and cultivate them. In a perpetual crunch for time, we spread our net wide and try to make as many positive acquaintances as possible. Soon we mistake popularity for connectedness—and then we can't figure out why we still feel so lonely.

Most of us know individuals who are always the life of the party, the popular men and women who seem to know everyone by first name, yet who seem strangely distant and hollow. Perhaps we are such individuals.

Things won't change until we recognize that a huge gap lies between being popular and having a genuine connection with other human beings.

Popularity may offer an abundance of superficial, shallow acquaintances, but true friendship provides deep heart-to-heart connections that, over time, can mature into kinship.

Opting for the Best

It's no sin to be popular, of course. Everyone wants to be liked. If heaven frowned on the idea of popularity, then what would we be forced to say about Jesus? As a young boy, he grew "in favor with God and men" (Luke 2:52). At the beginning of Jesus's earthly ministry, "all spoke well of him" (Luke 4:22). And just days before Jesus's crucifixion, his enemies saw the crowds thronging him and exclaimed, "Look how the whole world has gone after him!" (John 12:19).

The danger lies not in popularity *per se*, but in mistaking popularity for friendship. And by pursuing popularity in lieu of genuine human connection, we only compound the error. Popularity can act like potent wine, delighting the palate while blinding the drinker to an onrushing bus. It was the popular Jesus, remember, who told the crowds, "Woe to you when all men speak well of you, for that is how their fathers treated the false prophets" (Luke 6:26). Jesus knew popularity comes far more easily when you say only what people want to hear. True friendship, however, prizes truth even when it hurts.

While friendship may be harder to cultivate than mere popularity, it also pays far greater dividends. Let's consider five ways in which genuine connectedness surpasses the benefits of popularity.

Popularity	Connectedness
• Gives Ego Boost	• Provides Reservoir of Strength
• Flavor of the Day	• Perennial Favorite
• Craves Compliments	• Seeks Truth
• Known Widely	• Known Deeply
• Seeks to Be a Star	• Desires to Be a Friend

Gives Ego Boost vs. Provides Reservoir of Strength

No doubt about it: Popularity makes a person feel good. We might get a certain kick out of playing the role of the outcast, the solitary villain, but if given the choice, most of us would choose popularity in a heartbeat. When we know that lots of people like us, our ego breaks into a gigantic smile.

But ego boosts, no matter how frequent or potent, have little power to sustain us when real trouble or discouragement hits. You need a true friend, not an autograph-seeking fan, when life turns hard. A genuine and deep connection to another human being provides a reservoir of strength that popularity cannot match.

As a young woman in the Philippines, Evelyn Fernandez was popular—especially among the young males who longed to be with her. "We all wanted to marry her when we were young," one man told me. But Evelyn would have none of it. "With all the abandoned children here in our city," she asked, "why would I want to get married and have *more* children? I'm going to adopt children and bring them up as my own."

So that's exactly what she did. She became a primary school teacher, and over many years she adopted *forty-two* children, all but four of whom ended up working for various Christian ministries. She never received any money from international relief and development agencies. Local people who knew her from childhood supported her. Despite the financial and emotional stress, Evelyn chose connectedness over popularity—and influenced hundreds of lives.

I met Evelyn when she served as chair of the children's committee of our campaign in Davau City. She captured my attention through another surprising act of generosity.

Our campaign in the Philippines took place during a severe economic downturn. Our meetings had ended, we had thrown a little farewell party, and we were saying good-bye to members of the executive committee. As we finished the reception, Evelyn gave me a card. I figured it thanked us for coming to her country. But later, when I opened the envelope, I found three one-hundred-dollar American bills earmarked for our ministry. "Thank you for coming to our country," her note said. "We know that you didn't ask for any money from the committee, but I felt like I should give something."

I've always considered myself a giving person, but her example pushed me to become even more generous, more open, more sensitive and sacrificial. Imagine! A single Filipino woman—a school teacher who reared forty-two adopted children—gives me, a rich American (by Filipino standards), three hundred dollars! I consider Evelyn a living example of the grace of God. And I know her generous spirit didn't develop by accident; it blossomed when she consciously chose intimate connections with other human beings.

You might not feel able to adopt forty-two homeless youngsters, but how can you make vital, personal connections with the men and women around you? Please don't confuse popularity with friendship; they really have little in common.

Every Wednesday when I'm home, I get together at 6:30 in the morning with a group of nine men. We pray together and encourage one another. Most of these men have become my close, personal friends.

A few years back our group began to pray for a man who then served in the United States Senate. We sent him a letter and told him he was in our prayers. Terrible family problems hounded him, and eventually he felt as though everyone had abandoned him. On a visit to our area he asked us, "May I visit your prayer meeting?" For most of his political career he had enjoyed tremendous popularity. But because he never spent the time to forge deep, lasting connections with caring individuals, he found himself with nowhere to go when his world caved in.

People feel lonely in America. Some pay enormous amounts of money to feel less alone. They run up huge tabs for memberships in exclusive country clubs, for lavish parties, for escort services. Others, without great financial resources, feel confused about where to turn. Because the Lord knew this, he created his own club, his own society, to address the need:

the church, the Body of Christ, the family of God. It is there that God encourages us to connect at a deep level with others in his family.

Just a few days ago a friend told me about his friend's tragic loss. While driving with the couple's three children to visit members of her family in another state, his wife lost control of the car and died in a violent rollover. The crash severely injured two of the children.

Were you the husband in this tragedy, would you know where to seek help? To whom could you turn? Who would come to your aid? When this grieving man informed his church of the fatal accident, his pastor immediately accompanied him to the out-of-state hospital caring for his injured children. Other members of the congregation made travel plans to join them a few days later, and Christian friends from across the nation received briefings on the disaster and learned how to best help.

Nothing will restore the life of that man's wife—but how much better to endure such a tragedy with close friends at hand! Deep, heart-to-heart connections provide a reservoir of strength in dark times. And popularity? It offers not even a thimbleful of tepid water.

Flavor of the Day vs. Perennial Favorite

Popularity comes and goes, depending upon the mood of the day and the fashions of the moment. You can be popular one minute and forgotten the next. Off the top of your head, can you name the members of the rock group Boston, the most valuable player of the 1975 World Series, or the 1988 presidential and vice presidential nominees of the Democratic Party? No? Well, at one time, they all enjoyed substantial popularity. Now you need a good encyclopedia or Internet connection to find out their names.

Close personal connections, however, survive the passage of time. Tastes may change, but we'll always possess a sweet tooth for good, long-term friends.

My wife, Pat, and I treasure our long-time friendship with a couple from Bellingham, Washington. They're not popular speakers; they're not rich. They're just "ordinary folks." But Pat and I seldom feel more comfortable than when we spend time in their home. We've known them for almost forty years and they feel to us like "old shoes." We don't have to put on a show with them. If we're visiting at their home and want something to drink, we go to the kitchen and get it. We feel accepted, completely at home. We count both the husband and the wife a great blessing.

How many friends do *you* have, I wonder, with whom you can feel comfortable and relaxed, at ease and happy, with no need for putting on airs or pretending to be something you're not? No masks, no games, no pressure—just the satisfied feeling of being yourself and "at home"?

With such friends, you feel no need to impress, no need to preserve false expectations about how a "serious Christian" should conduct himself. You can make freewheeling comments or off-the-cuff statements that you would never want repeated in the newspaper (or even at the elders' meeting). You know that your good friends see you as part of themselves.

One word of caution, though: Long-term friendship doesn't mean nonstop contact. You can connect with people without hanging out on their doorstep day and night. Friendship demands wisdom. Some of the worst moral and sexual failures occur among "best friends," when couples get *too* close to each other.

Friendship has its limits. We need to set clear demarcation lines and establish appropriate fences and boundaries. Proverbs 25:17 says, "Seldom set foot in your neighbor's house—too much of you, and he will hate you." Boundaries create healthy friendships. Sexual temptation often hits among those who open up too much. If you've gotten too thick with each other, it's easy to slide into dangerous areas. Set boundaries around your conversation and how often you get together. Then don't cross those boundaries—you can't afford the risk.

Craves Compliments vs. Seeks Truth

Most individuals believe that to remain popular they have to hide their "ugly side." They live in fear that if the truth were ever discovered, their popularity would vaporize (and most of the time, they're right). So they inhabit a fantasy world of airbrushed facts, sugar-sweet flattery, and ego-inflating compliments.

While true friends speak kindly to one another, they don't hide the truth. Avoiding unpleasant facts may help to sustain one's popularity, but it acts like a cancer on true friendship. "Wounds from a friend can be trusted, but an enemy multiplies kisses," says Proverbs 27:6.

The truth can frighten us, however, and I suspect that's one reason some individuals collect a lot of acquaintances but few close friends. They refuse to take the risks required by honest friendship.

And risks there are. What if your honesty angers your friend and he slams the door in your face? What if the truth forces your friend to make unwanted changes? What if your honesty makes you a stench in the nostrils of others? What if you're wrong in your perception of "the facts"? What if you tell a friend the truth, thinking she'll feel grateful, but instead she attacks you for meddling?

Honesty with a friend can indeed entail risk—but without it, you can never develop personal connections capable of sustaining you in the tough times and delighting you in the good ones. Friendships based on truth grow stronger in the jungles of reality, but acquaintances addicted to flattery survive only while the bubble over fairyland remains.

How many "friends" deserted basketball superstar Kobe Bryant when he was charged with sexual assault in late 2003? How many stuck with fighter Leon Spinks after he lost his heavyweight championship belt? How many "friends" did Bill Clinton lose once he left the White House in 2000? A decade earlier, how many "friends" could Rob Pilatus and Fab Morvan count on when the press in 1990 exposed their act, Milli Vanilli, as a musical fraud? Apparently not many, for despite selling ten million albums and scoring five Top Five singles (including three number ones),

Pilatus tried to commit suicide in 1991 by jumping out of his Beverly Hills Hotel suite.

True friendship gets its toughest test after failure. It's then you discover your real friends. Genuine friends will tell you to your face that you messed up, then put their arm around you and figure out how, together, you can recover.

Fans just walk away.

Let's face it: friends make mistakes. More than once close friends of mine have made mistakes in interpreting my words or actions. They made me angry, but I knew that they loved me. Although they barked up the wrong tree, they barked well, and God used it. I knew their words came from pure love and nothing else.

Do you want your friends to put on an act for you? Friends don't always see or say things right, but you don't throw them out because they've ticked you off. Even if they goof up and make you look bad, you stand up for them.

Some time ago Pat and I stayed for a few days with some friends. At one point our hosts suffered a major marital blowup. To our eyes it seemed childish and embarrassing, but the incident also revealed the intense anger that had been building for years. The wife disappeared into the couple's bedroom for four long, uncomfortable hours.

In her prolonged absence, I got alone with my friend in the living room and tried to draw him out. He knew he had provoked his wife's explosion and seemed both eager and yet reticent to talk. I made some simple comments about husband-wife relationships, about how we all go through cycles when we can't explain why we lose self-control. Suddenly, to my surprise, this proud man who doesn't like to show weakness began to pour out his story.

Not everyone responds to truth in the same way. Sometimes a friend opens up, you offer help, and the friendship dies. It's not that you spoke improperly, but rather that your friend said things he or she later regretted. An instant and prolonged distance results.

Another friend once visited our home for a few days and said things he later regretted. From that moment on, our friendship more or less ended. Friendships can disintegrate; that's part of the risk. But why would anyone choose the alternative?

A friend of mine lives in a world where insincere compliments darken the air like overgrown vultures. He knows he needs truth amid these swarms of flattery, so he invites honesty from his closest friends.

We first met when he agreed to serve as chairman of one of our campaigns. I think he wanted not only to assist the campaign, but also to find help for his own troubled family. His work as a high-powered lawyer strained his relationships with both his wife and children. I sensed his need for a friend outside of politics and law, someone who wouldn't use personal information against him. Over the months he came closer to the Lord through our friendship.

Some time after the campaign, the president of the United States asked my friend to take a key federal position. He called me immediately to talk and pray. I counseled him to accept the job as a way to open doors, sow the gospel seed, and raise a light for the kingdom of God. He took the post and soon realized he had to dismiss several individuals from their jobs—including some who were his friends. When I read in the newspapers about the mess facing him, I called his office.

"You must be under heavy pressure," I said. "I just wanted to pray with you."

"Oh, man," he replied, "I was at the Kennedy Center last night, sitting next to a guy I have to dismiss this afternoon. You'd better believe I need prayer."

To this day he and I remain close. I could phone him right now and I imagine he'd take the call, even if he were leading an important meeting. Although we interact less often these days than we used to, no distance has grown between us. He would do anything for me, and I for him.

A word of caution here: Don't expect from friendship more than friendship can deliver. If you're looking to a human friend for what only God can supply, you're going to be disappointed. Don't demand from your friend what only Jesus Christ can give you.

A merely human friend can't give you fulfillment, peace, or joy, but Jesus specializes in all three. He secured them for you on the cross, explaining before his death that "Greater love has no one than this, that one lay down his life for his friends" (John 15:13). Jesus could rightfully insist that we drop everything to serve his every desire, but he doesn't. Instead, he says to us, as he did to his disciples, "I no longer call you servants, because a servant does not know his master's business. Instead, I have called you friends, for everything that I learned from my Father I have made known to you" (John 15:15).

Friends. On the lips of Jesus, it has a nice ring, doesn't it?

Known Widely vs. Known Deeply

If one intimate friend is good, would twenty be better? Thirty? Fifty? A thousand?

Not necessarily.

I don't believe you can develop a lot of close friends. Popularity may clamor for multitudes of adoring fans, but connectedness cannot happen without limit. While popularity opts for breadth, friendship thrives on depth.

Why the difference? Popularity doesn't need to spend time with its admirers; its interests lie primarily in receiving, not giving. The greater the number of fans, the better—and it doesn't much matter whether they're near or distant. So long as one can hear their applause, they serve their purpose.

Close friends, however, must be cultivated. You can't nurture an intimate friendship without spending significant amounts of time with your friend, one-to-one. Hearing a friend's applause doesn't interest you nearly so much as listening for his or her whisper of counsel, encouragement, or warning.

Experience tells me that we possess differing capacities for maintaining close friendships. Three or four is more than enough for some. The way their life boxes them in, the way their responsibilities clamor for their attention, they can't handle more than four good friends—and they shouldn't feel guilty about it.

Really, you don't need dozens of friends. You can befriend only so many people. Time doesn't allow for more; neither does life. Even Jesus, the Son of God, developed only a few close friends during his earthly ministry. You could think of his "friendship life" as a series of concentric circles.

In the outer ring stood the crowds, the multitudes, who surrounded him wherever he went. Jesus ministered to them and taught them and loved them, but he didn't choose them for his closest friends. In the next circle we see a smaller group of devoted followers, numbering anywhere from 72 (Luke 10) to 120 (Acts 1:15). The men and women in this group ministered with Jesus and represented him to others, but they couldn't be called close friends. Step another circle closer to the center, and we encounter the Lord's core group of twelve disciples. He ate with these men, traveled with them, challenged them, led them. He called them all his friends, even though one betrayed him.

Still, these men didn't qualify as his closest friends. That distinction went to three disciples in the circle just one ring from the center. Peter, James, and John knew Jesus better than anyone on earth. Only these three did Jesus Christ invite to the "Mount of Transfiguration" where he revealed his glory (Matt. 17:1–13). It was these three whose help in prayer he requested just before his arrest and crucifixion (Matt. 26:36–46).

But at the very center of all these circles stood one man, John, whom the Bible consistently calls "the disciple whom Jesus loved" (John 13:23; 21:7, 20). It was John to whom Jesus entrusted the care of his mother (John 19:25–27). John must be considered the Savior's closest earthly friend.

The example of Jesus suggests that if you value close friendships over popularity, you can't have many intimate friends. Life simply doesn't allow for it. Instead, resolve now to develop a few rich, heart-to-heart connections. My wife does not make friendships easily, but when she does, they last a lifetime. Whether her close friends come from socio-economic positions above or below her, she feels neither embarrassed by the one nor proud of the other. They're her friends, and she doesn't give a second thought to their social status.

So where can you find the person who will become your closest friend? First, look for someone whose heart beats like yours on many fundamental issues. For a close friendship to develop, there must exist a commonality, similar dreams and ambitions and goals and views of life. Think of close friendship as a form of teamwork. "If one falls down, his friend can help him up," says Ecclesiastes 4:10. "But pity the man who falls and has no one to help him up!" The book of Proverbs adds, "A friend loves at all times" (17:17), and most tellingly, "A man of many companions may come to ruin, but there is a friend who sticks closer than a brother" (18:24).

We all crave a few companions with whom our friendship goes so deep, with roots so strong, that nothing can break the connection. Solomon spoke of such an indestructible bond with his wife and best friend: "Many waters can never quench love," he said (Song of Songs 8:7). We all need a few friendships like that.

And how do we nurture them, once we've made the connection? You have to spend a lot of time talking about the deep and serious things of life: Intimacy cannot develop without opening up to each other and exposing your heart.

My closest friends all are Christians. I counted the late Ray Sted-man as one of my most intimate friends. Though two years could go by without seeing each other, if I picked up the phone or he called me, it was as if we had spoken to each other the day before.

How did we get to that point? Through his selfless love. From the moment he met me during a missions trip to South America, he took the initiative to cultivate our friendship. I knew he would stand with me if I had done the worst thing in the world. He never walked out on me, never gave up on me, but habitually went out of his way to help and encourage.

You may not have a Ray Stedman in your life, but if you're married, do you realize that your spouse could become your best friend? Many years ago I bought a book for Pat called *My Best Friend*. As I scribbled a few words to her, I realized for the first time: Pat *is* my best friend! Until then, I had buddies whom I considered soul brothers, while I thought of my wife as, well . . . just my wife. I loved Pat, I would do anything for her, we had four children together—but I considered her almost an appendage.

On that day, however, it struck me: My best friend is Pat, right here, right with me. While our personalities differ greatly, we share the same basic outlook, the same goals, the same mission. Out of such shared commitments develop best friends!

Could your spouse become your best friend, too? Sure—if you choose to make it so.

Seeks to Be a Star vs. Desires to Be a Friend

The other day I read an article about Judy Garland, perhaps the greatest entertainer of the twentieth century. With her golden voice and magnetic screen presence, the woman who portrayed Dorothy in the film classic *The Wizard of Oz* commanded worldwide attention. Yet she told a writer for *Forbes* magazine, "If I'm such a legend, why am I so lonely?"

A legend? You bet. Famous? All over the world. A star? Certainly. Popular? No question. And yet Judy Garland died in the middle of the night from an accidental overdose of drugs—a broken and lonely woman.

Stardom may shine brightly for a while, but its light remains fitful and icy cold. Genuine connectedness may not attract the glare of the media, but its arms provide a comforting, steady warmth. Which do you choose?

If you opt for friendship, realize that you're going to need help in developing the solid connections you really want. If you genuinely desire to knit yourself to others at the deepest level, you can't do it alone. The media can't help you; money can't help you; not even the most insightful psychiatrist can help you. The deepest form of friendship develops only with divine help.

As a little boy I used to sing, "The best friend to have is Jesus." I believed it then, and I heartily believe it today. When Jesus lives in your heart, other friendships become more meaningful, more valuable, more fulfilling. Why? Because you feel at peace. You don't depend upon some flawed human to be your closest friend.

I personally live by this philosophy. Without question, Jesus Christ is my best friend. If everyone else let me down, I'd be horribly disappointed and sad, but I wouldn't grow desperate. I know I have a friend who will never leave me and never forsake me. I know I can depend on him completely.

Jesus improves all my friendships. I don't have to cling to my friends, and I don't want my friends to cling to me. I'm really not worth being clung to. There is a limit to how much I can take of my friends, no matter how wonderful they may be. And there's certainly a limit to how much they can take of me, no matter how marvelous I may be.

Jesus gives purpose to my friendships. If I'm convinced in my heart that I'm on the right track, I don't need to hear from a friend, "You're doing the right thing, buddy." I get my approval from Jesus Christ; therefore my friendships can be unselfish.

Now, don't get me wrong; it's nice to hear a friend say comforting things. But when Jesus is your best friend, you don't get desperate when nobody speaks pleasant words to you. If I were stranded on a deserted island, I'm quite sure I wouldn't lose my mind. I'd miss my loved ones terribly, but I wouldn't feel desperate.

Did you see Tom Hanks in the movie *Castaway*? His portrayal of a man stranded alone on a tiny South Pacific island earned him an Academy Award nomination. Hanks's character couldn't stand the isolation, so when a volleyball washed up on shore, he used his own blood to paint a face on it, gave it hair of weeds, named his creation "Wilson," and made it his best friend. He spoke to it, yelled at it, stroked it, embraced it, and almost lost his life for it when it drifted away on strong ocean currents.

Hanks unforgettably illustrates the human need for friends. But he also makes me wonder: Would I need a Wilson if I were marooned on a forgotten chunk of rock in the middle of the wide, blue ocean? Honestly, I don't think so. I'd feel achingly alone, sure, and I'd try my best to get home. But I don't think I'd need a Wilson; I already have a best friend named Jesus. And I'd much rather talk to him than to a volleyball with bad hair and a bloody nose.

At the age of forty-four, Elvis Presley booked his last show in Las Vegas. A newspaper reporter came to his hotel room and asked, "Elvis, when you started out you said you wanted three things out of life. You said, 'I want to be rich, I want to be famous, and I want to be happy.' Are you happy?"

And Elvis Presley—"the king of rock and roll"—replied, "No, I'm not happy. I'm lonely."

"The king" died a few months later.

During his life, crowds of fans mobbed Elvis wherever he went. He had to hide out to enjoy any kind of privacy. Elvis had all the money in the world. Women screamed his name and tried to grab handfuls of his clothes. Yet at the end he said he felt terribly lonely. Why was that?

I believe he was talking about an inner loneliness, a spiritual loneliness. You see, Elvis grew up in a good Christian church. His father and mother used to take him to worship services. He did his first public singing in church. But there is a huge difference between going to church and meeting the Lord Jesus. You have to solidify your friendship with Jesus Christ, because only he can give you inner peace, real rest, and a sense of balance.

A Few Guidelines

What should you do if you really want to develop a few close friends, but you're not sure how to start? What should you keep in mind? Allow me to sketch out a few guidelines in your quest to get connected.

Be a friend to win a friend.

Don't go around looking for friends; just be friendly. Remember the maxim, "He who would have friends must show himself friendly." People will then feel drawn to you and will say, "I could enjoy this person as a friend."

At the same time, realize that friends don't just show up on your doorstep. In rare cases friendship begins instantly, but even then it takes genuine give-and-take. It isn't a one-way street. You must cultivate friendship; it doesn't grow automatically.

Don't try to push friendship.

Friendship can't be pushed or forced. You can't demand friendship or manufacture it. It's not contrived; it can't be planned. You can enrich it, water it, develop it, but it happens naturally, one step at a time.

I bumped into most of those who became my friends; our relationship developed from there. I remember a businessman who tried to force a close friendship between us, but the nature of his personality made that impossible. One day he approached a good friend of mine and said, "I believe God wants me to be Luis's personal friend and mentor"—even though he's much younger than I. Nothing ever happened.

Don't expect instant connections.

Friendships aren't like instant coffee; they develop one step at a time. Even after spending four years with a college roommate, you may not know much about the person. So see how the friendship goes. Observe how he or she responds in a variety of situations. Then ask yourself, "Is this going to be worth pursuing? Is this going to be a lifelong connection, or just a passing thing—good but momentary?"

Make sure you're trustworthy.

Friendship demands trust. Can your friends trust you? If they tell you a secret, does the information stay just between you two? If you make a promise, do you keep it? If you say you're coming at 8:15, do you come at 8:15? If you must be late, do you call and explain why? Don't expect real friends to bear with your untrustworthiness. That's a friendship killer.

Look to give more than you get.

Friendship is more of a giving thing than a getting thing. You don't make friends in order to get something. If you try it, you're bound to fail. Many individuals don't have friends because they want only to receive, not give. They feel a lack in their inner person and want someone to fill it. True friendship is a give-and-take. Make up your mind to give more than you take.

Recognize that healthy friendships elevate you.

A healthy friendship elevates you; a sick friendship drags you down. While you look to encourage and raise up the person you befriend, also make sure you pick friends who encourage you and make you a better person.

Make sure you have realistic expectations.

What do you expect of a friend? What do you need? What are you looking for? Probe deeply. Answer the question, "What am I looking for, and why?" Above all, realize that your friend can't give you everything you need. Never expect a friend to supply what only Jesus Christ can deliver.

Identify potential friends within your normal sphere of activity.

Make a list of the people in your sphere of activity with whom you believe you could develop close friendships. Begin to show respect and love for them. Friendship happens where you live, where you go to church, where you work. Look around and ask, "Who are the kind of people to whom I'd like to feel close? Where can I enrich them and they me? How could we be mutually healthy for each other?" Certainly you can't go shopping for friends like you're looking for fresh vegetables at the supermarket, but you can keep your eyes open.

Look for men and women with big vision.

It's fun to have friends with big vision, with huge dreams. I enjoy friends who aren't satisfied with the way things are, who want their lives to make a difference in the world. I also enjoy people who don't see life as one big party, who don't always insist on having fun. My kind of friends enjoy the moment, the nice things of life, a good party, but they concentrate on how to do the most good in the least amount of time.

Look for spiritually serious friends.

Look for morally honorable and spiritually serious friends. Someone with a reputation as "the life of the party" may be a lot of fun during the good times, but lifeless otherwise. Those who take seriously their commitment to Jesus Christ, but who can poke fun at themselves, provide your best bets for potential friends.

Don't test your friendship.

You don't test a friendship. A friendship either exists or it doesn't. You don't need to spend your life trying to figure out if someone is really your friend. You're either a friend and you know it, or you aren't. Never try pushing the boundaries in order to test the strength of your friendship, to see whether your friend will stick by you. That's a test you can fail just by handing it out.

Pray.

Ask God to open your eyes to the friendships he has for you.

The Cure for Spiritual Loneliness

God created us to live in the company of others. All of us long for the sort of companion the Bible speaks about, a friend who sticks closer than a brother (Prov. 18:24). I believe that friend is Jesus Christ. He is the only one who can fill the profound vacuum at the level of spiritual loneliness.

You may be Catholic, you may be Protestant, you may be any or no religion, but until you open your heart to Jesus Christ, you will continue to feel lonely when you allow yourself time to think.

During a midnight television broadcast a young boy with a high-pitched voice called our program. "Mr. Palau," he said, "I'm all alone, and it's so scary out here."

"Why are you alone?" I asked.

"My dad is in the bar, gone somewhere."

"And where's your mom?"

"She left us four years ago when I was eight."

"Don't you have brothers and sisters?"

"Yes, I have two sisters. One has two babies, but she's not married and lives in another town. The other one's on drugs and she never comes home."

"You're all alone at home? What time will your dad come back?"

"Probably four in the morning. And I'm so lonely and so scared."

How many kids today feel this kind of deep loneliness? How many adults? I felt a profound sadness as I spoke with my young caller. "Tomorrow night you come to the crusade at the stadium," I told him. "I'm going to introduce you to a bunch of people who are going to love you."

When the boy showed up the next day, I gave him a big hug and we prayed together. What a loveable kid! And so lonely. But this twelve-year-old gave his life to Jesus Christ, and we introduced him to a local youth group. The church took the boy under its wing and cared for him. Today he no longer feels so lonely.

Loneliness can be cured. Jesus Christ died and rose again so that we might call him "friend" and so that we might be linked together as brothers and sisters in God's family. Everyone has moments of being alone, but we never have to feel isolated and lonely again.

Jesus sees to that.

How to Get Connected According to the Bible

1. *Admit your need for others.*
   "If one falls down, his friend can help him up. But pity the man who falls and has no one to help him up! Also, if two lie down together, they will keep warm. But how can one keep warm alone? Though one may be overpowered, two can defend themselves. A cord of three strands is not quickly broken" (Eccles. 4:10–12).
2. *Develop a few close friends rather than a boatload of acquaintances.*
   "A man of many companions may come to ruin, but there is a friend who sticks closer than a brother" (Prov. 18:24).
3. *Be gently honest with others, and genuinely value their honesty in return.*
   "Wounds from a friend can be trusted, but an enemy multiplies kisses" (Prov. 27:6).
4. *Recognize that true friendship will require self-sacrifice.*
   "Be imitators of God, therefore, as dearly loved children and live a life of love, just as Christ loved us and gave himself up for us" (Eph. 5:1–2).
5. *Remember that no one likes to hear you talk incessantly about yourself.*
   "Do not be conceited" (Rom. 12:16).
6. *Be more concerned about a person's humanity than his or her social status.*
   "Do not be proud, but be willing to associate with people of low position" (Rom. 12:16).
7. *Throttle your selfish instincts and look for ways to show respect to others.*
   "Honor one another above yourselves" (Rom. 12:10).
8. *Refuse to give bitterness any place in your soul.*
   "Be kind and compassionate to one another, forgiving each other, just as in Christ God forgave you" (Eph. 4:32).

9. *Don't concentrate merely on your own fun, but think of ways to reach out to others.*

"And let us consider how we may spur one another on toward love and good deeds" (Heb. 10:24).

10. *Find a good church and build God-centered friendships there.*

"Let us not give up meeting together, as some are in the habit of doing, but let us encourage one another—and all the more as you see the Day approaching" (Heb. 10:25).

4

A Fresh Start

Acceptance or Forgiveness?

If you forgive men when they sin against you, your heavenly Father will also forgive you. But if you do not forgive men their sins, your Father will not forgive your sins.

Jesus, in Matthew 6:14

Fernando Montero had the world by the tail—wealth, prestige, power, influence. He had it all. With an internationally acclaimed artist for a father and armed with an MBA from Harvard University, Fernando had climbed the political ladder to become secretary of defense for Colombia at thirty-seven years of age. He ran the nation's army and directed its attacks against the powerful Cali drug cartel.

And then something went terribly wrong.

He was accused of using drug money to finance the political campaign of the president. Montero landed behind bars in a military penitentiary. Prison officials cut him off from all contact with the outside world. No journalist could speak with him; no friends could see him. Neither his father nor his wife even tried to visit him in jail.

Eventually a friend managed to smuggle a Bible into Montero's cell, urging him to read the book of Romans. Fernando had never heard the gospel of Jesus Christ, and while the ancient book intrigued him, it also confused him.

A few years ago Promise Keepers invited me to Bogota to speak on its behalf, and during our visit an associate of Fernando asked me to try to visit his jailed friend. I agreed. We thought the guards would turn us away at the gate, but to our surprise, they let us in. "Just leave your passports here," they ordered.

We entered the compound and spent forty-five minutes with a weary and confused Fernando. He told us that he had read the book of Romans, but said, "I don't get it. I just don't get it." It quickly became clear to me that Fernando's main problem was the load of sin he carried. He confessed that he had committed a lot of sins—he admitted he had been imprisoned partially because of his misconduct, partially because friends had betrayed him; he hid nothing. He just couldn't see how God could possibly forgive him.

I drove home the first verse of Romans 8 ("Therefore, there is now no condemnation for those who are in Christ Jesus") and emphasized the absolute and total forgiveness God offers to those who place their faith in Jesus Christ. "All of it can be forgiven right now," I declared repeatedly. "All of it, right now, forever." At the end of our short time together, God totally broke this man. We got on our knees and Fernando asked the Lord for forgiveness—still amazed that God could forgive him so completely.

Some time later, after his release from prison, Fernando moved to London. During one of our trips to England, Pat and I invited him over to our hotel for tea. When Pat went down to the lobby to meet him, he greeted her with the words, "The thing that got me was that your husband assured me from the Bible that ALL my sins were forgiven in one moment, forever, never to be brought up again." He could not get over the forgiving heart of God.

A few days after this visit, Fernando told his story to a group of English businessmen. "I never would have listened to the message of Jesus Christ if I hadn't been in jail," he admitted. "I was too arrogant, too proud, and wouldn't even have talked to Palau had he come to see me when I was in power. I wouldn't have received him for three minutes. But in jail I was desperate, I was in a crisis—and God used it."

I'm So Unworthy

You can't imagine how many individuals all over the world have told me, "I feel exactly like Fernando. I have committed so many sins. I am so unworthy."

Most of us admit to feelings of unworthiness. Maybe we grew up in church, went to mass, did first communion, spent a week at Bible camp, attended Sunday school, or memorized some Bible verses. But somehow we got off track, married wrong, walked out of the church, got divorced, and now feel so guilty that we believe God will never take us back. *I'm finished,* we think. *God is through with me. Jesus is fine for good people, but not for me. For church people, but not for me. Good for people who believe like I did when I was a kid, but now there's no hope for me.*

We're surrounded by men and women who feel as though God is through with them. Many of them faithfully attend church, but have never fully understood the grace and forgiveness of God.

While the Bible insists that Jesus Christ offers forgiveness as a free gift, many of us think, *I've got to become religious first. I have to pay my dues. I've got to make a special effort. I have to make difficult promises and get my act together.*

None of that is true. The Bible says God longs to set you free, if you open your heart to Jesus Christ and say, "Lord Jesus, I am unworthy. You know the thoughts I've thought. You know the deeds I've done. But if you really died for me, Lord, and you rose from the dead—then please cleanse my conscience. Forgive my past. Set me free!"

By asking for Jesus Christ's forgiveness you can fly again. There's no need to live in fear of dark secrets.

Every one of us, if we're honest, knows that we've done disgraceful things. We all need forgiveness. Yet many times we don't seek out what we really need. Too often we settle for a substitute that doesn't go quite far enough. We settle for acceptance when we really need forgiveness.

The difference isn't as subtle as it might first appear. Forgiveness wipes the slate clean, while acceptance merely covers it. The first says, "forgive me"; the second says, "excuse me." Forgiveness fully acknowledges the wrong that has been done, while acceptance often minimizes the offense just to keep the relationship going.

Nobody likes to walk around with a cloud hanging over his or her head. That's probably why our culture so strongly emphasizes "tolerance" and "accepting" others—and that's good, so far as it goes. Yet to feel fully whole, what we really crave is forgiveness, a wiping clean of the slate.

Forgiveness outperforms mere acceptance in at least five important ways:

Acceptance	Forgiveness
• Offers a Way to Continue	• Permits a Fresh Start
• Supplies Emotional Respite	• Provides Emotional Release
• Based on Technique	• Based on Truth
• Manages Guilt	• Removes Guilt
• Stops the Bleeding	• Fosters Healing

We ought to accept others for who and what they are, but when by our actions we injure or damage a cherished relationship, we need more than mere acceptance. "Excuse me" can never fully substitute for "forgive me."

Offers a Way to Continue vs. Permits a Fresh Start

We like to hear a friend say, "Just forget about it," when we pull some boneheaded move. And very often, nothing more is required. Friends accept their friends and understand that everybody makes mistakes. If we called in the road repair crew for every relational bump in the road, we'd never get anywhere. "Just forget about it," "It's okay," "It's no big deal," and "Let's just move on" work fine much of the time. An attitude of acceptance allows us to continue, to keep plowing ahead.

Sometimes, however, we don't need a way to continue so much as we require a fresh start. Some patterns need to be broken—but they'll never come to an end if we don't stop dead in our tracks, name them for what they are, express genuine sorrow for the pain we have caused, and ask for forgiveness.

Did you know that *repentance* is the most positive word in the English language? I never thought of it like that until I heard my friend John Hunter make the claim. We usually think of *repentance* as a sad, dark, and horrible term; actually, it's the greatest term in the world. It's the beginning of a new life. It's leaving the past behind. It's starting over. It's a very liberating word.

To repent means simply to admit the truth and to start moving in a different direction. The way out is to admit the truth: I've failed; I have caused pain; I have done wrong. Repentance doesn't mean beating your breast and burning a candle. Repentance doesn't mean groveling in the dirt and acting weird. Repentance is a deep conviction that I did wrong, I hurt other people, I offended God—and I want to change. That's really the only way to start over. Repentance means taking responsibility for our actions and saying, "Yes, I've sinned against my spouse [or my neighbor], I am sorry for it, and by the power of God I intend to start behaving in a healthier way."

Many years ago I heard a sermon on forgiving others as Jesus Christ forgave us (Col. 3:13). The speaker explained how a father could alienate his children and forfeit an adult relationship with them by something he did years before. "Maybe it's as small as a broken promise," he said.

That sermon burned a hole into my soul. I returned home quickly and separately called in my twin sons, who were then about nine years old.

"Kevin," I said to the first, "have I ever promised you anything that I haven't fulfilled? Or have I ever said anything to you that hurt your feelings, but never asked you for forgiveness?"

"Yes, Dad," he immediately replied. "Last Christmas you promised Keith and me a special toy that I really wanted and you never gave it to me."

I hugged my son to my chest and said, "Kevin, please forgive me."

"I forgive you, Dad."

"Okay, Kevin, we're going to the shopping center today and I'm going to buy you that toy. Anything else I promised you but never delivered?"

"No, I can't remember anything."

"Have I ever offended you and never asked you for forgiveness?"

"No, Dad, I don't think so."

I dismissed Kevin and called in Keith. "Keith," I said, "have I ever promised you anything that I haven't fulfilled?"

"Yes."

"What?"

"Last Christmas you promised me a special toy"—the same toy Kevin wanted—"but you never gave it to me."

Apparently, I had blown it big-time with my boys—and I didn't even know it.

"Okay," I said, "I'm going to buy you one today. Will you forgive me?"

"Yes, I forgive you."

"Have I ever really hurt your feelings, Keith, but never asked you for forgiveness?"

"Yes."

I didn't expect *that* answer.

"What did I do?" I asked.

"Do you remember when Stephen was born?"

He had appeared on the scene six years earlier.

"Yes, I remember when Stephen was born. What happened?"

"Do you remember when Mom was going to have Stephen, you jumped in the car and took off for the hospital in Mexico City?"

"Yes, I remember that."

"You came back a half hour later. You had forgotten the suitcase for the baby."

"I don't remember that."

"Well, I remember."

"And what happened?"

"The suitcase was all messed up and you spanked me because you thought I had messed it up."

"But you didn't mess it up?"

"No. One of the neighbor boys did it."

Boy, I felt so rotten. Six years! Keith had never forgotten that I spanked him unjustly. I immediately drew him close and said, "Keith, I spanked you for something you didn't do. Will you forgive me?"

"Sure, I forgive you."

Twenty years later we were talking about this incident and Keith said, laughing, "You know, Dad, you took advantage of us. We were only nine years old and didn't realize the goldmine you offered us. Why don't you ask us *now* if you made any promises you haven't kept?"

Acceptance provides a good and necessary service, but it will never heal the wounds that only repentance and forgiveness can treat. Sometimes we hurt someone and quickly forget the incident—but the injured party never does. Multiply forgotten toys and undeserved spankings by a thousand, and you soon begin to see the necessary place of repentance and forgiveness.

Supplies Emotional Respite vs. Provides Emotional Release

When we have wronged a person, acceptance allows the relationship to continue by providing an emotional respite from the pain. When the aggrieved person decides to forget the matter and "let bygones be bygones," we can maintain our interaction at a certain level.

But unless the aggrieved party forgives—until we bring the problem into the light of day and fully and finally deal with it—we're only shooting Novocain into an infected foot. The treatment brings some relief from the pain and allows us to continue walking, but the infection never gets any better.

An emotional respite feels nice, but emotional freedom feels a whole lot better. Parole may brighten our day, but freedom brightens our life. And freedom really is the issue.

During his boyhood days, a friend of mine noticed that an uncle seemed always to hang around the family farm. One day this uncle offered to take my friend's mom shopping. My friend, who was only five-and-a-half, thought, *Hey, this is fantastic! I'm going to hide in the back of the car. At the shopping center, I'll pop my head up and then they'll buy me something.*

So the little boy threw himself on the floor in the back of the car before it zoomed away. But instead of heading toward a shopping center, the car stopped in a park. My friend grew frightened when he heard a commotion from the front seat. After several minutes of odd noises, the curious boy poked his little head over the backseat—and there was his mother, lying on her back, with the uncle carrying on.

The mother panicked. Both she and the uncle jumped up, and the uncle threatened the boy, "If you ever tell your dad about this—if you ever tell a soul—I'm going to get you." My friend never saw this uncle after that day.

Years later, my friend, a successful businessman, took care of his elderly parents until they died, his mother succumbing six months after his father. At age fifty-seven, my friend confessed to me, "Luis, you know the thing that really hurt? As the years went on, my mother never apologized. She never said, 'I'm sorry.' She never talked about it. My father never found out, and I didn't have the heart to tell him."

Although my friend faithfully attends church and everyone considers him a great guy, he suffered a massive breakdown shortly after his parents died. He never forgave his mother, and memories of their unresolved problem demolished him. Imagine—a bright guy, an inventor, a millionaire who collapsed emotionally because he never resolved the festering anger in his soul. He needed the emotional release of forgiveness, not the emotional respite of acceptance.

In Matthew 18 Jesus told a parable about the necessity of forgiving others. Those who refuse to forgive, he said, would only slam the door on their own prison cell. Unforgiving people can expect only "anger" and "torture," Jesus said. And he ended his story with the sobering words, "This is how my heavenly Father will treat each of you unless you forgive your brother from your heart" (v. 35).

But Jesus wants us to walk free!

A young Scottish woman made this discovery after spending several years behind emotional bars. Her father abandoned the family and took off to work in Saudi Arabia. Bitterness gripped her heart, and over time a nasty grudge against her father grew ever larger. Eventually she gave her life to Jesus Christ, but still she refused to forgive the old boy.

One day she heard the words of Jesus: "If you forgive men when they sin against you, your heavenly Father will also forgive you. But if you do not forgive men their sins, your Father will not forgive your sins" (Matt. 6:14–15). She took her Lord's warning to heart and wrote a letter to her father, telling him that, because of Jesus's love, she forgave him for walking away and never returning.

To her surprise, the heartbroken old man immediately wrote a reply, asking for her forgiveness . . . and asking her mother if he could come home.

Forgiveness sets you free. If you allow yourself to grow bitter and angry in your heart, you are the one who pays. My wife and I were talking recently about some friends from England. Five years ago the husband announced to his wife, "I'm tired of you. You talk, talk, talk. You're pushy. We're never separated from each other. You're a good cook, but my mother was better . . ."

He rattled off all sorts of hurtful lines. He left his wife and took off with a woman he knew when both were teenagers. For the first few months after the split, the wife felt terrible anger—and rightly so. It hurts to be abandoned for someone else. At first she told us she could have shot her husband. But one Christmas Day she called my wife from England.

"I'm free!" she cried. "I'm free!"

Pat mistakenly thought she had gotten a divorce. "No," our friend explained, "I didn't divorce him. I forgave him."

Ten days before Christmas, this woman finally decided that her bitterness and anger were destroying her. So she declared, "Just as God in Christ has forgiven me, I forgive him. And I feel so free!" Since that day—and it's been several years—she has enjoyed true freedom. We are free when we forgive!

Based on Technique vs. Based on Truth

While we all instinctively recognize our need for forgiveness, human beings have developed hosts of techniques to deal with guilt apart from forgiveness. We deny it. We dull its pain through drugs or alcohol or sex. We try to ignore it, pacify it, redefine it through expensive psychological procedures. We ask spiritists to remove the curse we imagine rests on us. We adopt atheism, hoping that our feelings of guilt will go away if we make God go away. We try to counterbalance our evil deeds with good deeds. And some who grow weary of the struggle commit suicide.

But none of these techniques ultimately work, because they never deal completely with the truth of our guilt. You cannot do enough penance to remove your guilt. Only Jesus Christ can remove it, because only he has the power and wisdom to oppose it at its source. As the apostle Paul said, "When you were dead in your sins and in the uncircumcision of your sinful nature, God made you alive with Christ. He forgave us all our sins, having canceled the written code, with its regulations, that was against us and that stood opposed to us; he took it away, nailing it to the cross" (Col. 2:13–14). Jesus provides forgiveness through truth.

During an encounter with the communist party secretary of Ecuador several years ago, I had only the truth of Jesus Christ to offer.

This woman, a bitter revolutionary, came to see me after she'd watched one of our call-in television programs. She cursed me out and my mother too, insulted me repeatedly, and proudly described herself as an atheist. She said she came from an upper-class, Catholic background, but had long ago abandoned the church. When her mother died, she attended the funeral primarily to mock the archbishop, who did the honors. She'd married and divorced three times. She seethed with anger. But I could tell she felt profoundly guilty for her revolutionary activities.

So I thought, *What Bible verse shall I quote?* Hebrews 10:17—and *only* Hebrews 10:17—came to mind: "Your sins and lawless acts I will remember no more."

"Well, I don't believe the Bible is the Word of God," she spat at me.

"You may not believe it," I said, "but God says, 'Your sins and lawless acts I will remember no more.'"

"Oh, you priests and Saint Paul are all alike! Cheats and liars every one."

"Even if that were true," I repeated, "God still says, 'Your sins and lawless acts I will remember no more.'"

Our wrestling match went on for an hour and a half. I counted how many times I quoted the verse: seventeen. Toward the end she began to cry. "If there is a God," she said, "do you think he would forgive a woman like me?"

And I repeated one last time, "Your sins and lawless acts I will remember no more."

She paused, then said slowly, "If God can forgive me, he can forgive anyone in the world." And right there she asked the Lord Jesus to forgive her sins and make her clean. She gave up her party membership and was marvelously and completely converted to Jesus Christ.

How does Christ forgive us? First, he forgives us while we are still guilty: "God demonstrates his own love for us in this: While we were still sinners, Christ died for us" (Rom. 5:8). Christ died on the cross to forgive us when we were still rebels. He forgives us out of his own free will. All he asks is that we come to him with sincere hearts and say, "God, please forgive me and make me your child." Believe that he died on the cross for you and that he rose again from the grave to give you life. As the apostle Paul said, "If you confess with your mouth, 'Jesus is Lord,' and believe in your heart that God raised him from the dead, you will be saved" (Rom. 10:9).

Jesus deals with our guilt not by applying some sophisticated technique, but by taking our sin upon himself. "God was reconciling the world to himself in Christ, not counting men's sins against them," Paul tells us. How? "God made him who had no sin [Christ] to be sin for us, so that in him we might become the righteousness of God" (2 Cor. 5:19, 21).

When we visited Russia just before the fall of the Soviet Union, we met thousands of men and women who longed to be free of personal guilt. For seventy years their atheistic masters had told them that sin did not exist, that guilt was the figment of a sick religious imagination and nothing but a priestly tool to keep them in bondage. But they knew better. I'll never forget the tears of regret we saw everywhere—constant, abundant, and freely flowing. We didn't stay for long, visiting five cities in nine days. But it was enough to witness a national outpouring of grief, especially when I talked about forgiveness. When I started naming promises from the Bible, the crowds just broke down and sobbed. It touched me deeply. As I stood behind the pulpit a voice in the audience would call out something in Russian.

"What is she saying?" I'd ask my interpreter.

"They are all saying, 'Am I forgiven? Am I forgiven?'" he would reply. They kept asking that one question over and over again, no matter where in the country we went.

On the cross Jesus dealt decisively with our guilt. The Bible says his blood keeps on cleansing us from all sin, as long as we are living in the light of God's presence (1 John 1:7). And it doesn't matter what sins we might have committed.

My wife and I were having breakfast at the home of some friends whose daughter had just endured a messy divorce. When the daughter and her Marine husband lived in Hawaii, a friend arrived for a three-week visit. While her husband left for work, this fellow walked over to the beach and swam, then came back to chitchat with the wife. After about a week and a half, he began to make little jokes and coy passes. Eventually he got a little more brazen—and she accepted it. In a moment of weakness, he threw himself at her, she surrendered, and they committed sexual immorality.

When she realized what she'd done, she fell apart. She told the man to leave, but he hung around until the end of the third week. She didn't know whether to tell her husband, but finally she felt so guilty and miserable that she said, "I have to tell you something and I need your forgiveness." Hearing his wife's confession, this young husband got so upset that he threw her out and immediately filed for divorce. And just like that, the marriage ended.

The young woman suffered a massive breakdown and moved in with her parents. Neither psychologists nor psychiatrists could do a thing to help her. So when Pat and I arrived, her parents asked, "Would you talk to our daughter? Maybe you can do something to help."

We agreed, and when their daughter told us her story she began to weep uncontrollably.

"You know, there's forgiveness," we said. "The beauty is that the Lord Jesus will forgive you. The Bible says that the blood of Christ will cleanse you from all sin—every sin is forgiven."

"But I did it!" she kept repeating. "I did it! I knew it was wrong. I knew it wasn't right, but I did it anyway. It was my fault. Now my husband's remarried and I'm a wreck."

She spoke the truth. It *was* her fault, and she *was* a wreck. She had completely fallen apart.

"God will *never* forgive me!" she insisted. "Look at what I did to my home!"

For an hour and a half we read passage after passage from the Bible, assuring her of God's love. Finally God's Word started to penetrate the fog around her tortured mind. The tears dried up and understanding began to glow in her wet eyes. That day this young woman, only twenty-six, opened her heart to the Lord Jesus. Of course, she needed further counsel to help her remake her life, but she took the first step that day by asking Jesus Christ to forgive her and take away her guilt.

That was many years ago. This woman is now fifty but still lives in the grace and forgiveness of Jesus Christ. She enjoys peace with God. She's a happy woman again. The memories remain, but they have forever lost their power to terrorize. Why? Because when the Lord Jesus forgives, he forgives *completely*.

Manages Guilt vs. Removes Guilt

Most psychologists will tell you that unresolved guilt accounts for about 80 percent of all psychological and psychiatric problems. Men and women are desperately looking for relief from guilt.

The late English writer Somerset Maugham once said, "If I wrote down every thought I've ever thought, and every deed I've ever done, people would call me a monster of depravity."

Thousands of individuals live in fear of being discovered. *Any day this thing is going to jump out and catch up with me,* they think, *and I'm going to pay a steep price.* So they live in despair. More than once when I have quoted the line, "Most men live lives of quiet desperation," I have seen guys burst into tears.

Even the best among us have skeletons in our closet, secrets known to no one else. Maybe you had an affair. Maybe you cheated with money. Maybe you lied about some qualification or experience. You're smart enough to cover it up, but inside you feel rotten and guilty.

The question is, How can we best deal with guilt? What are we to do with it? A growing number of men and women today try to *manage* their personal guilt—keep it under control, under wraps. They've tried and failed to deny it; they can't see how to rid themselves of it, so they learn little tricks to try and keep the guilt penned up inside (as much as possible).

They're right about one thing: Guilt *is* real. We all grapple with guilt. But Jesus Christ wants to do more than *manage* guilt; Jesus wants to *remove* it:

Jesus stepped into a boat, crossed over and came to his own town. Some men brought to him a paralytic, lying on a mat. When Jesus saw their faith, he said to the paralytic, "Take heart, son; your sins are forgiven." At this, some of the teachers of the law said to themselves, "This fellow is blaspheming!" Knowing their thoughts, Jesus said, "Why do you entertain evil thoughts in your hearts? Which is easier: to say, 'Your sins are forgiven,' or to say, 'Get up and walk'? But so that you may know that the Son of Man has authority on earth to forgive sins . . ." Then he said to the paralytic, "Get up, take your mat and go home." And the man got up and went home.

Matthew 9:1–7

We all grapple with guilt, but left to ourselves, we remain down on the mat. Jesus gives us a way to *get rid of it* altogether. The Bible says that guilt can be removed by God, our Creator, and eradicated from our conscience through faith in his Son, Jesus Christ. Jesus died on the cross to provide forgiveness and remove our guilt. The Bible says that when we come to him in faith, Jesus Christ will "cleanse our consciences from acts that lead to death, so that we may serve the living God!" (Heb. 9:14). We can try to manage our guilt, but only Jesus can remove our guilt and cleanse our conscience.

Hurting individuals with terrible guilt need to hear that God is a good God, a loving God. He knows all about our guilt and he wants to take it away. The Bible tells us frankly that we all have wandered away from

God and gone our own stubborn way, but in love God has made it possible for us to return to him—not by sweeping our sins under the table, not by ignoring them, not by managing them, but by removing them through faith in Jesus Christ. Jesus can remove our guilt and cleanse our conscience, something infinitely beyond the ability of even the most gifted psychiatrist or psychologist. They can help by pinpointing problems, but none would dare to say, "I can remove your guilt."

Jesus does say it.

> "But that you may know that the Son of Man has authority on earth to forgive sins . . ." [Jesus] said to the paralyzed man, "I tell you, get up, take your mat and go home." Immediately he stood up in front of them, took what he had been lying on and went home praising God.
>
> Luke 5:24–25

The writer to the Hebrews celebrated Jesus's ability to remove guilt and urged his readers, "let us draw near to God with a sincere heart in full assurance of faith, having our hearts sprinkled to cleanse us from a guilty conscience" (Heb. 10:22).

Of course, not everyone celebrates Jesus's work. Several years ago I appeared on a call-in radio program in England. The host told me about a good friend of his from a strict religious home, a man with "an A-grade in guilt."

"I believe that revealed biblical principles help you walk out of the guilt and the knots that tie you up, that A-grade in guilt," I said. "Christ comes into your life and cleans your conscience and lets you know, 'Yes, you are guilty. Yes, you are wrong—but I truly forgive you. You are cleansed.'"

The host didn't buy it.

"Sorry, Luis," he said. "That's an easy way out, it seems to me."

"What do you mean 'an easy way out'?" I asked.

"Yes, I've sinned, but I'm okay now because I'm forgiven. It's too easy."

"But you know," I insisted, "that *is* the way out."

It may be "easy" for us to rid ourselves of guilt, but it wasn't easy at all for Christ. To make our forgiveness possible he had to give up for a while the glories of heaven, take on human flesh, suffer at the hands of cruel enemies, die on a Roman cross, and rise from the tomb on the third day. It was no "easy way out" for him! "He died for us," wrote the apostle Paul, "so that . . . we may live together with him" (1 Thess. 5:10).

And live without guilt!

Still, as I said, not everyone celebrates. A caller to the radio program that same day, who identified himself as a member of the National Secular Society, strenuously objected to my take on guilt and forgiveness.

"Religion says that suffering is out there and it's bad," he said, "but also says it has the explanation for it: you are guilty, you are the sinners, you have original sin inherited from Adam and Eve—who are, incidentally, fictional. All religion does is transfer the guilt for everything that goes wrong in the world onto human beings, which I think is a terrible thing to do. The priests have done this for their own purposes. I mean, if you can convince people that they're guilty, that they need Jesus or the church or whatever to save them, then you have control over them. A famous humanist once said that Christianity not only has the unique advantage of turning men and women into slaves, it also teaches them to love their chains—and this is what Luis Palau is doing here. He is teaching them to love their chains, to accept that they are guilty, and then spend their lives groveling in the dirt, saying how wonderful it is that they've been relieved of their guilt."

But this is all wrong. Jesus does not want us to grovel in the dirt; he wants to lift us from the dust (where we put ourselves) and help us to soar high into the skies. If my humanist friend were correct, then the only people struggling with guilt should be those with some connection to church—but I know from traveling the world that the phenomenon of guilt penetrates every culture, every nation, every community, every human heart.

Not too long ago in Guam I helped a man in his eighties to find forgiveness in Christ. People called him Dutch. He fought in World War II and in Israel's Six Days' War in 1967. He was a pilot of fortune with an incredible story. But by the time I met him he was almost blind and getting close to the end.

"I want to have eternal life," he said to me as we sat in the lobby of a hotel. "I need forgiveness of sins, but I don't want to stop being Jewish. How can I do it?"

"This is the way it works," I said. "You receive Jesus Christ, he'll forgive your sins, he'll give you eternal life, and you'll go to heaven."

"But I want to still be Jewish."

"You can be a completed Jew," I replied, and I explained the way of forgiveness through Jesus Christ.

By the end he burst into torrential tears. It was amazing; all I said to him was, "Your sins and evil deeds I will remember no more," quoting Hebrews 10:17 from the Bible.

"Hey, I've done a lot of things," he declared.

"Dutch," I replied, "I don't want to hear them. You know them. God knows them. Christ took them away on the cross."

"I believe that," he said.

"You're one step from the kingdom of God," I replied.

"But you can't just shove all that under the chair," he objected.

"No," I explained, "God didn't shove it under the chair. He shoved it on his Son on the cross."

And Dutch started bawling again. By the end of our conversation, he had accepted the forgiveness that Jesus Christ offered to him. A few days later when I passed through Guam on my return home to Portland, I called a friend of Dutch to see how he was doing.

"He is so thrilled and at peace with God," the friend reported.

Don't settle for "managing" your guilt. And don't bother trying to deny it. Let Jesus Christ remove it, once and for all.

Stops the Bleeding vs. Fosters Healing

When we hurt someone or someone hurts us, acceptance can act as a kind of relational tourniquet. The decision to accept someone despite an offense stops the bleeding in a relationship and allows us to carry on.

Yet it's no final solution, for stopping the bleeding isn't the same as fostering healing. We use tourniquets for emergencies, as a stopgap measure, not as a permanent solution. Once we get the bleeding stopped, we need to start the healing process—and in relationships, that occurs only through forgiveness.

If your home is hurting, breaking up, or suffering through something you have done, what can you do? Let me tell you what the Bible says.

First, put aside pride and humble yourself. Colossians 3:12 says, "As God's chosen people, holy and dearly loved, clothe yourselves with compassion, kindness, humility, gentleness and patience." How can you build up a home that appears to be breaking up? The first step is humility. Most of us don't want to humble ourselves. But if your home is hurting, or if your home isn't what you want it to be, humbly admit your failure, your fault, or the hurt you've caused.

Second, the Bible says we are to forgive one another. The very next verse in Colossians says, "Bear with each other and forgive whatever grievances you may have against one another. Forgive as the Lord forgave you."

One of the best ways for a family to start over and mend its problems is for its members to forgive one another from the heart. It works!

I remember an engineer and his wife from Central America, an attractive, well-educated, and well-traveled couple. The husband cheated on his wife, and when she discovered his unfaithfulness, she decided to pay him back in kind. They both felt terrible, but didn't know how to undo the damage.

They came to our crusade in San Salvador and visited me one afternoon in our hotel. "We want to forgive each other but we don't know where to begin," he told me.

"Well, one of you start," I suggested.

And the man did. Dropping to his knees in front of his wife, he said, "Please forgive me! I was the one who started it."

They both started weeping; I soon joined them. She quickly fell to her knees beside her husband and said, "Please forgive me for trying to pay you back. I'm so sorry." Then they hugged each other.

"All right," I said, wiping away tears, "the next step is this: Go home, and from tonight on, seek God every day on your knees. Get together by your bed before going to sleep at night. Put your arms around her," I said, now directing my counsel to the husband. "Read a chapter from the Bible, then lead your wife in prayer."

"Goodness gracious," he protested, "how can I do that?"

"Just start," I said, "and in the morning, gather your three children and open the Bible with them. You're the head of the home—you read a chapter, explain it, and lead in prayer."

I called him up a week later to see how things were going. His mother-in-law also lived in the house, along with a maid, so I knew it wouldn't be easy.

"Luis," he said, "you can't believe it. The first day, my mother-in-law stood in a corner, looking at me as if she were going to kill me. Suddenly I had become a Bible reader, a Holy Joe? But three days later she sat down with us, then went to the bookstore and bought herself a Bible. Now even the maid sits around at the table. We're having a great time!"

I checked on them again many years later when I returned to El Salvador. There they were, still walking with God. First they humbled themselves, then they forgave each other, and then they began to study the Word of God together. It works!

The road to healing doesn't always rumble along so smoothly, of course. Many times restitution must accompany the forgiveness package. Those who have truly received the forgiveness of God naturally want to make things right, so far as they can, with those they've hurt. When Zacchaeus received the forgiveness of Jesus in Luke 19, he immediately turned around and said, "Look, Lord! Here and now I give half of my possessions to the poor, and if I have cheated anybody out of anything, I will pay back four times the amount" (v. 8).

Remember the English radio show I described earlier? Restitution became a sticking point in our discussion. I had a difficult time helping listeners to see the difference between getting right with God and getting right with those they had wronged.

"Luis," said my humanist friend, "you are saying to people, 'Don't take responsibility for your actions. Give them to God.' You are depriving people of ultimate responsibility for their actions. As a secular humanist, I would say to people, 'If you have done harm to people and you feel guilty about it, then make it good in this life. There's no afterlife to make it good in.' Belief in an afterlife, and Jesus and God making it right in the hereafter, stops people from being responsible for their own actions in the here and now."

I tried again to explain that we must distinguish between the two issues. First, our conscience needs to get clear with our Creator. The idea that somehow we have no responsibility to God may seem like a neat way to run away from deep personal guilt, but it won't work. But neither should we mix up our debt to God with our responsibility to the person we've offended.

The message of Jesus Christ does not teach irresponsibility. We are to ask forgiveness from one another, and if necessary, make restitution to one another. If you walked out on your wife, then humble yourself and ask her to forgive you. Maybe it's too late to repair the marriage, but the gospel impels us to make things right, to whatever degree that's feasible. "If it is possible," says the apostle Paul, "as far as it depends on you, live at peace with everyone" (Rom. 12:18).

Lee Atwater discovered just how difficult this could be after he came to faith in Christ. Atwater ran George Bush's successful 1988 presidential campaign against Massachusetts governor Michael Dukakis. Atwater, you might remember, was the brash but brilliant Republican campaign manager who often won by "going negative." Some said Atwater "made politics into a blood sport." More than one pundit called him "the guru of dirty politics." On the day of Bush's inauguration, Atwater stood with an old friend at the inaugural ceremonies. "Lee," the friend noted, "you said you wanted to be a millionaire by age thirty, and you were. You said you wanted to run a successful presidential campaign—and Bush is being sworn in. What now?"

"I want to be chairman of the Republican Party," Atwater replied.

A few weeks later, Atwater got his wish. He felt on top of the world—and then he began to feel some pain. Medical tests revealed an inoperable brain tumor. And Lee Atwater—banjo player, party boy, big campaigner, political dirty trickster—suddenly thought, *I'm going to die!* Like many of us in a crisis, he despaired. Like never before he began to think of God and eternity and heaven. He arranged for a meeting in Washington with some influential people who really love Christ, who showed him how to be forgiven. He received Christ and forgiveness of sins—and skeptics around the capital expressed their cynicism. "He's dying," they said, "so of course now he's going to straighten out. But is it real? Or is this just the despair of a drowning man?"

The proof came soon enough. The Lord had forgiven Lee Atwater; now he realized he needed to ask many people to forgive *him*. First on the list: Michael Dukakis. Atwater had taken a lot of nasty shots at Dukakis, including widespread publication of a photo of Dukakis popping his head above a tank, looking for all the world like Snoopy. When I saw that picture, I said, "Dukakis is finished."

Atwater phoned Dukakis and said, "Governor, this is Lee Atwater. I know you're probably going to hang up on me, but please give me a second. I'm dying of cancer; I'll be dead in a few months. I've repented. I've asked God to forgive me and he has. And now I want you—I beg you—to please forgive me for the dirty deeds I did to you. I'm the one who said your wife was an alcoholic. I'm guilty. Would you forgive me?"

Dukakis already had learned of the tumor and said, "Lee, you're forgiven. Don't worry."

Then Atwater said, "May I talk to your wife?"

Dukakis hesitated. "That's going to be another story," he said. But Atwater pressed his request, and Kitty Dukakis eventually came to the phone.

"Mrs. Dukakis, I apologize," Atwater said. "I ask you to forgive me. I'm the one who spread the word that you were drinking. It's my fault, and I was wrong. Would you forgive me?"

To his surprise, Mrs. Dukakis graciously said, "I forgive you."

Then Atwater began to call individuals all across the country whom he'd wronged. He spent thousands of dollars in phone calls to ask men and women to forgive him. A few months later, he died—at peace with God and at peace with those he had wronged.[1]

That's the power of genuine forgiveness.

A Fresh Start in Minnesota

A few years ago I was staying with a friend who owns a cabin on a Minnesota lakeshore, across the border from North Dakota. My friend fished regularly with a neighbor, an elderly gentleman named Aaron who fought in World War II. Five years prior to my visit, Aaron's wife had gone to live in a rest home.

The day I met Aaron I said to him, "Aaron, it's a pleasure to meet you. My friend has told me about you."

But this no-nonsense Norwegian American had little time for niceties. "You're a preacher, are you?" he asked.

"Yes sir, I am."

"Is it true that if you believe on the Lord Jesus Christ, you will never have to face the judgment of God?" he asked.

"You're absolutely right," I replied. "Aaron, if you believe on the Lord Jesus Christ, you'll never have to face the judgment of God. What made you think of that?"

"I'm getting old. My wife is old. My World War II buddies are old. And the other day I heard Billy Graham on television. I wrote him for a little cassette. I listened to it. The subject was 'Life after Death'—and I want to get ready."

"Tomorrow morning I'm preaching in a church near here," I said. "Will you come?"

He did come, along with his friend. I preached my heart out, if for nobody else, for Aaron. At the end, when I gave the invitation, Aaron—this tough old bird—beat everyone else to the front. He dragged one of his old military buddies with him as he came forward.

That night I went to see him at his cabin. "Aaron," I asked, "are you sure now that Jesus Christ has forgiven your sins and given you eternal life?"

And this tough World War II veteran, a Norwegian American who doesn't like to talk much, replied, "You'd better believe it. I know that I've got eternal life."

Do you have the same assurance? You can, so long as you come to the same Lord for forgiveness.

How to Receive Forgiveness According to the Bible

1. *Realize that forgiveness flows from God's love, not your worthiness.*
   "In accordance with your great love, forgive the sin of these people, just as you have pardoned them from the time they left Egypt until now" (Num. 14:19).

2. *Recognize that God's mercy holds back his judgment.*
   "Yet he was merciful; he atoned for their iniquities and did not destroy them. Time after time he restrained his anger and did not stir up his full wrath" (Ps. 78:38).

3. *Understand that God wants to grant you forgiveness through Jesus Christ.*
   "For he has rescued us from the dominion of darkness and brought us into the kingdom of the Son he loves, in whom we have redemption, the forgiveness of sins" (Col. 1:13–14).

4. *Confess your sins to God.*
   "If we confess our sins, he is faithful and just and will forgive us our sins and purify us from all unrighteousness" (1 John 1:9).

5. *Turn away from your sins and determine to walk in a new direction.*
   "I preached that they should repent and turn to God and prove their repentance by their deeds" (Acts 26:20).

6. *Believe that Jesus died and rose again to give you forgiveness.*
   "[Jesus] is the one whom God appointed as judge of the living and the dead. All the prophets testify about him that everyone who believes in him receives forgiveness of sins through his name" (Acts 10:42–43).

7. *Declare your dependence upon Jesus.*
   "If you confess with your mouth, 'Jesus is Lord,' and believe in your heart that God raised him from the dead, you will be saved" (Rom. 10:9).

8. *Once you receive forgiveness, practice forgiving others.*
   "Bear with each other and forgive whatever grievances you may have against one another. Forgive as the Lord forgave you" (Col. 3:13).

9. *Don't "keep score" of the offenses committed against you.*

   "Then Peter came to Jesus and asked, 'Lord, how many times shall I forgive my brother when he sins against me? Up to seven times?' Jesus answered, 'I tell you, not seven times, but seventy-seven times'" (Matt. 18:21–22).

10. *Don't allow resentment to derail your forgiveness.*

    "When you stand praying, if you hold anything against anyone, forgive him, so that your Father in heaven may forgive you of your sins" (Mark 11:25).

5

A Priceless Gift
That Costs Us Nothing

Relief or Peace?

Do not be anxious about anything, but in everything, by prayer and petition, with thanksgiving, present your requests to God. And the peace of God, which transcends all understanding, will guard your hearts and your minds in Christ Jesus.

The apostle Paul, in Philippians 4:6–7

Comedian and late-night talk show host Jay Leno once suggested how he might try to impress the judges if he were somehow to compete at a famous beauty pageant: "As Miss America, my goal is to bring peace to the entire world and then to get my own apartment."[1]

We laugh at the incongruity, but sometimes apartments are just what one needs to get peace—if not world peace, then at least some personal peace. My maternal grandmother lived for many years with a mean-spirited, spiteful husband. He habitually let loose with hurtful words and seemed to look for ways to spew his venom. Because of him, my grandmother provided me with some of my earliest and greatest pictures of peace.

Grandma was French, and whenever her surly husband started ranting and raving, she would grab a piece of cheese, a loaf of French bread, and a bottle of wine. She'd head off to her bedroom, close and lock the door, and say, "Bread, cheese, wine—and peace."

We all need peace in a world so overflowing with strife. We long for tranquility, for quiet, for harmony, for serenity and calm. Unfortunately, it just doesn't seem easy to find.

Some time ago I met an emergency room doctor who worked in a Michigan hospital. "All my life," he told me, "I knew I was missing something. I had no peace and I hated people."

As he worked night after night with the bloody and the wounded, he turned cynical and hardened. He told me he "frankly despised" many of those who came in for treatment, especially the ones beaten up in drunken brawls or the drug addicts who vomited all over the facility.

"I just hated those people," he admitted. "I patched them up because it was my job, but I didn't even wish them well."

That is, until he met Jesus Christ. Then he suddenly realized the problem was *him*. Although he still doesn't like what many of his patients do to get so torn up, now he has compassion on them because Christ had compassion on him.

"What was the major change in your life after you met Jesus Christ?" I asked him.

"Peace, instantly," he replied. "I'd never had peace in my life. I used to hear people talk about it, but I never knew what they were talking about. The moment I met Jesus Christ, however, I had peace."

Peace is one of the tremendous benefits of coming to know Jesus Christ. When you find peace with God, you gain peace with others, and you begin to experience great peace in your soul—the amazing peace of God. You learn how to put aside the agitation and turmoil and unrest that once troubled you and replace it with a quiet confidence. Your peace bubbles up from within, out of a gentle spirit energized by the living God.

Peace or Relief?

We all want peace, but in a world so torn by rancor and unrest, it's all too easy to mistake genuine peace for an attractive counterfeit or to settle for a less comprehensive alternative. And we have many of both to choose from!

Every day many of us opt unknowingly for counterfeit peace. We convince ourselves that peace comes through "spiritual" experiences, controlled finances, toned bodies, downsized possessions, fewer responsibilities, green lawns, long vacations, or ignored problems. Some of us, certain that authentic peace cannot be attained, opt for simple relief. So we flee a good part of our pain through the use of alcohol, drugs, sex, or psychological therapy. Relief may not be peace, but it feels better than stress or pain.

It seems to me, however, that the fundamental question facing all of us is this: Does genuine peace really exist? And if so, can we find it and secure it for ourselves? Is it really possible to leave behind the half-measures of relief to enter into the overflowing blessings of peace?

Not only is it possible, but I maintain that millions of men and women throughout the ages and across the globe have come to understand and enjoy the message of the psalmist: "The LORD gives strength to his people; the LORD blesses his people with peace" (Ps. 29:11).

Real peace, the kind that God places in the hearts of his children, earns superior marks to mere relief in at least five ways:

Relief	Peace
• Comes and Goes	• Remains Steady
• Dulls Anxiety	• Lends Quiet Confidence
• Delivered from Outside	• Drawn from Inside
• Requires Increasing Dosages	• Enjoys Growing Calm
• Expensive	• Priceless

It saddens me that so many of us settle for relief when what we really want, what we really need, is peace. We all want this: "I will lie down and sleep in peace" (Ps. 4:8). But too often we have this: "I have no peace, no quietness; I have no rest, but only turmoil" (Job 3:26). Travel or meditation, tranquilizers or therapy can bring a measure of relief—but why settle for a mere reprieve when God offers us real, genuine, personal peace.

Comes and Goes vs. Remains Steady

Relief comes and goes. We feel relief only so long as our muscles ripple or alcohol flows through our veins. The pain subsides only so long as we feel distracted by something else. But as soon as that distraction ceases, the pain returns—quite possibly with greater intensity than before. The peace of God, however, remains steady and firm regardless of circumstances. Why? Because the infinite God supplies it: "You will keep in perfect peace him whose mind is steadfast, because he trusts in you" (Isa. 26:3).

Nothing can take away a growing Christian's peace, *if* the Christian chooses to trust God. Though circumstances may shake you up, no outside force can strip away your peace. What if your paycheck doesn't cover all your expenses? What if you're mugged? What if your doctor tells you that he's sorry, but you have an inoperable form of cancer? Those things naturally cause a lot of anxiety, but believers who keep their minds steadfastly focused on the solid rock of Jesus Christ can (and often do) say things like, "Lord, this could be a great opportunity to tell others about you."

On April 20, 2001, missionary Jim Bowers lost his wife, Veronica "Roni" Bowers, and their newly adopted seven-month-old daughter, Charity, in a terrifying tragedy. As the Bowers flew to their post on the Amazon River, a Peruvian jet mistook their pontoon plane for a drug-trafficking vessel and opened fire. During the attack, a single bullet instantly killed both Veronica and Charity. Jim, his son Cory, and the pilot survived the crash into the Amazon River.

When memorial services for his loved ones received international media coverage, Jim did not express vengeance or bitterness; instead, he glorified God. "Obviously it hurts," he said, "but God works mysteriously to give me comfort so that I don't have to be sad all the time. . . . One sign that God was responsible for what happened is . . . the effect on missionary work now. I'm hoping it will result in an increase in missionaries in the future. I'm sure it will; people are challenged now to go do what Roni did. . . . Cory and I are experiencing an inexplicable peace, and to me, that's proof that God is in this. Our attitude toward those responsible is one of forgiveness."[2]

The peace of God doesn't mean that you feel no terror or pain in horrifying circumstances; it simply means that God's peace can overwhelm anything thrown at it from the outside.

No outside force can take away the Christian's peace. Not your government. Not your boss. Not even your in-laws! Only two things can rob a Christian of God's peace: lack of trust in the Savior, and unconfessed sin.

In 2 Thessalonians 3:16 the apostle Paul wrote, "Now may the Lord of peace himself give you peace at all times and in every way. The Lord be with all of you." When Paul ended with, "The Lord be with all of you," he didn't merely mouth a religious platitude. He meant that his friends needed to depend on the Lord and consciously make him part of their day-to-day lives. Only then could they expect to enjoy his peace.

Make no mistake: While God offers us all the resources we need to enjoy his peace, many of us never take him up on his offer. Why not? Because we try to fix things by ourselves—but the proverb "God helps those who help themselves" is *not* in the Bible. Or we choose the fleeting pleasures of some favorite sin. We forget that the Lord tells us, "He who conceals his sins does not prosper, but whoever confesses and renounces them finds mercy" (Prov. 28:13). And it somehow slips our minds that God insists, "The mind of sinful man is death, but the mind controlled by the Spirit is life and peace" (Rom. 8:6).

Do you want God's Holy Spirit to flood your mind and heart with his all-encompassing peace? Do you want to free your soul from unending inner turmoil? You really can have God's peace . . . if you want it. Jesus

Christ is the Prince of Peace. Isaiah says that Jesus "was pierced for our transgressions, he was crushed for our iniquities; the punishment that brought us peace was upon him" (53:5). Jesus took the punishment that humanity's sins deserved, thereby making peace possible between us and our Holy God. All it takes for you to receive his peace is to commit your life to Jesus Christ through faith. Then the Prince of Peace himself has promised to bless you with the peace of salvation he won at the cross.

And yet I need to make an important clarification: The peace of God doesn't shield any of us from life's unpleasant moments, like some sort of supersedative. Those who know and love Jesus Christ—even those happy men and women who make Jesus a daily part of their lives—can be rocked by tragedy and hardship. God's peace doesn't enable faithful believers to march through life with vacant eyes and frozen smiles. Nor does it act like a perpetual "upper," allowing them to bubble their way through life as though no troubles ever touch them. But it does give them a confidence and calmness of spirit that allows them to deal with whatever comes their way.

For the longest time my wife could not understand why I harped on the Bible's picture of human beings as creatures with body, soul, and spirit (1 Thess. 5:23; Heb. 4:12). "So what?" she'd ask. "How does that knowledge help anyone?"

Then she came down with cancer, had major surgery, and started chemotherapy. "You know, at last I understand the value of your hammering home that business about body, soul, and spirit," she told me. "My body is in pain and I'm not sure whether I care much for it. My spirit is absolutely at peace. I'm ready to die, though I don't want to die; I really want to see our sons grow up. Still, I'm ready. I'm at peace. I have no fear. At the same time, however, my soul is a yo-yo. One day I wake up and I'm happy because I'm alive. Another day I wake up and I feel depressed because the cancer could have spread undetected."

That's the reality we all have to face. The peace of God doesn't mean the absence of distress. So then, are Christians duplicitous by saying, "I have absolute peace with God, although I'm horrified that the cancer could be in my liver"? Not at all. To say such a thing simply means that the one speaking is a complete human being with body, soul, and spirit. Even when we belong to God, our emotions go up and down and our feelings teeter-totter.

- The *body* is hurting and sick (it's going to die anyway).
- The *spirit* is utterly at peace (secure and assured of eternity).
- The *soul* will fluctuate emotionally, depending on circumstances (and one day it, too, will be completely redeemed).

So long as we live in these disintegrating bodies, our emotions tend to run hot and cold and skitter up and down, depending on circumstances. Without God, those emotions take control and quickly put us in chains of fear and dread. But with God, the peace we enjoy in our spirit greatly influences the fluctuating emotions of our soul. We do not have to be ruled by our feelings.

When we move through life with God, we can count on the promise of his Word: "I will listen to what God the LORD will say; he promises peace to his people, his saints—but let them not return to folly" (Ps. 85:8).

Dulls Anxiety vs. Lends Quiet Confidence

No fortune ever amassed and no alcoholic beverage ever brewed has even once eliminated the anxiety felt by a human soul. The best they can do is dull the pain for a little while. Riches and shot glasses can briefly take the edge off the knife, but in the end they often wind up sharpening the blade to a razor's edge.

Peace, on the other hand, means not so much the absence of anxiety as the presence of quiet confidence. It is "God's holy presence in every experience of our human existence."[3] The peace of God lends a calm and an assurance that leaves witnesses marveling.

Quiet confidence naturally blooms in the heart of an individual who lives in the peace of God. "The fruit of righteousness will be peace," said Isaiah, "the effect of righteousness will be quietness and confidence forever" (32:17). Those who snuggle deeply into the peace of God have no need either to swagger or cower, for they believe God when he says, "Have no fear of sudden disaster or of the ruin that overtakes the wicked, for the LORD will be your confidence and will keep your foot from being snared" (Prov. 3:25–26).

I saw the peace of God at work in an amazing way in my mother. She became a widow at age thirty-four, quickly lost the family business, and had to find a way to feed seven children on almost nothing. Yet to my eyes she seemed to float through life primarily on two verses from the lips of Jesus: "In this world you will have trouble. But take heart! I have overcome the world" (John 16:33); "Peace I leave with you; my peace I give you. I do not give to you as the world gives. Do not let your hearts be troubled and do not be afraid" (John 14:27).

Mom never suffered a breakdown and never let our extreme poverty get to her. While she didn't enjoy our circumstances and did what she could to improve our lot, I still remember the warm smile that overflowed from the depths of a heart at perfect peace.

God's peace does far more than dull anxiety. It lends a quiet confidence that can sustain your spirit through the worst of times. Just today I was thinking of a favorite verse in Isaiah. God tells his people, "So do not fear, for I am with you; do not be dismayed, for I am your God. I will strengthen you and help you; I will uphold you with my righteous right hand" (41:10).

Tremendous peace can be yours when you walk with God!

Delivered from Outside vs. Drawn from Inside

Those who seek relief rather than peace run into another major problem: They have no inward source from which to get relief, but must seek it from the outside, from sources exterior to themselves. Whether exercise or alcohol, exotic travel or never-ending therapy, the relief they seek has to come from without. So what happens when the body wears out, the booze dries up, the vacation ends, or the therapist takes off? What then?

"Aha!" someone might say. "Luis, now you've painted yourself into a corner. All along you've been saying that we need to look to God for peace—but he's outside of us."

Well, yes and no.

Without question, God exists forever and infinitely beyond us and above us. As Paul said, God is "the blessed and only Ruler, the King of kings and Lord of lords, who alone is immortal and who lives in unapproachable light, whom no one has seen or can see" (1 Tim. 6:15–16). God "himself gives life and breath to everything, and he satisfies every need there is" (Acts 17:25 NLT). So yes, he certainly is outside of us.

On the other hand, one of the greatest mysteries and blessings of the Christian faith is that God himself has chosen to live *within* his people, inside their very bodies. "Do you not know that your body is a temple of the Holy Spirit, who is in you, whom you have received from God?" asks Paul (1 Cor. 6:19). Since God is the God of peace (Rom. 15:33; 1 Cor. 14:33; Phil. 4:9), that means God's peace dwells within us and does not need to be supplied from the outside. Wherever a Christian goes, God's peace tags along. This is why Jesus could say, "Whoever believes in me, as the Scripture has said, streams of living water will flow from within him" (John 7:38). John explained that, "By this he meant the Spirit, whom those who believed in him were later to receive" (v. 39).

That "later" is *now*. The moment someone invites Jesus into his or her heart, the Holy Spirit takes up residence in that individual's body. From that moment on and for all eternity, the peace of God is available from *within*.

Despite that, we often try to find peace (or at least relief) from the outside. Sometimes we try to get relief from the pain of living, not by popping pills or ingesting some other chemical substitute, but by striving to achieve more than the other guy. But it doesn't work. If we really do excel beyond our peers, satisfaction and peace still elude us; and if others yet remain "above" us, we get depressed.

When we compare ourselves with others, we are not wise (2 Cor. 10:12). Somebody will always be better than us in some area of life, often exactly where we covet the top spot. Someone will always rise above us in looks, or height, or education, or talent, or expertise—and that can devastate whoever feels the need to be number one. Such individuals can have everything they need, all the money a human could spend responsibly, and yet they lack peace.

A lack of peace often reveals itself through anger at the world, anger at more successful people, anger at the past. Such angry individuals forever rehearse their bad luck and mistreatment at the hands of others, real or imagined. Some lose their peace for the rest of their life. When others see them coming, they flee. They know these bitter people continually repeat the old story everyone already knows by heart.

To experience God's peace, we must adopt God's goals, not the diseased goals that end up destroying us. God's goals come from within, not from without, and they don't depend upon comparisons with others.

Do you know why many of us live lives of quiet desperation? It's because we have adopted goals unworthy of a human being. Human life lasts only seventy, maybe eighty years, and most people (especially in the West) have everything it takes to enjoy life. And yet how many peaceful people do you know?

I know women who have reared amazing families, but lack peace. They listen to the constant putdowns about their choice to remain home and wonder if they made the right decision. My wife stayed home with our four sons, and every so often I had to remind her of her enormous contribution. "Hey," I'd say, "let's wait ten years and see what happens to the kids of all these people who put you down." A mother who rears godly children, healthy sons and daughters who go on to marry growing Christians and have godly kids of their own—that's success! Your peace deserts you when your goals differ from those of God. And bogus goals can afflict anyone.

For evangelists like me, the great temptation is to want to be "the biggest." Who's the biggest, who's the best, who leads more people into the kingdom of God, who draws the biggest crowds, who writes more books, who gets quoted the most, who gets asked to appear on *Larry King Live*? You can get all wrapped up in that stuff and lose your peace. No one can enjoy peace while pursuing godless goals.

The current chairman of our board, businessman Dave Hall, tells a funny story about how chasing unworthy goals can rob a man of peace. He retired as a millionaire before he was fifty and today owns part of the Phoenix Suns of the National Basketball Association. He's always been supercompetitive. While speaking last year to a group of professionals in Evansville, Indiana, he explained just how competitive.

"I didn't eat my whole lunch today," he said, "but if I had, the chances are that I would have been the first one to finish. I have always been a pretty fast eater. Today it means nothing to me, but there was a time when people would see how fast I ate and they would say, 'Boy, you eat fast.' And my response would be, '*Yes!*'—like it was a victory. If you and I crossed the street, I never said anything, but I assure you that I would have touched the curb before you did. It was important for me to beat you. When I was in college, getting a high grade wasn't as important to me as being the first one to finish the exam. So when I was done with the test, I took it up and turned it in well ahead of anybody else, regardless of the grade. Winning was very important to me. I *wanted* to win; I wanted to win at everything, and I won quite a bit."

After graduating from college, Dave took a job as a salesman with IBM; in his first year, the company named him top rookie salesman in the West. His second year he did even better, and his third year he won a promotion from Los Angeles direct to New York (the normal track would have led him first to San Francisco).

"I was able to achieve virtually everything I wanted to achieve," Dave said. "I had a Porsche, a Jaguar, I had little animals all over my shirts. I had Maytag, KitchenAid. Everything I was working for that I thought was going to make me happy, I had, and I had very early. But it didn't give me what I thought it was going to give me."

At that stage of his life, Dave put his priorities in the following order: job success; happiness (which included his job success, money, and how much fun he was having); his children; and his wife and marriage. It seemed appropriate to him, because after all, *What could be a greater gift to give my wife than for me to be successful?*

One day Dave's wife announced she thought they should start taking their family to church. It sounded like a good idea to Dave; wasn't that what every all-American family did? Besides, he'd probably make a lot of good business connections there.

At church, Dave eventually found the peace he'd been missing. Life suddenly started to "click" for him with Jesus Christ in the driver's seat.

"It used to be that I worked to please only myself," he admitted. "But after that day in 1979 when I committed my life to Christ, very shortly my priorities changed. They became: To love and serve God; my wife and my marriage; my children (and now my grandchildren); and my job and my business and financial success. And I'll say this: My business and financial success has been ten times greater as my fourth priority than as my first priority. When I wasn't paying as much attention to my business and financial success, but was paying attention to my relationship with God, the Father who created me and knows me better than I know myself, my life changed immeasurably."

Dave discovered that true peace comes not from without—not from competing and winning against the best—but from within, as the Holy Spirit took up residence in his heart. And that's an enduring kind of peace that can survive even the worst drought.

Requires Increasing Dosages vs. Enjoys Growing Calm

When we seek relief from emotional pain through drugs or alcohol or self-destructive behaviors, we discover that our bodies quickly adjust, demanding ever-increasing dosages to maintain the same level of relief. What worked a year ago to bring some measure of relief now has no effect at all.

God's peace works in exactly the opposite way. The more we allow his peace to bring tranquility to our hearts, the more steady and calm our lives become. What used to upset us a year ago now barely causes a ripple. The more his peace infuses our day-to-day lives, the more confident and assured and balanced we feel. And everyone notices.

Still, we shouldn't think God's peace magically appears in our lives. Certainly many men and women have told me how God instantaneously lavished on them a deep feeling of peace the moment they trusted Jesus Christ for salvation. Even in their lives, however, God continues to build his peace gradually, over time. One of the most important ways he does this is through the fourth commandment:

> Remember the Sabbath day by keeping it holy. Six days you shall labor and do all your work, but the seventh day is a Sabbath to the LORD your God. On it you shall not do any work, neither you, nor your son or daughter, nor your manservant or maidservant, nor your animals, nor the alien within your gates. For in six days the LORD made the heavens and the earth, the sea, and all that is in them, but he rested on the seventh day. Therefore the LORD blessed the Sabbath day and made it holy.
>
> Exodus 20:8–11

God intended the Sabbath to make us happy, joyful, and rested, but through the centuries we have managed to make it a severe, religious day. What a tragedy! The Lord tells us, "Work for six days, but give me this one day of rest. Use it to be happy and free and relaxed. Enjoy it, have some laughs, be with your family, and spend time with me in worship."

It makes all kinds of sense, doesn't it? For six days you work hard. You feel tense. You put everything you have into your job. But one day out of seven you give to the Lord. That day you are to rest from labor.

Do you do that? If not, is it any wonder that you lack God's peace?

The fourth commandment is the only one among the ten that doesn't appear to be repeated in the New Testament—and yet it has never been rescinded, either. It's a love gift from the Lord. He wants us to take one day in seven and thoroughly enjoy it.

The Lord says, "I want you to be free. I want you to enjoy peace. This command is just one of my fences. I'm giving you a big, broad piece of land, an enormous estate. Within the fences around this estate, you can work and have fun. Just don't run into the fence, and certainly don't try to jump over it, because if you do, you will fall apart. Stay within this big fence, and you can have a great life."

Doing things God's way brings such liberation and excitement. You don't have to worry. You don't have to beat your breast. You don't have to continually search your soul. And you experience God's peace at the deepest levels.

The fourth commandment reveals God as a peaceful Lord who wants a hardworking and restful people. In this commandment God is not just "laying down the law," as we tend to say. The law reveals his loving character. Jesus told us, "The Sabbath was made for man, not man for the Sabbath" (Mark 2:27). In other words, it is an expression of God's love that our Lord commanded us to set one day aside in the week where we don't have to feel guilty about not working or worry about getting a reputation for laziness. "You can work six days," says the Lord, "but on the seventh day, rest."

How does this commandment bring us God's peace? First, it liberates us from feverish, endless financial preoccupation. We tend to become slaves of whatever captures our unceasing attention, and God intends for the Sabbath day to break our obsession with finances.

Second, this commandment frees us from the greed of living for work only. The Lord intends for the Sabbath to cut the feet out from under workaholism. An executive who refuses to rest in the Lord because he is determined to do whatever it takes to hit the top and stay there cannot know God's peace. Many workers wreck their families by not finding freedom in this area.

Third, the commandment protects your health. "Oh, that their hearts would be inclined to fear me and keep all my commands always, so that it might go well with them and their children forever!" said God to Moses; "Walk in all the way that the LORD your God has commanded you, so that you may live and prosper and prolong your days" (Deut. 5:29, 33).

Of course, rest doesn't mean only that you lie on the beach. Rest also brings a confidence that God controls your life. When you live with integrity and keep God as your main priority, you enjoy a quiet rest and confidence that the Bible calls peace. "My gift of the Sabbath is inner rest," God says. "Rest of spirit. Rest of mind. Rest of conscience."

My mentor, the late Ray Stedman, told me years ago that at his funeral he wanted the congregation to sing a beautiful hymn titled, "Jesus, I Am Resting, Resting." The first stanza of this great song reads, "Jesus, I am resting, resting, In the joy of what Thou art; I am finding out the greatness Of Thy loving heart. Thou hast bid me gaze upon Thee, And Thy beauty fills my soul, For by Thy transforming power, Thou hast made me whole."[4]

Ray illustrated for me what it means to rest in Jesus Christ and live by his peace. When I first came to the States I didn't understand this inner rest that comes from knowing one is indwelt by the living Lord Jesus. Oh, I often heard about the "indwelling Lord Jesus." I got it intellectually. I understood the point. I even preached to others that Jesus Christ lives in us, that all his resources were available to us, that his resurrection life was our life, and that we live because he lives. I insisted that we were united to the Lord, one spirit with him, and that as the Father is one with the Lord Jesus, so we were one with the Lord Jesus.

And yet, for some time I never rested in the finished work of Jesus Christ. I never seemed able to rest in the indwelling presence of the Lord Jesus—and that produced a restlessness and confusion and an incessant nervousness. I didn't enjoy the peace of God until I thoroughly came to rest in the promises of God, in the character of God, and in the indwelling presence of his Holy Spirit.

Then one day I heard Major Ian Thomas speak in chapel at Multnomah Bible College (then called Multnomah School of the Bible). In
a talk on Moses and the burning bush, this English gentleman turned
the key that opened my spiritual understanding.

Before he came, one of my professors opened every class in the same
way. He would walk into the room, stand there and quote Galatians
2:20: "I am crucified with Christ, nevertheless I live. Yet it's not I, it's
Christ living in me. And the life I now live in the flesh, I live by faith
in the Son of God who loved me and gave himself for me."

I despised that old man. I still had the arrogance of a young man
and thought I knew doctrine pretty well. So when this frail old man
started teaching basic doctrine, in my pride I sat there thinking, *I can't
believe this. I came all the way to this country to listen to* this? *In my
church even the children know this.*

This man did the same thing in all his classes, regardless of the subject. And I just sat there, thinking, *This old man knows only one verse.
He's gonna repeat this verse all the time!* It began to enrage me.

But over time, the Holy Spirit used that verse to dig deep into my
heart. Here was his question: "Are you crucified with Christ?" And I
knew the answer: "No, I'm not." I finally realized that while I knew a
lot of Bible doctrine, I didn't have any idea what it meant to be crucified with Christ. And the Holy Spirit began to say to me, "Look, you
arrogant little boy. You think you know so much! But you know nothing
of the power of the living God. You despise other people, just because
I've given you a sharp mind and the privileges of a good education.
But you know nothing of the power of God."

The thought crushed me . . . until that day in chapel. I felt in total
despair. I knew my lack of power. I had no spiritual authority in my
life; it was all intellectual. I knew nothing of the power of the risen
Christ.

That day, Ian Thomas talked about the burning bush. "It's not your
education that counts," he said. "It's not your connections that count.
It's not your privileges that count. Any old bush will do, so long as

God is in the bush." Then he quoted Galatians 2:20: "I am crucified with Christ."

And suddenly it all came together for me.

I ran to my bedroom and skipped my other classes. I fell on my knees and said, "Oh God, at last I get. it. It's not I, but Christ living in me. The life I now live in the flesh, I live by faith in the Son of God, who loved me and gave himself for me."

I stayed on my knees for nearly two hours. I had been trying for seven or eight frustrating years to serve God in my own power, in my own knowledge, experience, and education. I thought I was sharp. But the Lord had shown me, "Luis, as long as you trust yourself, I can't use you. But if you will rely on the indwelling Christ—if you let Christ live in you and through you—then, Luis, I can use you. All the dreams you've had as a teenager? They're from me. I will bring them to pass. But you must learn to live according to this word: 'It's not I, it's Christ living in me.'"

It was a revolutionary thought, a revolutionary time. I was twenty-five years old and felt as though I had just been converted all over again. Finally I realized that the secret is not what we do for God, but what God does in us and through us. Oh yes, we obey—but not by relying on our power. Rather, we rely on the power of the risen Christ.

Soon I started preaching the same basic messages I had given before—but this time, to my surprise, people were converted. I saw a power in the messages I had never seen before. I began to enjoy a freedom and a joy that I had never experienced. It suddenly felt exciting to serve the Lord; it was no longer a burden.

How delightful it is when a believer in Jesus Christ finally comes to rest in the certainty that the Son of God indwells him or her! How wonderful to realize, *All his resources are mine! Everything he is, is available to me!*

The Lord says to us, "Enter my rest and enjoy my peace." Have you entered that rest? Do you have peace in your inner soul? If Jesus Christ lives in you, you can and you should.

Expensive vs. Priceless

The bills really pile up when you depend on material resources and human techniques to grab a little relief from the pain of life. On the other hand, God's peace costs us nothing—and yet no one can set a value on its worth. The peace of God is simply priceless.

Two businessmen were among those who came to some meetings we held in Australia. Both felt under terrible pressure. Both suffered tremendous business problems. Neither got along with their wives, and both felt the burden of nasty family troubles. When I gave the invitation to receive Jesus Christ, one of the businessmen opened his heart to the Lord. The other businessman became extremely angry and left the meeting, stomping all the way. He blasphemed and walked out, cursing me as he went.

Three years later I returned to that city and inquired about these two men. The first went home, settled affairs with his wife, and began to repay his debts and repair his business. Friends told me he learned to really love and obey God—and had a joyful family to prove it. This man discovered the peace of God.

The news about the second man broke my heart. A few weeks after our meetings, he climbed outside a tall building and jumped to his death. He had rejected Jesus Christ, refused to bow to the Savior, and snuffed out his life. This man never discovered the peace of God, for as the prophet Isaiah said, "'There is no peace,' says the LORD, 'for the wicked'" (48:22).

The Bible says you can find peace with God through faith in our Lord Jesus Christ (Rom. 5:1). You can burn incense for generations and never enjoy peace with God. You can offer sacrifices at the altar and yet never find peace with God. You can even read the Bible for twenty years and still have no peace in your soul. The Bible says Jesus Christ is our peace. It calls the gospel "the good news of peace" (Acts 10:36). But to experience this peace you must open your life to Jesus Christ and receive him into your heart. It's a priceless gift that costs you nothing.

Yet it's also a gift we can refuse, even as believers. Colossians 3:15 says, "Let the peace of Christ rule in your hearts." Did you notice the first word? "Let." God does not force his peace on anyone, not even his own children. We can have the peace of God . . . if we want it. We can allow his peace to rule in our lives and make us into a sweet aroma to those around us.

But we must choose it.

Christians living day by day in the peace of God can have a tremendous impact on those around them. "Through us," the apostle Paul said, God "spreads everywhere the fragrance of the knowledge of him. For we are to God the aroma of Christ" (2 Cor. 2:14–15). God considers growing Christians the perfume of Jesus Christ—believers with an unforgettable influence.

A friend of mine, Odice Amyett, died suddenly a few years ago. I went to see Odice's widow, Billie, a short while later. Now, when you walk into a home after a sudden death, you often don't know what to expect, even with believers. But when Billie opened the door, she greeted me with a big hug and we sat down and talked and prayed for several minutes. She seemed to be at perfect peace. Don't misunderstand—the shock of Odice's unexpected death still hadn't worn off and she missed her husband terribly. He was a loveable guy, and we all missed him. But I felt a palpable peace in that home. Billie didn't look desperate, she didn't pull her hair out, she didn't seem about to fall apart. She gave no indication of thinking, *God, why did you do this?* No. She was utterly at peace, both with herself and with God. The perfume of Jesus Christ in that house smelled absolutely beautiful.

While God doesn't sell that perfume, he does give it away. "Do not be anxious about anything," Paul counsels us, "but in everything, by prayer and petition, with thanksgiving, present your requests to God. And the peace of God, which transcends all understanding, will guard your hearts and your minds in Christ Jesus" (Phil. 4:6–7).

Does that kind of sweet aroma permeate your home? It can. It's a priceless fragrance, but cannot be bought for all the gold and diamonds in the world. Some may choose perfumes with names like "Obsession" or "Beautiful" or even "Destiny." As for me, only one name will do.

"Peace."

Promoting the Prince of Peace

A few years ago the *New Zealand Herald* published an article on me under the headline, "Promoting the Prince of Peace." I couldn't have said it better myself. I love to promote the Prince of Peace.

Some time ago I was in upstate New York for a week of prayer with several Presbyterian churches. One night it snowed so heavily that only a few hearty souls braved the weather to attend the meeting. An older gentleman approached me just before the service, limping and walking slowly with a cane.

"Young man," he said—he couldn't pronounce my name—"can I talk to you before you leave the area? You're staying with friends of mine from college days. May I see you?"

"Yes," I said, and we set a time.

After the service I rode home with my host. "Luis," he said, "that was Dr. Smith. He's the most famous ophthalmologist on the East Coast. He's always been in the church, but he's never been happy. And now he wants to talk to you? This is marvelous."

On the day of our meeting, we all sat down and began to chat. After a cup of tea, he asked my hosts to leave the room.

"Young man," he said gravely, "I've got to ask you a question. When I was at university, John R. Mott, the well-known missionary, came to our school and challenged medical students to go and help the poor in certain parts of the world—in the Middle East and in Afghanistan. I felt the Lord sending me out, as well as my brother. But when I told my family and my fiancée, they all made fun of me, booed me down. When I graduated from university, I came out with really good prospects. I turned down the Lord's call and married my sweetheart—we've been married now for forty years.

"But you know something, young man? I've now retired, I've made my little money, I've written my books—but my son is going to hell because of me. He's an atheist. For forty-two years I've never had a day of peace in my life. Now I'm an old man and on my way out, because my illness is serious.

"I want to go with my wife to Afghanistan to try and help the many people with poor vision. But my wife refuses to go. And now I want to ask you a question, and I'm going to act on your word: shall I go, or shall I not go?"

Oh, boy, I thought, *what a decision for me to make.* I felt an impulse that I hoped came from the Lord, so I put my arms around this gentleman and said, "Doctor, you go."

He clung to me and began to weep.

"Oh, Lord," he cried, "I'm going! I'm going and no one will stop me."

Then he prayed a prayer and left. And that was it.

The next day we visited another church. Again the snow fell, again just a few showed up for prayer, and again there was the doctor. About ten minutes after I began to give my little message on prayer, this retired physician stood up—in a Presbyterian church, mind you, not a Pentecostal one—and said in a loud voice, "I'm going. I'm going, and no one will stop me!"

All the Presbyterians turned, looked, and their startled expressions said wordlessly, "*What* is going on?"

"Doctor," I said, "why don't you explain to the crowd where you're going and who's not going to stop you."

That was the end of the meeting. The good doctor took over and began to tell his story. His wife wanted to stay home so badly that she slipped in the snow and claimed she had broken her leg. "But I'm a doctor," he said. "I looked at the X-rays and there's no broken leg. She just didn't want to go."

Six months later I called up my former hosts and said, "How are you doing? And how is Doctor Smith?"

"Haven't you heard?" my friend asked.

"No."

"He's in Afghanistan with his wife. He's like a teenager all over again! He is so excited. He returned to the States once already to visit the big pharmaceutical companies, pick up tons of medicine, and take it all back to Afghanistan. He's working for a while with a missionary, and he says he's never been so happy. But his body's falling apart."

The following Easter I visited New York for a week of evangelism. There was the doctor, his body a wreck. He could hardly talk by now, but he came to a luncheon we put together.

"Luis," he whispered to me, "thank you for making me go to Afghanistan. I redeemed all the lost forty-two years *in just one year*! I'll never see you again except in the presence of the King, and I'll see you there."

About two months later the faithful physician went to be with the Lord.

Have you ever heard the call of God, like this doctor? Perhaps you heard him call at some time in your life, but you resisted. Maybe the Lord spoke to you about going some place or doing some thing, or maybe he spoke to you about something else. But you didn't respond—and you haven't enjoyed a day of peace for years. If that's you, then listen: It's never too late to plunge back into the stream of God's will for your life. Never!

If the Master has spoken to your heart, don't let another week go by without answering. And if the Lord is speaking to your heart right now, say, "Yes, Lord," because you will never have a day of peace if you remain outside of God's will. If you've been running away from the Lord, come back to him immediately and say, "I'm going. I'm going, and no one will stop me!"

How to Find Peace According to the Bible

1. *Recognize that peace eludes everyone who remains estranged from God.*

   "'There is no peace,' says the LORD, 'for the wicked'" (Isa. 48:22).

2. *Believe that God wants to give you his peace.*

   "Now may the Lord of peace himself give you peace at all times and in every way" (2 Thess. 3:16).

3. *Accept that the way to peace is found by trusting in God.*

   "You will keep in perfect peace him whose mind is steadfast, because he trusts in you" (Isa. 26:3).

4. *Find peace with God through faith in Jesus Christ.*

   "Therefore, since we have been justified through faith, we have peace with God through our Lord Jesus Christ" (Rom. 5:1).

5. *Realize that the peace of Jesus must be consciously accepted.*

   "Peace I leave with you; my peace I give you. I do not give to you as the world gives. Do not let your hearts be troubled and do not be afraid" (John 14:27).

6. *Look for peace in Jesus, not within yourself.*

   "I have told you these things, so that in me you may have peace. In this world you will have trouble. But take heart! I have overcome the world" (John 16:33).

7. *Listen to what God says in his Word and turn away from thoughtlessness.*

   "I will listen to what God the LORD will say; he promises peace to his people, his saints—but let them not return to folly" (Ps. 85:8).

8. *Make sure the Spirit of God guides your mind.*

   "The mind of sinful man is death, but the mind controlled by the Spirit is life and peace" (Rom. 8:6).

9. *Habitually bring your concerns to God in prayer.*

   "Do not be anxious about anything, but in everything, by prayer and petition, with thanksgiving, present your requests to God. And

So that was it—the last sport I thought I could play, and they just sent me off. (I still think I could play cricket. But since I've never played in England, I don't know how bad I really am.)

Why doesn't anyone want me on his team? And why don't I enjoy playing such sports? The fact is this: we love to win and hate to lose.

We love to win in athletics. We love to win in business. We love to win in school. We love to win in love. We love to win, period. Why? Because we feel great when we win, and depressed when we lose.

We love success. And why not? We're wired for it. God himself wants us to succeed. Before Joshua led the ancient Israelites into the Promised Land, God gave his servant explicit instructions to help him "be successful" wherever he went and to make him "prosperous and successful" (Josh. 1:7–8).

Do you think the Lord wants anything less for us?

A few years back I gave a graduation speech at a Christian college. I urged the graduates, "Leave here to be successful for God. Get out of this place and be a success. God has given you a fantastic education in a Christian context with a biblical base. Everything is before you to excel for the glory of God. So go do it!"

Judging from the looks I received from some of the faculty, I think the "be a success" part of my message irritated a few professors. But I look at it like this: what are your options? I see only three: success, mediocrity, or failure. Which do you pick?

I'll take success any time—but not society's version.

The beautiful thing is that true success isn't about money. True success does not mean beating the other guy. It does not mean surpassing your peers. It has to do with pleasing God and partnering with Jesus Christ in the greatest adventure in history.

Ephesians 2:10 teaches, "For we are God's workmanship, created in Christ Jesus to do good works, which God prepared in advance for us to do." God created specific works for us to do throughout our lives here on earth. If we seek God's will, he will lead us to the works he has prepared. It could be loving our children into salvation or becoming a medical missionary. It could mean becoming an evangelist and leading festivals or quietly making the most of every opportunity to serve others and share the gospel. The purpose isn't achievement for our own sake; it's succeeding at what God has prepared for us to do. If we accomplish what God wants, we are successful.

Spiritually, every one of us can be a winner in Jesus Christ.

Choose Success, Not Achievement

It's only natural to desire success and to shun failure. I have yet to meet anyone who would rather fail in life than succeed. No one makes it a goal to fail as many times as possible.

And yet too often we settle for mere achievement when we could enjoy real success. What's the difference? Achievement focuses on goals and tactics, while success emphasizes purpose and strategy. Achievement takes the short view, while success maintains the long view. Achievement concentrates on personal triumphs while success opts for community victories. In the end, achievement leaves the heart hollow and the soul gasping for more, while success expands the spirit and leaves the individual deeply contented.

All of us can choose to succeed or fail. One can achieve many things and yet wind up a spectacular failure. Since I prefer success, I try to keep in mind at least five ways that genuine success towers over mere achievement:

Achievement	Success
• Earns Rewards	• Brings Fulfillment
• Gains Fame	• Wins Respect
• Gratifies the Flesh	• Makes the Spirit Content
• Meets Goals	• Enjoys Purpose
• Builds an Empire	• Builds a Legacy

To see how true success shows its superiority over simple achievement, let's take a closer look at the foregoing comparisons.

Earns Rewards vs. Brings Fulfillment

Hard work, perseverance, and determination can lead to great achievements that in turn yield impressive rewards. Some individuals spend their whole lives chasing those rewards: corner offices, expensive cars, designer clothes, big houses, sleek boats, a position on the board of directors. Yet most folks dedicated to achievement eventually discover that the rewards and toys they worked so hard to earn don't satisfy for long.

True success, on the other hand, brings something that no material benefit can ever deliver: fulfillment. "The deepest, most satisfying delights God gives through creation are free gifts from nature and from loving relationships with people," says one author. "After your basic needs are met, accumulated money begins to diminish your capacity for these pleasures rather than increase them. Buying things contributes absolutely nothing to the heart's capacity for joy."[1]

Author David G. Myers said it another way in his book *The American Paradox: Spiritual Hunger in an Age of Plenty*. "When sailing on the *Titanic*," he wrote, "even first class cannot get you where you want to go."[2] Everyone saw the *Titanic* as quite an achievement when it sailed on its maiden voyage in April 1912, but before it could reach New York, it sank to the bottom of the frigid North Atlantic, a watery tomb for some of the wealthiest men and women of the day.

Achievement just will not get you where you want to go.

Many years ago I had a friend who owned a pool-cleaning business. His company did all right, but it was nothing outstanding. One year he asked if his daughter could visit us on the mission field in Colombia. We wondered how he could manage it financially, but he did.

Some time later, just before we returned to the United States, he wrote me a letter. "I'll wait for you at the San Francisco airport," he said. "I have a nice car, I'll take you home, we'll have fun. I'll take you to the spa."

Spa? I thought. *A pool cleaner?*

When I arrived in San Francisco, there he sat in a Mark IV Lincoln Continental, sleeves rolled up, suntanned, muscled, that look of somebody not working too hard. *Wow*, I thought, *something's really happened to him.*

We left for the spa, sweated it out, then visited a coffee shop. I noticed he'd picked up all the mannerisms and tastes of the wealthy.

"Gerald," I said, "what happened?"

"Well, let me tell you," he replied.

In four years he'd gone from pool cleaning to owning expensive property outside of San Francisco atop the hills overlooking the Pacific. He ran fifteen radio stations and a computer company.

"Man," I said, "now you can really help me with evangelism."

"That's exactly why I brought you here," he said. "I really want to help you. Right now I have a few deals to finish off—I have to buy another station in Modesto and one in Fresno—but as soon as I hit it, you're going to the top of my list."

I looked forward to seeing what God would do through Gerald's new wealth.

He bought the stations in Modesto and Fresno, then said he needed just three more. When he acquired those, he promised the money would start rolling in. But the months kept going by and it was always just one more deal—that's all, one more deal.

In 1978 the country went through a major recession and his company began to fail. He had to sell the radio stations. He had to sell the land. He and a business partner began to fight.

"You know," he once told me, "the thing that really eats me up is that I didn't pass on the money that I said I was going to give to the Lord. And now a bunch of bankers in San Francisco have it."

Today Gerald has lost his authority and his joy. Why? Because he opted for achievement rather than true success.

God earnestly desires that his people enjoy fullness of life. Jesus said, "The thief comes only to steal and kill and destroy; I have come that they may have life, and have it to the full" (John 10:10). God wants us to live an abundant, successful life in the spiritual realm, so that it spills over into the physical realm. God wants to bless his people and put responsibility in their hands. He says to us, "I'm giving you this so that you can honorably use it for the extension of my kingdom."[3] It is part of the package God desires for his people.

Maybe you remember Paul Jones, lead singer for the pop group Manfred Mann in the 1960s. He set a lot of teen hearts on fire with tunes like "Do Wah Diddy Diddy." His good looks and versatility shot him to the top of the entertainment industry. In the early 1980s he costarred with Fiona Hendley in *Guys and Dolls* and *The Beggar's Opera* on a London stage. The two hit it off and soon moved in together.

Paul fancied himself a brilliant debater, often using his wit and oratorical skills to skewer the beliefs of those he believed to be hypocritical Christians. For twenty-five years he considered himself a staunch atheist. And yet something kept bothering him.

While on tour in Germany, he visited an art gallery. "I was particularly struck by the paintings of a German artist, Caspar David Friedrich—a contemporary of Beethoven," he said. "What impressed me was his ability to create a kind of 'spirituality' out of landscapes and scenes of nature. It's funny, really, that I used the word spirituality, because I'd have said, as an honest atheist, that this word was pretty meaningless. Still, the paintings did speak to me about the values beyond the simple visible object."[4]

His live-in girlfriend believed herself to be a Christian. "I was convinced that a Christian was somebody who believed there was a God, was pretty moral, and was quite a good person, and probably went to church every now and again," Fiona said. She grew up in a broken home and saw her mother seek relief in spiritualists and the occult. She herself tried to seek God through a cult. But none of it worked, and she said she felt "in a muddle."

"I thought the way to escape all this pain was to make it in my career," she said. "I thought, I'm going to do everything I can to be the best in what I can do, and I'm going to make it and no one's going to get in my way and no one's going to stop me."

One day Fiona inexplicably walked into a church in central London. Even though she'd "sort of given up on God," she picked up a Bible, opened it, and her eyes alighted upon John 3:16 (KJV): "For God so loved the world that he gave his only begotten Son, that whosoever believeth in him should not perish, but have everlasting life."

"I was just absolutely astounded at this verse," she said, "because I thought, If this is true, it's amazing and wonderful. If it's a lie, how dare it be written!"

To see whether the verse might prove true, she and Paul started attending Sunday services and studying the Bible with a pastor. The exploration both thrilled and frightened Fiona, because she thought, *Now hang on. If I follow this fully to find God, what happens if God takes something away from me that I want?* She wanted her career more than anything and felt desperately afraid that God might send her to Africa instead. Paul, on the other hand, worried that he might have to stand up in front of a crowd some day and say, "Remember me? I'm a Christian now."

One day, pop singer Cliff Richard phoned Paul and Fiona to ask them to come with him to Queen's Park Rangers Stadium.

"Who are they playing?" Paul asked.

"No, no, it's not football," Cliff answered. "It's a man called Luis Palau. I think it will improve your life to hear him speak."

At first Paul hesitated, but when Cliff offered to buy dinner, the couple accepted. The message of Romans 1 struck home with both Paul and Fiona. Lost in a crowd of sixteen thousand, Fiona said, "We felt like we were the only people there. It was like this spotlight was on us and we were kind of caught in the headlights."

At the invitation, Fiona got up to move to the front, but Paul grabbed her arm.

"Just a moment," he said. "Where are you going?"

"Well, it's time to stop with this half-baked stuff," she replied, "and Jesus is going to be my Lord from now on."

"That's terrific," Paul said. "Where am I sleeping tonight?"

Fiona sat back down. But before the night was up, both had committed their lives to Jesus Christ.

"I've just been so happy ever since," Fiona said. "The change is amazing. God has given me such a peace about that whole career thing. Now I have a purpose that I didn't have before. I shudder to think what our marriage would be like after fourteen years if we hadn't both come to Christ."

Achievement or success? Paul and Fiona have had both, but they discovered the former can't hold a candle to the latter.

Gains Fame vs. Wins Respect

Outstanding achievement can certainly get a person noticed. Achievement often leads to fame. Who in our media-saturated culture hasn't heard the names of Tiger Woods, Julia Roberts, Oprah Winfrey, Stephen King, or Billy Graham? They have all performed at a high level in their chosen fields of expertise and have, in the process, become household names.

But what, exactly, is fame worth? Mark Twain didn't think a whole lot of it. "Fame is a vapor; popularity an accident; the only earthly certainty is oblivion," he said.[5] Actress Marlo Thomas offered a less abstract critique: "Fame lost its appeal for me when I went into a public restroom and an autograph seeker handed me a pen and paper under the stall door."[6]

Achievement can win tenuous fame that waxes and wanes according to changing public tastes, but success earns lasting respect. When someone gives another respect, he or she is really saying, "I know you and I trust you. I have seen you at work and you have earned my confidence. You have won my loyalty."

I know a gentleman in Paraguay who will never be famous, but he has forever earned my respect. He volunteered several years ago to help out in the counseling ministry of one of our missions. We train local churches to counsel the hundreds who come seeking help for their marriages, families, and other personal problems. Even though this man was a pastor, he was very poor, his appearance unkempt, and he didn't read well. He sat in class all day, listening, as his twelve-year-old nephew took notes for him. A little exam followed the training. Again, the boy wrote for the pastor. This worried our director of counseling, but when he read the man's answers, he found them excellent.

A local church let us use its facility as a counseling center; about seventy counselors staffed the place. One day all seventy were busy with counselees, while this humble brother sat there, awaiting his turn. In walked a well-dressed man—we learned he was a medical doctor—who said to the secretary at the door, "I need to talk to somebody. I have a problem with my wife. We're about to be divorced. I hear on television that you give counsel here. With whom could I speak?"

Immediately the humble brother jumped up and said to the doctor, "I will counsel you." About half an hour later this illiterate pastor emerged, arm-in-arm with the doctor.

"Doctor, is there anything I can do for you?" our director of counseling asked when he caught sight of them. "I'm available if you need me."

"No, thank you," the doctor replied. "This gentleman has just helped me very well. I know what I must do when I get home. I just said a prayer and opened my heart to Christ." He then hugged the pastor and walked out.

The next day the place again was jammed, all the counselors were tied up, and there sat this pastor, waiting for another opportunity to counsel. The same doctor returned, this time with two of his colleagues.

"Doctor, could I give you a hand?" the counseling director asked. "Could I talk to you?"

"Thank you very much," the doctor replied, "but this brother here helped me to receive Christ yesterday. My two friends want to receive Christ, too, and I want them to talk only to him."

So these three professionals headed into a classroom, led by the pastor, and in a few moments the man led the other two doctors to Jesus Christ. The next day all three physicians showed up with a fourth doctor. All of them had serious marriage problems and knew one another from the country club. They insisted on talking to only one person. And the poor pastor with a scraggly beard and rumpled clothes led all four to Jesus Christ.

After the mission, the four doctors got together with their wives and threw a big party. Whom do you think they invited? The evangelist whose name appeared on publicity posters all over town? They didn't even know me. Our counseling director? No, thank you. They asked the pastor and his nephew. Those professional men all became dedicated followers of Jesus Christ, active in a local church, and put their families together again—thanks in large part to a poor, illiterate pastor. He'll never be famous, but do you think he's earned some respect? That man has enjoyed more success than 90 percent of all the Fortune 500 CEOs who ever lived.

After I heard this story I just had to meet this man. On the closing day of the mission, it was a privilege to have my picture taken with *him*.

Gratifies the Flesh vs. Makes the Spirit Content

Achievement feels good and gratifies our desire for victory, but the feeling never lasts. As I write, the playoffs are winding down in both the National Hockey League and the National Basketball Association. In just a couple of weeks both leagues will crown new champions. Although I'm no prophet, I can guarantee that one scene will occur just moments after the final buzzer. Some reporter will shove a microphone into the face of a jubilant athlete and ask something like, "Do you think you can repeat this next year?"

The athlete will respond with some version of, "We just want to savor this for a while," but the damage already will have been done. Some portion of the winner's gratification will have vanished forever.

True success involves gratification, but it goes far beyond that to contentment. When you succeed at helping others overcome some persistent problem, you feel a contentment that just doesn't fade. When you succeed at the things that make God smile, the contentment you feel lasts and lasts. And that's true success.

In Newcastle, Australia, we spoke with students and professors at four universities. At one school a young woman, around twenty years old, told me, "Mr. Palau, there's something missing inside. My boyfriend and I have talked about it many times. There's something missing inside us and I can't put my finger on it."

"Listen," I said, "what is missing is eternal life. What is missing is Jesus Christ."

"Is that all?" she asked. "Well, how do I find him?"

And right there, standing in the middle of the University of New South Wales, surrounded by several dozen other students all waiting to talk, this beautiful girl bowed her head and we prayed together. She found what was missing inside, the contentment that comes only through Christ.

Three days later I saw her again and asked, "That element in your life that was missing inside—is it still missing?"

"No, Mr. Palau," she answered, smiling broadly. "It was filled by Jesus Christ."

Could that be your situation right now? You don't lack for money; you're a likable person; you live a clean life. And yet, deep inside, you feel something's missing.

That "something" is the contentment only Jesus can bring, as Joy Stevens can tell you.

Ten days after Joy gave birth to her second son, her husband walked out on her. In response, "I determined I was going to give my boys the best life possible," she said. She became a realtor and quickly made a lot of money. "But I became bitter and angry," she admitted. "In a few years my boys were in bad shape; one of them got into drugs."

Every day, on her way to the office, Joy noticed a sign posted at the front of a church: "Come back to God."

"I can't come back to God," she'd say. "I was never there in the first place." The church never changed the sign, and this ritual went on for years.

Through a series of events, Joy eventually made a profession of faith in Jesus Christ, but she didn't really understand what God was doing in her life. When she revealed her conversion to her new husband, whose mother had once worked with the Salvation Army, he exclaimed, "Oh, how fun! Now I've got a Christian wife!"

To celebrate, they stopped off at a pub to get a drink. At home that night, with her husband asleep, Joy remembers, "My mind was in turmoil. As I lay there in the dark, I said, 'Okay, God. What now?' And I felt as if the Lord said to me, 'I'll show you.'"

The next day when her husband awoke, he said to Joy, "You know, now that you're a Christian, we should buy a Bible, shouldn't we?"

So they bought a Bible. That very week she started attending services at a little chapel down the street. In time her husband committed his life to Jesus Christ; the Lord freed her son from his drug addiction; the other son and her husband's two children trusted Jesus Christ; and her eighty-two-year-old mother also came to Christ. Today the whole family loves and serves the Lord.

Eventually Joy decided to attend church with her daughter—and do you know what church it was? The church with the sign that still urged passersby to "Come back to God."

Joy's search for contentment began with a career and money. She thought that was what her family needed. But only in Jesus Christ will you ever find true and lasting contentment. Other things might gratify for a while, but only the Lord Jesus can make you eternally content.

Meets Goals vs. Enjoys Purpose

Even today you can witness their astonishing ability to meet aggressive goals. Yard after yard, mile after mile, you can still see the amazing fortifications they built—strong, imposing, and deeply impressive. They used concrete thicker than anything known previously, armed themselves with huge guns, and built air-conditioned areas for troops, recreation areas, living quarters, supply storehouses, and underground rail lines connecting various portions of the fortification. It took the

French several years in the early 1930s to construct the Maginot Line against a German invasion—and it took the Germans no time at all to outflank the fortifications by invading France through Belgium, thus rendering the line useless.

Everyone today recognizes the Maginot Line as a great achievement, but no one would call it a success. While its builders met all their goals, their shortsighted purpose doomed the whole enterprise.

What benefit is there in meeting goals that don't serve a worthy purpose? How can that be called "success"? You could read and slavishly follow the advice in a book like *Power, Money, Fame, Sex: A User's Guide*—a book intended for "the unabashedly ambitious," according to the publisher—but where will it get you, ultimately?

I meet many wealthy individuals who get excited to use their financial blessings for evangelism, but never really follow through on their God-given potential. They have enjoyed incredible spiritual experiences, amazing business capacity, extensive education, a broad worldview—and yet they don't live to one-tenth of their full capacity. So far they've rejected the slogan of the U.S. Army: "Be all you can be."

To "be all you can be" requires purpose, not merely the ability to meet goals. It's possible to go with the flow, not rock the boat, avoid great sins—just pursue the goal of being nice—and end up a failure.

Are you just floating along? I consider a missionary friend one of the most godly men I have ever known, and I've seen him from inside out. But only three of his six children have a serious commitment to the Lord. The others seem nice enough—nice lifestyles, nice children of their own, nice church, nice people—but have no fire, no power, no cutting edge. They just go with the flow.

When this man's wife was dying, she said to my wife, Pat, "The great agony of our lives is to see half of our children not counting for anything. It's not that they're evil. It's not that they're into sin; they're perfectly okay in that area. They're just not *counting* for anything. They're nice people, floating along."

I realize not everybody can be a statesman or a politician or a loud evangelist. But if we live with an eternal purpose rather than living to meet a few shortsighted goals, we are bound to work on the cutting edge. Men and women will feel the touch of God when our lives touch theirs.

But woe to us if we're only meeting goals! Without an eternal purpose, meeting even great goals doesn't count for much in the end.

My friend, Bob Waymire, used to be an engineer with Lockheed Martin, where he helped develop the Polaris and Poseidon weapons systems, forerunners of the Trident. He came home from work one day to discover a note from his wife: she had left him for another man and had taken their three children with her. Soon after, she divorced Bob.

Devastated, Bob gradually acquired an alcohol problem. He continued to work hard, but he was more interested in his vivacious secretary. To Bob's frustration, she was a married Christian who was more interested in him getting his life together by accepting Jesus Christ. She and another secretary regularly prayed for him. She told Bob, "Maybe *your* god isn't big enough to cure your drinking problem, but mine is."

After a typical afternoon of drinking, Bob faced an angry secretary. "It's one thing to throw your life away, but you're throwing your children's lives away!" she said. Bob shot back bitterly, "How can I be throwing my kids' lives away when I can't even see them?"

The bold woman pointed out that Bob's children needed to receive eternal life. "If you will trust my friend Jesus, you can lead your children into the kingdom of heaven. It isn't God's will that they stay lost; they need someone to explain Jesus Christ to them."

Finally having Bob's attention, she went on to tell him that he himself needed to receive Jesus as his Savior, and to let Jesus Christ—not alcohol—control his life. By the end of their long conversation, Bob yielded control of his life to Jesus Christ in prayer.

Bob's conversion quickly and dramatically changed his life. He had always known how to meet goals, but for the first time in his life he now had an eternal purpose.

Today, Bob is thoroughly committed to world evangelism. He used his scientific training to start Global Mapping International. His business develops products and programs that enable Christian leaders to better utilize strategic missions information. He is remarried to a wonderful Christian woman, and they have two children. Bob has a great relationship with his ex-wife and all five of his children. God's grace is fulfilling his converted goals.

The ability to meet goals just won't cut it if you're after real success. To enjoy success at the highest level, you need an eternal purpose. Fortunately, that's just what Jesus Christ supplies.

Builds an Empire vs. Builds a Legacy

On either coast of the United States, visitors can witness grand tributes to colossal financial empires. Those on the East Coast can travel to Asheville, North Carolina, to view the spectacular Biltmore Estate, a sprawling complex built by George W. Vanderbilt in the Blue Ridge Mountains. It features the largest house in the United States, its two hundred and fifty rooms filled with fine art and period antiques. Those on the West Coast can visit the Hearst Castle, featuring one hundred and twenty-seven acres of gardens, terraces, pools, and guest houses, built by famous newspaperman William Randolph Hearst. The crown jewel of this estate, the 137-foot-high Mediterranean Revival Mansion called "Casa Grande" ("Big House"), sits 1,600 feet above San Simeon Bay in northern California, about five miles inland from the Pacific Coast.

One look at either of these impressive compounds removes all doubt that their builders controlled enormous assets and built mighty empires. Yet that same look reveals something else: nobody really lives there anymore. Both estates function basically as museums intended to draw gawking tourists.

Not much of a legacy, in my book. When I think of "homes" and "legacies," I can't help but think of my dad.

I love to visit Argentina because each time I go there I get to hear new stories about my dad. It gets better each time I visit, although the old-timers are all dying. The oldest couple still alive who served with my parents in their little church are now both in their late seventies. The husband sat in church the night my dad received Jesus Christ; he himself came to faith only a few months before.

My dad, a homebuilder before he died at age thirty-four, built houses for nine couples who he thought showed potential for starting local churches. He built a home for the couple I just mentioned—a little chalet type of thing—and it's still in super shape. It boasts the same shiny, red tile roof my dad installed fifty-five years ago.

These folks told me that three weeks before my dad died, he came to the house and gave them the title to the property. "It's yours," he said. "You pay me any way you can. If you can't pay, that's all right, so long as you start a church in this town." And they did. They showed me photos of the first bunch of children with whom they started. This is how they used to do it in Argentina: they'd start with children; then get to the mothers; then the dads; then finally start a little congregation. The nine villages where my dad built homes all host active churches today. He maximized his potential in his own way, appropriate to his own style.

What's keeping you from maximizing your own potential? Could it be that you're out to build an empire rather than leave a legacy?

A rich young power broker once approached the Lord Jesus and asked him anxiously, "Good teacher . . . what must I do to inherit eternal life?" (Mark 10:17). The gospel makes it clear the young man had social standing, wealth, an attractive personality, sincerity, courage, humility, religious training, and led a clean life. Yet he felt desperate. Why?

It's not that he thought of himself as a bad person. Jesus didn't challenge him when he said he had kept God's commandments (Mark 10:18–21). It appeared this young man had everything going for him. Then why did he feel so desperate? If we had been there, I'll bet we would have asked, "If you are young, wealthy, with good social standing; if you are attractive, sincere, courageous; if you have kept the commandments and know all the religious jargon—*then what in the world is your problem?*"

His problem was that he felt a desperate hunger for life. He was searching for satisfaction, for something more than an empire. He was searching for life with a capital *L*.

At that decisive moment, Jesus "looked at him and loved him. 'One thing you lack,' he said. 'Go, sell everything you have and give to the poor, and you will have treasure in heaven. Then come, follow me'" (10:21).

Jesus told the young man that he lacked only one thing. But what a thing to lack! If you lack that one thing, you lack everything.

Suppose you or I were to go to the airport tomorrow morning and get on a flight to Madrid. Let's imagine that it is a new Airbus A 340–600, a beautiful, big plane. It's just been painted with a brilliant logo. The flight attendants wear snazzy new uniforms. The pilot looks "first class" and can hardly contain his excitement. You board the airplane and it looks and smells brand new. You hear orchestral music over the speakers and someone hands you a magazine. You sit down and buckle up, then are offered a complimentary soft drink or glass of wine. You hear the safety spiel, the engines roar, and the plane takes off.

When you're cruising at about 30,000 feet, the pilot comes on the intercom and says, "Ladies and gentlemen, we want you to know that you've boarded the maiden voyage of this beautiful A 340–600. Listen to those Rolls Royce engines! They are running beautifully. Look at the exquisitely decorated interior, feel the comfortable seats. Everything is just right. We do, however, have just one little problem. The paint job looks great, the engines are running fine, the music sounds tremendous, we have plenty of food—but in the excitement of launching this plane, the ground crew forgot to refuel it. But don't worry! That's the only thing wrong. Everything else is just fine."

What is going to happen to your airplane? Without fuel, it will crash—and you're finished. The airplane needed only one thing, but it was the most important thing.

Could it be that way with you? Everything seems all right. Your bank account is full. Your cars run great. The kids seem fine. Everything appears good—except one thing. You don't have God in your life. You don't have Jesus Christ living in you. Listen, without his divine fuel, you are dead, finished. You may build an empire, but you'll leave no legacy.

Jesus told the rich young man that only one thing stood in the way of receiving eternal life. One idol blocked his access to God: money. So Jesus told him, chuck the idol and join me.

As I travel around the world, the people who consistently respond most eagerly to the gospel seem to be those with empty stomachs. People from poor countries recognize their need for God much more quickly than those from prosperous ones.

Do you know why many men and women lack assurance of eternal life? It is not because they are immoral or ungodly. It is because they have never taken the action that God demands. The Bible calls for action. You must *do* something. Jesus gave this young man five simple commands: Go, sell, give, come, and follow (10:21). Jesus said, in effect, "I will give you eternal life and you can build a true legacy, if only you will do what I say."

Life means making basic decisions. Do you know what happened to this young man—powerful as he was, handsome, humble, rich, moral, and religious? The Bible says he got up off his knees, dusted off his clothes, and walked away, crestfallen. He refused to do what Jesus asked of him and ambled away, sad. And Jesus let him go.

He still lets men and women walk away. During our festivals, in the midst of thousands of happy endings in which individuals settle their affairs with God, I've seen hundreds of "rich young power brokers" walk away sad. Many hear the voice of God, hear the demands of Jesus Christ, but respond, "I'm sorry, but I can't go through with it. I would rather build my empire than leave a legacy for God. I'm more concerned with what my neighbors and relatives think than what God thinks. I'm sorry." And they leave with their heads bowed and their faces sad.

Do not walk away like the rich young man! Don't leave with a sorrowful expression, lost and sad. Surrender to Jesus Christ. By faith say,

"Oh, Lord God, I'm just like the rich young man. I feel a great emptiness inside. I want to receive Jesus Christ. I will follow Christ. I trust him. I believe him."

When you accept Jesus's offer, the Bible says you become a king and priest (Rev. 1:6; 5:10). Through Jesus, you can begin to reign in life (Rom. 5:17; 2 Tim. 2:12; Rev. 20:6).

When kings and presidents walk into a room, they stride in with a sense of confidence. Whether it's the president of the United States or the ruler of the Palau Republic, the smallest kingdom in the world, you sense a certain confidence. When the Scripture says we are kings and priests, God intends to give us a sense of dignity, authority, and confidence. And that's true no matter the socioeconomic standing of the believer.

When you visit the poorest Christians in the world, such as those in the remotest villages of Guatemala or Bolivia, even illiterate believers can enter the room with dignity and confidence. Jesus Christ takes even those without shoes and causes them to walk with the bearing of kings and queens.

That's part of the legacy of Jesus Christ, and it far outstrips any human empire ever built.

Be a Winner

One afternoon, years ago, someone gave me tickets to the Wimbledon tennis championships. I had the pleasure of seeing Chris Evert Lloyd win one of her titles. And it got me to thinking: *In life, as in tennis, there is really no tie. You either win or you lose.*

Every one of us playing the game of life will end up as either a winner or a loser, depending on what we do with Jesus Christ. Are you going to be a winner? Or when it's all said and done, will you be a loser?

God made the game of life and its rules, and one of his rules is this: "Love the Lord your God with all your heart and with all your soul and with all your strength and with all your mind" (Luke 10:27). All of us play in this game of life. No one can say, "Hey, I'm not signing up." We are on the roster of one team or the other. We can't stand on the sidelines and say, "I'll play referee and watch everybody play." No, God is the referee, and we play on either one or the other team. We can win or we can lose. The choice is ours.

God wants us all to be winners. He made each one of us to enjoy life here and to wind up in God's Hall of Fame in heaven. So don't settle for mere achievement when you can enjoy true success. Jesus asked us, "What good is it for a man to gain the whole world, and yet lose or forfeit his very self?" (Luke 9:25). Don't give up your place in God's Hall of Fame. Choose success!

How to Be Successful According to the Bible

1. *Never set yourself up in opposition to God.*
   "There is no wisdom, no insight, no plan that can succeed against the LORD" (Prov. 21:30).

2. *Make sure that you and God are walking the same path.*
   "In everything he did he had great success, because the LORD was with him" (1 Sam. 18:14).

3. *See to it that both your methods and goals honor God.*
   "He sought God during the days of Zechariah, who instructed him in the fear of God. As long as he sought the LORD, God gave him success" (2 Chron. 26:5).

4. *Gain a thorough grasp of God's Word, the Bible.*
   "Do not let this Book of the Law depart from your mouth; meditate on it day and night, so that you may be careful to do everything written in it. Then you will be prosperous and successful" (Josh. 1:8).

5. *Pray for success.*
   "O LORD, save us; O LORD, grant us success" (Ps. 118:25).

6. *Spend whatever time is necessary to gain whatever skills you may require.*
   "If the ax is dull and its edge unsharpened, more strength is needed but skill will bring success" (Eccles. 10:10).

7. *Seek out wise counselors and ask for their advice.*
   "Plans fail for lack of counsel, but with many advisers they succeed" (Prov. 15:22).

8. *Don't fly by the seat of your pants, but devise a plan.*
   "The plans of the diligent lead to profit as surely as haste leads to poverty" (Prov. 21:5).

9. *Commit your plans to the Lord.*
   "Commit to the LORD whatever you do, and your plans will succeed" (Prov. 16:3).

10. *Realize that God may have a different idea for your success than you do.*

"Many are the plans in a man's heart, but it is the LORD's purpose that prevails" (Prov. 19:21).

7

A Lifelong Source of Thrills

Excitement or Adventure?

One thing I do: Forgetting what is behind and straining toward what is ahead, I press on toward the goal to win the prize for which God has called me heavenward in Christ Jesus.

The apostle Paul, in Philippians 3:13–14

There's nothing like a bit of excitement to add a little zip to your life.

You know the glorious feeling: that awesome rush of adrenaline as you prepare to . . .

- Kiss the long-distant object of your affection
- Claim a last-second victory
- Cash your first paycheck
- Meet your lifelong hero
- Step on the plane for your dream vacation

Jason Hale and Dixie-Marie Prickett certainly know that sweet feeling. Jason, a neurotrauma nurse, and Dixie-Marie, a kayak instructor, lived their dream summer in 2001. The twenty-something couple from Asheville, North Carolina, spent four months kayaking, romancing, and "checking out lots of waterfalls and lots of exciting places" across the United States.

Interviewed by National Public Radio's Susan Stamberg, Jason said, "I love surfing a wave and 'dropping' a twenty- to thirty-foot waterfall early in the morning. . . . The lighting is better . . . and you can always have more time to go back and do it two or three times again in the afternoon." He likened "dropping down" off the lip of a waterfall into the basin pool below to a very fast elevator ride.

Dixie-Marie described the "perfect waterfall" near Hood River, Oregon: gorgeous moss-covered rocks, a perpetual rainbow off intensely blue glacial waters—and a thirty-four-foot drop. When she realizes how far a drop really is, she coaches herself through the fear: "It's going to be two seconds at most and it's done."

Both admit that kayaking waterfalls involves risks similar to NASCAR driving. Jason has even broken his back once and is still haunted by "evil dreams" of his accident. Now recovered, he strives to perfect his landing and rejoices each time he runs a waterfall correctly. "I come up and '*Whooee*! I didn't break my back this time!' It's just awesome."[1]

Despite the risks, the excitement of whitewater kayaking defines Dixie-Marie and Jason's lives. It may have been their favorite summer so far, but both believe upcoming years will be even better.

The Many Faces of Excitement

Fortunately, excitement comes not only when we avoid breaking our backs, but also in a wild variety of shapes and flavors.

Look for "adrenaline rush" in a popular electronic encyclopedia, and up pops a picture of a pair of skydivers drifting to earth in what's called a "two-person stack." The caption reads, "Because of the sensation of leaping into the air and free-falling some distance before opening their parachutes, skydivers usually experience a rush of adrenaline and then a peaceful sense of well-being."[2]

Turn to the wider net of the World Wide Web, and you can find not only skydiving, but also bungee jumping, tornado chasing, and running with the bulls in Pamplona, Spain.

The Travel Channel recently aired a program called "101 Things You Should Do to Have a Full Life." Besides suggesting a parachute jump (a universal favorite), the show counseled excitement seekers to attend space camp or take a deep-sea voyage to the *Titanic*, where the disintegrating Cunard liner lies a frigid two and a half miles down on the bottom of the Atlantic Ocean. "Thirty-five thousand dollars is a lot of money," the host admitted, "but you'll only do it once and you'll never forget it."

Neither will your pocketbook, I bet.

The Physiology of Excitement

Why do we crave excitement? What urges us on to outrageous expenditures of money and time in its frenzied pursuit? Mostly, because of the way it makes us feel.

The human body responds to excitement much as it does to stress. When we get excited, the autonomic nervous system directs the adrenal glands to secrete epinephrine (also called adrenaline) and norepinephrine into the bloodstream, causing the heart to beat more rapidly, blood pressure to rise, breathing to accelerate, the pupils to dilate, perspiration to increase, and blood to flow to the brain and muscles from the internal organs and skin. Then the hypothalamus prompts the body to burn more fats and carbohydrates, further fueling the "fight or flight" response.

Our bodies also produce abnormally high levels of endorphins during periods of intense stress or excitement. Endorphins play a huge role in producing the feelings of ecstasy or pleasure we experience when excited—whether that excitement comes from sexual arousal, a business triumph, or athletic competition.

Because we crave the intense feelings generated by excitement, increasing numbers of us pursue the ever-escalating thrills provided by "extreme sports." Bungee jumping is probably the most popular, while other extreme sports such as sky surfing and BASE jumping (hurling one's body off of *b*uildings, *a*ntennas, *s*pans, *e*arth—illegal in most jurisdictions) are gaining in popularity. And a lot of folks are opting these days for "adventure vacations."

Some psychologists see this fascination with extreme sports as a modern substitute for vision quests and traditional rites of passage found in other cultures. Other experts believe such sports indicate a reaction to the relative safety of modern life. As writer Hope Winsborough noted, "Lacking a feeling of danger in their everyday activities, people may have felt compelled to seek out danger or risk."[3]

Maybe. But I think most enthusiasts of extreme sports get involved simply for the thrill of it, for the heart-pounding, blood-pumping, face-flushing adrenaline rush that leaves them with "a peaceful sense of well-being."

Who doesn't love the goose pimples that race across our flesh when a wave of excitement hits? We're designed to enjoy that which stirs up our emotions or feelings. Excitement makes us feel good, brightens our outlook, and puts a smile on our face. We're naturally drawn to whatever can animate us, kindle our sleeping affections, stir us to action, and inflame our built-in desire for *adventure*.

Ah, adventure! The very word suggests excitement—but also something more, something beyond, something extra. My dictionary declares adventure to be "an undertaking involving risk, unforeseeable danger, or unexpected excitement."[4] When I think of adventure, my mind fills with electrifying images of dangerous quests in exotic lands undertaken for a worthy purpose. Excitement may raise my pulse for a moment, but real adventure supplies me with a lifelong source of thrills generated by commitment to a noble mission.

In other words, excitement's good, but adventure's better.

How's It Better?

Of all possible adventures, the Christian life is the greatest. A more exciting adventure simply can't be found. It qualifies at every point: it's exciting; it lasts a lifetime; it's rooted in a noble cause; and unexpected danger accompanies it everywhere. While earthly adventures may tempt death, the Christian life actually affects life *after* death.

Now, understand I'm not talking about the insipid, apathetic Christian life of too many couch-potato believers in these La-Z-Boy days. I'm talking about the robust brand of Christianity that inspired first-century pagans to say of their Christian neighbors, "These men who have turned the world upside down have come here also" (Acts 17:6 RSV). I'm talking about the risk-taking kind of faith that has prompted believers throughout the centuries to sail uncharted waters, cross dangerous borders, confront powerful kings, give away fortunes, minister to the sick, and eagerly offer their very lives in hazardous service to the King of Kings.

The Christian life truly is the grandest adventure of all—despite what some commentators say. Too many of them try to temper a believer's natural enthusiasm with grim warnings. "Adventure?" they ask. "Surely. But never forget that Jesus told us, 'In the world you'll have tribulation,'" or "Don't think it's going to be easy," or "Satan's just around the corner!"—as if we didn't know it. Of course, we know it perfectly well. Who's ever heard of an *easy* adventure? Overcoming obstacles and facing dangers *make* adventure wonderful.

We're not frightened because the devil's lurking around the next bend. He's always been there. He prowls around comfortable, low-risk lives as well. I say let's deal with Satan by tapping into the power of God—that's part of the adventure, too.

Real adventure, the kind offered by a full-throttle Christian life, touches the deepest part of our souls and opens up a world of wonder, while mere excitement quickens our pulse for a few moments and then leaves an internal vacuum that demands a bigger rush next time. Adventure "works" over the long haul, while excitement offers the life span of a mayfly. I like to get excited, but I love adventure. Excitement, as good as it is, comes in second to adventure in at least five important ways:

Excitement	Adventure
• Appetizing	• Satisfying
• Physiological	• Spiritual
• Inward Focus	• Outward Focus
• Event-oriented	• People-oriented
• Momentary	• Lifelong

Appetizing vs. Satisfying

Compare excitement to an appetizer but adventure to a full-course meal. Buffalo wings or fried mozzarella sticks may taste delicious, but you wouldn't want to try to fill up on them; you need chicken fettuccine alfredo or beef wellington for that. Excitement provides spice to life, but who can live off of spices? Think of adventure as the main course, spiced up with excitement.

Unfortunately, many people mistake the sizzle for the steak. Tom Landry, former coach of the National Football League's Dallas Cowboys, made exactly that error before he discovered true adventure in the middle of his celebrated life.

Landry won all-pro honors as a defensive back with the New York Giants in the fifties, then coached the Cowboys for twenty-nine years from 1960–1988. He led his team to five Super Bowl appearances, winning in 1972 and 1978. When he died on February 12, 2000, he still ranked third on the NFL's all-time win list with 270 victories.

The coach spoke briefly at one of our mission events a number of years ago. He told the audience how for many years he mistook an appetizer for the main course—and then couldn't figure out why he still felt hungry.

He described getting a football scholarship to the University of Texas, then leaving college to fly B-17 missions over Germany in World War II. At the end of the war he reenrolled at the University of Texas. "I wanted to climb that ladder of success that's made America so great," he said. "I had great success at football at the University of Texas. We won the Sugar Bowl; we won the Orange Bowl my senior year. But each time we had the excitement of winning these games, there was something missing. I was empty and restless, and I didn't understand why that was. I thought that when you had success like that, you should be excited all the time. But that wasn't true. I thought, *Well, I just haven't reached the top.*"

After graduation Landry joined the New York Giants in the National Football League, where he earned further success. His team won the world championship in 1956 against the Chicago Bears, and played in one of the greatest professional games ever in 1958 against the Baltimore Colts. But again, the emptiness gnawed at him.

"I went to a friend of mine in Dallas and told him about my problem," Landry said. "I was empty and restless; I didn't understand why I wasn't getting the fulfillment I thought I should have."

His friend immediately identified the problem. He asked Landry to attend a Bible study that met in a Dallas hotel, but the coach resisted. "Heck," he explained, "I'd been to church every Sunday as long as I could remember. I knew the Christmas story and the Easter story, and I didn't think I needed any more."

But his friend finally persuaded him to go, and when Landry walked in to his first meeting, he heard the group discussing words of Jesus Christ from Matthew 6:25, 33: "Do not worry about your life, what you will eat or drink; or about your body, what you will wear. Is not life more important than food, and the body more important than clothes? . . . But seek first his kingdom and his righteousness, and all these things will be given to you as well."

And he wondered: *Could this be the adventure I've missed?*

Soon afterward, at age thirty-five, he committed his life to Jesus Christ. The next year he took over as coach of the Cowboys and immediately made it clear to players and coaches alike that he had adopted a new set of priorities: God first, family second, football third. When the rookies came into camp for their first team meeting, Coach Landry always began by laying out his philosophy. Bob Lilly, a future all-pro lineman, had a hard time buying his new coach's priorities; he just didn't think they could work. After retiring he admitted to Landry, "You know, Coach, when you told me that, I didn't think we'd ever win a football game." Landry just smiled—easy to do when you've been to five Super Bowls, won two of them, and "had twenty years of winning," in the coach's words.

Quite an adventure—and much more satisfying than mere excitement.

God offers all of us the adventure of a lifetime through a dynamic, thrilling, unpredictable, and yet satisfying journey with Jesus Christ. From the very earliest days of the church, that's always been true. When I consider the life of the apostle Paul, for example, I see one of the greatest adventurers in human history.

Paul lived an incredibly exciting, adventurous, dangerous existence, but it also qualified as the most fulfilling life possible. That's why we still feel the impact of his life some two thousand years later. He proves that following Jesus Christ is the greatest adventure on the market.

Paul never knew a dull day. Because he strove to introduce as many people as possible to Jesus Christ, he never found himself bored or fighting a sense of purposelessness. Meaning filled his life—almost overfilled it. In the words of the psalmist, his cup ran over.

But Paul also faced danger. Listen to his own account of his exploits:

> I have worked much harder, been in prison more frequently, been flogged more severely, and been exposed to death again and again. Five times I received from the Jews the forty lashes minus one. Three times I was beaten with rods, once I was stoned, three times I was shipwrecked, I spent a night and a day in the open sea, I have been constantly on the move. I have been in danger from rivers, in danger from bandits, in danger from my own countrymen, in danger from Gentiles; in danger in the city, in danger in the country, in danger at sea; and in danger from false brothers. I have labored and toiled and have often gone without sleep; I have known hunger and thirst and have often gone without food; I have been cold and naked. . . . In Damascus the governor under King Aretas had the city of the

Damascenes guarded in order to arrest me. But I was lowered in a basket from a window in the wall and slipped through his hands.

2 Corinthians 11:23–27, 32–33

Talk about adventure! Paul's life makes the celluloid exploits of Indiana Jones sound like an amusement park ride (which, I guess, it is). During one time of heightened religious tension in the Middle East, Paul made it clear he planned to visit Jerusalem. His friends pleaded with him not to go, but he insisted another adventure awaited him there. "Why are you weeping and breaking my heart?" he asked them. "I am ready not only to be bound, but also to die in Jerusalem for the name of the Lord Jesus" (Acts 21:13). And don't think his words reflected some hasty, ill-considered death wish. Earlier he had told another group of friends, "I am going to Jerusalem, not knowing what will happen to me there. I only know that in every city the Holy Spirit warns me that prison and hardships are facing me. However, I consider my life worth nothing to me, if only I may finish the race and complete the task the Lord Jesus has given me—the task of testifying to the gospel of God's grace" (Acts 20:22–24).

How could a man like that ever get bored? How could a believer with a mission that big, a passion that hot, and a God that great ever settle for mere excitement? He couldn't.

And neither should you.

Physiological vs. Spiritual

While excitement arises primarily as a physiological reaction to an outside stimulus—a matter of multiplied endorphins, flowing adrenaline, wide eyes, and increased pulse rate—adventure leaps far beyond the physical to embrace the spiritual. Excitement is a one-car locomotive, while adventure pulls a whole train speeding along a quarter mile of track from engine to caboose.

The best adventures always spring from a noble cause or mission. The greatest adventurers crisscross the world and interact with exotic peoples not only for the thrills, but also to accomplish a worthy purpose. Because the excitement they feel connects to a far greater objective, they enjoy a deeper, richer, and longer lasting pleasure than those who seek only an adrenaline rush.

That's another reason why the Christian life presents the best opportunities for adventure. Those who invest themselves unreservedly in partnering with God to extend his kingdom—whether they do so in the classroom, boardroom, lunchroom, or weight room—know an ongoing thrill unavailable to others. It's one thing to risk your life to set a (soon-to-be-broken) record in street luge; it's quite another to risk it in trying to bring eternal life to those who desperately need it.

When my four sons were younger and living at home, and I was getting ready to travel to a dangerous part of the world, I often explained to them that I might never return from that particular trip. I felt it was my duty to prepare them for whatever might come. Of course I didn't want to die, and I prayed privately that if it came to that, the end would come quickly and without pain. I'm a chicken like anyone else; I hope to live till I'm ninety-two. But the danger had to be faced, and in the power of the Lord Jesus Christ, it can be. The bottom line: if our Master died for us, what an honor it would be to die for him!

I almost had the honor thrust upon me several times.

In 1984, during a mission in the city of Arequipa, Peru, we felt high as kites because thousands of men and women had made a commitment to Jesus Christ. In South America it's traditional for people to give the speaker letters or notes as he walks out of the stadium, and I habitually put the pieces of paper in my pocket. When my team and I got back to the hotel on the next-to-last day of the crusade, we broke into a chorus of "Praise God from whom all blessings flow." As my guys continued to talk and sing, I took out an envelope and slowly read a note from the *Sendero Luminoso*, the Shining Path—Peru's infamous terrorist group. My singing stopped:

You leave the country within 24 hours, you criminal, or you're going to die like a dog. You deserve the worst, you thief, you murderer, you dirty capitalist.

They couldn't use enough epithets they considered insulting. The note threatened me repeatedly: "We're going to kill you, you swine, you pig, you thief."

Immediately we submitted the letter to the Peruvian secret police. Their faces turned pale as they verified the note's style and seal as that of the most murderous wing of the *Sendero Luminoso.* "Yes, this is real," they told us. "We'll have to protect you."

I couldn't sleep that night. You don't mind going to heaven when it's your time, but if someone is planning to send you there early, you hope their aim is impeccable so you die instantly.

The group had ordered us to leave Peru, but we had a mission scheduled for Lima afterward—with no safe way out of Arequipa. By car we would have to drive right through territory controlled by the Shining Path. By air we had our choice of one flight in the morning or one at night. So if they wanted to get us, they could get us.

After much prayer we decided that if we left it would be cowardly. What kind of Christian leader would I be if I quit just because I was threatened? Then everybody would say, "Palau took off because he was afraid—such a great, godly leader we have here." So we stayed.

We switched to a hotel with two underground exits, left the hotel from the basement, and often changed cars on the way to the stadium. We'd swap cars in the middle of the street—police stopped all traffic, we exchanged cars and scooted off a different way. And when we arrived at the stadium, nobody could talk to me.

On the last night of the campaign, police swarmed all over the place, using dogs to inspect the stadium. Of course, we knew committed terrorists could still get me. If gunmen could manage to assassinate three different presidents of the United States, they could easily get an evangelist like me. It wouldn't take much intelligence.

After our meetings ended, we snuck out at the last minute; police made all the arrangements. Still, we knew the Shining Path had people everywhere. Even when we finally boarded the plane for Lima, I couldn't help but look at every face and wonder, *Is there a killer in here?*

During such an adventure, you realize that only the Lord can protect you. And you're grateful that he can keep you safe not only from the Shining Path in Peru, but also from unknown enemies of all kinds.

Can serving Jesus Christ put your life at risk? It might. But what could be better than exchanging a few moments of danger for eternal dividends?

Inward Focus vs. Outward Focus

When something excites us, we can't help but get caught up in the bubbling emotions that engulf us. Our focus naturally turns inward, to how we feel, how we respond to this new thrill. We're happy if others share our excitement and feel it along with us, but mostly because their animated response intensifies our own sense of exhilaration.

Real adventure turns the focus outward, without diminishing in the slightest an individual's ability to enjoy events. It expands our field of vision, broadens our horizons, and enlarges our capacity for joy. And our excitement doubles when we see how our efforts bring delight to others.

I don't know that I have ever felt more excited than when I have seen God use my efforts to help "open up" a nation previously closed to the gospel of Jesus Christ. To witness the unbridled joy on the faces of men and women, boys and girls, when they hear about the spiritual riches offered them in Jesus Christ—my heart swells with gratitude to God.

I have prayed for the People's Republic of China since 1949, when the communists took over and stories of persecuted Christians started drifting into the West. I'd read the remarkable tales of Hudson Taylor, a pioneering missionary to China in the 1800s, so I had a fascination with that land. Even as a little boy, I thought, *Someday, I'm going to China and preach. And when I go, I don't want to enter through any other port but Shanghai.* Why Shanghai? Because that's where Hudson Taylor crossed the border. I know, I know—a crazy, sentimental desire. Who cares what port you come in? But to me it felt somehow meaningful.

For fifty years I continued to pray, "Lord, let me preach in Shanghai!" During that time I preached in Singapore, Hong Kong, and Taiwan—close, but not quite there. Everywhere I went in the Far East, I kept planting the seed: "I want to go to mainland China."

Not long ago I saw a video of my last message in Hong Kong during our "Hope for Eternity" mission in 1997. After giving the invitation I said, "Well, my dear Chinese, I'll see you in heaven, or I'll see you in Shanghai." I marveled that I actually said such a thing in public, because I knew that officials from mainland China sat in the audience. But I did say it. And three years later, I found myself entering China to preach—in Shanghai!

When you fly into Shanghai from the United States, you soar over green rice paddies that look much as they did in Hudson Taylor's day. But when you drive into the city from the airport (about twenty miles away), you see a modern metropolis like Chicago or Dallas or New York. In the last ten years more than 150 high-rise buildings have shot upward, all with reflective glass and modern architecture—shiny monuments and glittering globes. It took my breath away.

Nothing, however, could prepare me for the churches. I preached at three churches at the invitation of the Shanghai Christian Council. Each church was jammed with hordes of happy people sitting together in tight formations, singing with full voices to Jesus Christ. I tell you, there's nothing like it!

It's true that persecution still exists and China has a long way to go. But it seems inevitable that great changes are coming to the People's Republic of China. I base my conclusion not only on what I saw, but on personal conversations with key people. My prayers that God would completely open up that long-closed nation have become more fervent.

Do you crave adventure? I encourage you to look for opportunities to help open up a country to the staggering blessings of God. Research a closed country, then pray daily for its government and citizens. Support overseas missionaries financially—or go on a short-term missions trip yourself. God knows what thrills you and what is useful for his kingdom. Don't be afraid to ask God what adventures he has planned for *your* life.

Anyone can "grab for the gusto" if he or she will just determine to follow the Lord. Their experiences may not mirror mine, but they, too, can see lives saved and blessing bestowed upon cities and nations and whole generations.

Event-oriented vs. People-oriented

When we seek excitement for its own sake, events take center stage. We plan and gear up for a specific activity at a prearranged time. To a large extent, it doesn't matter whether another soul exists anywhere on the planet: It's just you and the event; not much else counts.

On the other hand, adventure features an unending succession of eye-popping events in which people dominate. That's why the Christian life offers the greatest adventure imaginable. What could be better than working with God through a high-stakes mission in which eternal lives hang in the balance?

Corrie ten Boom, the late Dutch evangelist, used to recite a poem I love:

> When I enter that beautiful city
> and the saints all around appear,
> I hope that someone will tell me,
> "It was you who invited me here."

It excites me when someone walks up and says, "Luis, something great has happened! For the first time in my life, I was able to lead someone to a personal relationship with Jesus Christ."

A few years ago a twenty-year-old college student from Glasgow University approached me. "Luis," she said, "I've been a Christian for two years; my family doesn't yet know Christ. I received training from your staff, became a counselor for the mission, and had the privilege of leading a number of people to Christ!"

"How many people did you counsel?" I asked.

"Ten," she answered.

"And how many of the ten were first-time decisions, opening their hearts to Christ?"

"Six."

"Are you excited?" I wondered.

"Am I excited!" she exclaimed. "My question is, what am I going to do *now*? I graduate in June, and there's only one thing I want to do in life, and that's win people to Christ."

If only more of God's children would discover that kind of excitement!

Something just as beautiful occurred in a Lanarkshire, Scotland, mission on a Friday night years ago. An elder from a Church of Scotland congregation accepted a friend's invitation to volunteer at the mission. "All right," he agreed, "and I'll take my children to help me."

At the mission the next day, after hearing my message, this man made his way to the front and admitted, "Lord, I'm an elder in our church, and I have never led one soul to Christ. Please use me. I dedicate my life to you. I am making my decision to serve you and follow you only. Make me a fisher of men."

After a few words of counsel, I prayed with everyone who had come forward to make a decision. Then I directed the whole group to the counseling tent. After spending a few moments with a trained counselor, this gentleman returned to the main tent to help clean up. When everyone had departed, an older woman approached him and said, "Sir, I'd like to get a cassette tape of tonight's meeting."

"Well, I don't think you can get it tonight, but I'll show you where the order forms are," the elder replied. "You can fill it in and they will mail it to you, or you can pick it up later at the book stall."

As she filled in the form, he noticed she looked terribly sad. Then this volunteer, who hadn't yet received training to be a counselor, said, "Madam, you don't look too happy. Can I do anything for you?"

"Yes," she broke down, "can you tell me how to become a Christian?"

And right then and there, this elder sat down with this broken lady and led her to Jesus. All this happened less than half an hour after he made his own decision to be a fisher of men!

Of course, you don't have to attend a mission to get excited about planting seeds that may help others cross from death to eternal life. Individual Christians faithfully make the most of their opportunities all the time.

Once, in Colombia, South America, we hosted an evangelistic reception for two thousand people. The president, Lopez Michaelson, attended, but his wife didn't, as she was traveling in Europe. Two days after the event, one of my British friends called me with an exciting report. During a flight from Rome to London, he had shared the gospel with the woman sitting next to him in first class. It turned out that she was the wife of Colombia's president!

While each of these events brought a tremendous amount of excitement to those involved, no one (other than God) orchestrated them. In each case, the events took a backseat to the people. That's genuine adventure, and it flourishes whenever and wherever enthusiastic followers of Jesus brag on their Savior.

Momentary vs. Lifelong

Because excitement is primarily a physiological response to an outside stimulus, it lasts only so long as high levels of endorphins and adrenaline course through the body. When they subside, so does the excitement. Only a pleasant, quickly fading memory remains.

Adventure boasts far more staying power. Because it follows the trail of a bigger-than-life mission, it doesn't fizzle out moments after the fireworks die. It doesn't have to go looking for the next buzz, because buzz is part of its very essence. Adventure dances long after excitement goes to bed.

But you don't have to travel to Shanghai or Rome or to any other exotic port to find adventure. God has provided more than enough adventure for you right where you live—*if* you're willing to accept the mission he wants to give you. The Bible says he'd like to appoint you to a lifelong post in heaven's diplomatic corps. He offers you an impressive title—ambassador (2 Cor. 5:20)—promises to provide you with all the resources you need to complete your assignment (Phil. 4:19), and gives you unlimited access to the Head of State for personal instructions, encouragement, or emergency insight (Phil. 4:6).

God loves to partner with his valued ambassadors to bring men and women, boys and girls, safely into his kingdom of love. When we're not acting foolishly, but strictly serious with God, the Lord always steps in—sometimes in amazing ways beyond anything we imagine.

One day two university students, both Christians, noticed two Chinese fellows who always seemed to stick together. The foreigners looked lonesome and appeared to speak only with each other. The two Christians befriended the Chinese students. Eventually they began to talk about Jesus Christ, and both of their Chinese friends fell in love with the Savior. Only later did it come out that these two expatriates were the sons of a powerful government official in the People's Republic of China.

The next summer, the new converts announced, "We're going home for vacation instead of staying in the States. We want to share the Good News with our father and with the rest of the family."

How's that for unexpected adventure? The Americans didn't know of the connection between these two Chinese students and one of the most powerful men on earth. They just served faithfully and God used them.

I get a particular thrill from accounts of powerful or influential people coming to faith in Jesus Christ. Not because it indicates a greater "catch" or makes for a more glamorous story, but because God's strategy involves benefiting "normal folk" through them. God cares about *all* humanity, not just the high and mighty. He wants *all* people to come to repentance and salvation. When community or government leaders come to faith, a trickle-down effect often brings salvation to multitudes of regular citizens—especially in closed countries. I have no doubt that China's attitudes toward the West, toward freedom and the church of Jesus Christ began to change because two young men at a university in the United States faithfully represented Jesus Christ.

But what if you're not a college student? What if you've never met the children of powerful world leaders? If you accept the ambassadorship that God wants to give you, there's no telling what kind of adventures await you.

Maybe you need to say, "God, I've sat around for thirty years complaining about the preacher and the deacons and hypocrites in the church. God, do something *through* me." Stop focusing on other church members' flaws and take your own light of Christ out to the world. Begin to look outside the church walls for opportunities to serve and evangelize. If you accept the ambassadorship God wants to give you, who knows what the Lord could do with your life? This is not hot air. This isn't pretty poetry. These aren't just nice little feel-good stories. This is serious business for ordinary men and women.

Bank on it: Come to God on his terms, and he will begin to open doors of adventure that you never envisioned.

Better Than Golf

Too many of us settle for excitement when we could grab adventure. We satisfy ourselves with a rush of adrenaline when what we really crave is a lifetime of wonder.

I'm sixty-nine years old. I know many individuals my age who dream about spending their "golden years" playing golf, traveling from one course to the next, trying to outscore themselves and their buddies. Personally, golf is not my thing. A retirement focused on golf sounds like punishment.

However, there are two courses I'd be curious to *see*. The one-hole course at Camp Bonifas at the demilitarized zone in South Korea, known as the world's most deadly as it is surrounded on three sides by land mines; and Elephant Hills Country Club in Zimbabwe, where crocodiles swim in water hazards and local rules provide for players chased by elephants—"He shall be allowed to return to his ball, which shall be played as it lies whether or not the animal had trodden thereon."

Now, even I might get an adrenaline rush on *those* courses. Golf can be a great hobby, but is striving to know every blade of grass on every course on the face of the earth the *best* use of your life? Why spend your days hitting a little white ball when you can be winning souls for eternity? What I really crave is a lifetime of continued adventures in winning more men and women to Jesus Christ. Knowing that their acceptance of Christ ensures their eternal happiness in heaven. That's real adventure. That's genuine excitement. And you can share in it fully the moment you take God up on his offer.

How to Find Adventure According to the Bible

1. *Choose the priceless over the expensive.*

   "Come, all you who are thirsty, come to the waters; and you who have no money, come, buy and eat! Come, buy wine and milk without money and without cost. Why spend money on what is not bread, and your labor on what does not satisfy? Listen, listen to me, and eat what is good, and your soul will delight in the richest of fare. Give ear and come to me; hear me, that your soul may live" (Isa. 55:1–3).

2. *Be certain you're chasing a worthy goal.*

   "Live lives worthy of God, who calls you into his kingdom and glory" (1 Thess. 2:12).

3. *Maintain a sharp, single focus.*

   "One thing I do: Forgetting what is behind and straining toward what is ahead, I press on toward the goal to win the prize for which God has called me heavenward in Christ Jesus" (Phil. 3:13–14).

4. *Be willing to forgo creature comforts.*

   "I consider everything a loss compared to the surpassing greatness of knowing Christ Jesus my Lord, for whose sake I have lost all things. I consider them rubbish, that I may gain Christ" (Phil. 3:8).

5. *Embrace a life of considered risk.*

   "I consider my life worth nothing to me, if only I may finish the race and complete the task the Lord Jesus has given me—the task of testifying to the gospel of God's grace" (Acts 20:24).

6. *Make sure the rewards are worth your sacrifices.*

   "By faith Moses, when he had grown up, refused to be known as the son of Pharaoh's daughter. He chose to be mistreated along with the people of God rather than to enjoy the pleasures of sin for a short time. He regarded disgrace for the sake of Christ as of greater value than the treasures of Egypt, because he was looking ahead to his reward" (Heb. 11:24–26).

7. *Admit your discomfort but keep in mind your future.*

   "Our light and momentary troubles are achieving for us an eternal glory that far outweighs them all" (2 Cor. 4:17).

8. *Keep fear under control.*

   "The LORD is my light and my salvation—whom shall I fear? The LORD is the stronghold of my life—of whom shall I be afraid? When evil men advance against me to devour my flesh, when my enemies and my foes attack me, they will stumble and fall. Though an army besiege me, my heart will not fear; though war break out against me, even then will I be confident" (Ps. 27:1–3).

9. *Find a way to replenish your inner resources.*

   "We do not lose heart. Though outwardly we are wasting away, yet inwardly we are being renewed day by day" (2 Cor. 4:16).

10. *Remember that God loves to beat the odds.*

    "No king is saved by the size of his army; no warrior escapes by his great strength. A horse is a vain hope for deliverance; despite all its great strength it cannot save. But the eyes of the LORD are on those who fear him, on those whose hope is in his unfailing love, to deliver them from death and keep them alive in famine" (Ps. 33:16–19).

8

A Shield All Day Long

Invulnerability or Safety?

Let the beloved of the LORD rest secure in him,
  for he shields him all day long,
  and the one the LORD loves rests between his shoulders.

Moses, in Deuteronomy 33:12

All of us need to feel safe and secure. Yet few of us go to the extremes of Hamilcar Wilts, the unfortunate subject of an old children's tale by Robert Yoder.[1]

"There never was a more careful man than Hamilcar Wilts," Yoder wrote. "Although the only river in his vicinity was two feet wide and looked badly in need of water, Hamilcar kept a rowboat on his roof in case of a flood. In the rowboat there was a raft, in case the boat leaked, and the raft's equipment included needles for sewing furs, in case Hamilcar was carried to the far north, and an augur for opening coconuts, in case he was carried to the tropics. There wasn't much against which Hamilcar wasn't prepared."

Hamilcar banished all poisonous or flammable materials from his home, and stocked his medicine cabinet with every potion known to man, including an ointment to treat "butter slicer's squint, which is a form of eyestrain affecting the pygmies who cut butter pats for restaurants." He filled his home with fire extinguishers, lightning rods, and an elephant gun. Sometimes he relaxed by sipping a sterilized glass of boiled beer. Within his fortress, Hamilcar felt safe.

Eight miles away, however, lived a dolt named Boggle. Boggle blew up his house one day while trying to open a can of gasoline with a blowtorch. The explosion threw him seventy feet into a warehouse of pillows, where he landed "so gently that it barely knocked the ashes off his cigarette." When Hamilcar heard the explosion he thought something had damaged one of his trees, so he quickly donned a pair of lineman's gloves (in case of live wires) and a bee veil, hurried out to the yard . . . and was promptly crushed by Boggle's plummeting stove.

The moral: "The chances of getting eaten by a leopard on Main Street are one in a million, but once is enough."

While few of us go to the lengths of Hamilcar Wilts, we all need to feel safe. We all look for security. If you were to ask a random group of passersby, "What do you most want in life?" you'd probably hear things like, "I want to be loved," or "I want to be rich," or "I want to be healthy." What lies behind and beneath all these wants? A powerful desire for security. Regardless of the words we use, we're all basically saying, "I want to feel safe."

Bulletproof or Safe?

We're built in such a way that we *need* to feel safe and secure. When we don't feel safe, we scramble after all manner of techniques to find security, some of them profoundly unhealthy. In an effort to feel safe, sometimes we try to wall ourselves off from all possible threats. We don't allow anyone to get too close. We obsess about building an impregnable financial portfolio. We spend inordinate amounts of time perfecting the "right" diet, the "right" exercise routine, the "right" medical regimen, the "right" home environment. We strive to feel bulletproof, invulnerable.

While such tactics can indeed protect us from some dangers, they also exclude us from real life. And in the end, they can't deliver real safety, anyway (remember Hamilcar Wilts?). Real security can't be found in a suit of armor, but in a Guardian who faithfully surrounds us with his protection.

One Scripture passage highlights two alternate ways of trying to feel safe. Proverbs 18:10 says, "The name of the LORD is a strong tower; the righteous run to it and are safe." Another popular option follows in verse 11: "The wealth of the rich is their fortified city; they imagine it an unscalable wall." The first way actually works; the second way doesn't.

How does the safety we enjoy in God differ from the invulnerability that some try to create for themselves? And why does God's security program outperform anything else? Let me suggest five areas of superiority:

Invulnerability	Safety
• Flees from Fear	• Frees from Fear
• Shuns Risk	• Embraces Risk
• Falls Back	• Forges Ahead
• Restrictive Outlook	• Expansive Outlook
• Focused on Danger	• Focused on Opportunity

Flees from Fear vs. Frees from Fear

No one wants to live in fear. We might go to the movies or rent a video to scare ourselves silly for a couple of hours with a popular horror flick, but nobody really wants to live out their days in the company of Count Dracula or Dr. Hannibal Lecter.

Some folks so hate the feeling of fear that they'll do anything to keep it at bay. They wall themselves off, whether physically or emotionally.

They flee any situation or opportunity that refuses to guarantee their safety. They run from all perceived dangers—but in fleeing fear, they become its prisoners.

True security comes not in fleeing fear, but in facing it and tearing free of its terrible grip. And how can we best do that? The best way I know of is to place ourselves in the protective hands of God. As the psalmist prayed, "Keep me safe, O God, for in you I take refuge" (Ps. 16:1).

During the Gulf War in 1991, I spoke to a good friend in California whose grandson had been ordered to the front lines.

"I tremble at night," he admitted. "I can hardly sleep, thinking of my grandson."

"That's completely understandable," I replied, "and we should pray for his safety." But I also wanted to encourage my friend with the words of an old British preacher named George Whitefield. Before the Revolutionary War, Whitefield made several mission trips to the colonies in America and frequently received death threats for his efforts. When friends would ask, "Aren't you afraid that you might be killed in America?" Whitefield would reply, "I am immortal 'til my hour has come."

That's true of every Christian. In fact, throughout my career I've banked on it. No one is going to kill me until the Lord says, "It's your time, son." Even if a hundred thousand enemies line up to my right and ten thousand wait on my left, I know I shall live until the moment God says, "Luis, come on up"—and then no one will be able to stop me from leaving. I am immortal until my hour has come. Scripture says it like this: "All the days ordained for me were written in your book before one of them came to be" (Ps. 139:16).

One of my favorite Bible portions is Hebrews 13:5–6: "God has said, 'Never will I leave you; never will I forsake you.' So we say with confidence, 'The Lord is my helper; I will not be afraid. What can man do to me?'" That was the verse my mother had given me when I left Argentina, and it served me well. Many times during evangelistic campaigns, enemies of the gospel had threatened to kill me—often describing their plans in gruesome detail. And every time I responded, "Lord, I will not fear; what can man do to me?"

A verse like this feels like a solid, massive rock under your feet. It tells you that God's unswerving presence will never leave you. It tells you he is constantly available and will never forsake you. He'll always be there. He will never leave. He's with your grandson on the front lines or in any other hotspot around the world. He's continually with all those who belong to Jesus Christ. Jesus said, "Surely I am with you always, to the very end of the age" (Matt. 28:20).

God's presence doesn't mean that you'll miss the storms, but that he will protect you through the storms until you arrive at his appointed destination. Many years ago, when we lived in Colombia, we often had to fly over the Andes Mountains, where ferocious winds bounce the plane up and down. Always. In those days I fell back on Deuteronomy 33:27, which promises, "The eternal God is your refuge, and underneath are the everlasting arms."

Underneath are the everlasting arms—there's great security in that! God remains in complete control. It's good on a bumpy trip to lay back and stretch out and refuse to let your body get tense. On those turbulent flights I used to consciously relax my body, beginning with my feet and going up to my head. "I am relaxing," I'd say. "My feet are relaxed, my legs, my neck. I am resting in the Lord."

Fear stalks all of us in a world filled with uncertainty and evil, and it does you no good to try to wall yourself off from it. When my sons were little, I used to pray for them at night. Often after they fell asleep, I'd lay my hands on them and pray for them, that they would become instruments of blessing to the nations. But since I traveled so much, I also prayed for their safety.

Even in those days, Colombia was a violent place—murder and mayhem erupted everywhere. As the only blonde-haired boys in the whole town of Cali, my sons stood out from the crowd. We had no guards as the governor general did. When I traveled, Pat often stayed home alone with our sons. And I'd think, *Why am I doing this? Why bring children into the world and then leave them?*

The day kidnappings took place not far from our neighborhood, I cried out to the Lord in despair, "I need a promise from you. I'm going back to the States. I can't just leave Pat alone without you giving me the assurance that you are going to protect her and the children. I feel like a criminal, leaving them like this."

And the Lord gave me Isaiah 54:13: "All your sons will be taught by the LORD, and great will be your children's peace."

I underlined that verse in all my Bibles, in both Spanish and English, and signed the date: 1966. Andrew was born that year in February. It gave me tremendous peace to know that because our family had come to live in Colombia for God's purpose, he had promised, "I will take care of your sons. I will give them peace."

I know of no better way to find freedom from fear. I suppose we could have fled to a safer community, but God had called us for that period of our lives to Colombia. And no safer place exists than the spot to which God calls you.

Shuns Risk vs. Embraces Risk

What kind of four-letter word do you consider risk to be?

In a frantic desire to shield themselves from pain, some men and women try to avoid all risk. They seek only "sure things." They opt out if they sense the slightest risk of failure. They imagine that by so doing they can steer clear of pain—but in fact they end up missing most of life, the good along with the bad.

I'm a firm believer in pursuing risks. How can we accomplish anything worthwhile without risk? Since we don't know the future, we can't know for sure how this or that specific venture might turn out—but that's half the fun! Barnabas and Paul, Priscilla and Aquila, these are some of the honored heroes of Scripture who "risked their lives for the name of our Lord Jesus Christ" (Acts 15:26; see also Rom. 16:4).

I learned a lot about risk from my mother, who started me out on the journey I've been enjoying now for more than forty years. Except for a risk she encouraged me to take, I might have settled for a career in international banking.

I was working as a teller at a branch of a foreign bank doing business in Argentina. One day a city official came to my line, asking about getting funds to purchase six street sweepers from a company in America.

"I have to transfer the payment to Detroit," the official told me. "So what's it going to cost me in pesos?"

I told him I would check and return with the answer. I went to a back room and called headquarters in Buenos Aires. They kept me waiting, pretending to check on availability and exchange rates. In a few minutes the bank representative came back on the line and said, "It's thirty-eight pesos to the dollar, but let's say it's forty."

I went to my manager and said, "Buenos Aires is selling us the transfer funds at forty pesos to the dollar, though it's really thirty-eight."

"Okay," he said, "tell the man it's forty-two."

In ten minutes we made 10 percent on the deal, plus charging a 3 percent service fee. But I felt we weren't telling the truth. *This is my city,* I thought. *They're really taking money from me, because I pay taxes. And we're just doing ourselves in to send money to these foreigners who milk innocent Argentines.* The incident got my conscience going.

Soon afterward, at a street meeting, I preached from the Gospel of John. I vividly remember the text, because it sparked a dramatic moment in my life. As I repeated Jesus's words, out of your "innermost being will flow rivers of living water, and this he spoke of the Spirit" (John 7:38–39 NASB), I felt the Lord saying to me, as clearly as if he were sitting on my shoulder, "You hypocrite!" I had been telling the crowd, "If you receive the Holy Spirit, you will overcome temptation, you will speak the truth," knowing that tomorrow at the bank I'd lie to people over the counter.

So I talked to my mom. I was single and nearly twenty-five years old. My mom always wanted me to leave the bank for a ministry of preaching and teaching the Bible, but how could I? I had five sisters, one brother, and a widowed mother, and I was our family's primary support. That didn't matter to Mom.

"Leave the bank," she said. "You can't go on like this."

Although the bank had given me a lot of freedom and a good salary, I approached the manager and said, "You know, I just can't do what we do over the counter. I feel that I'm lying."

The man hardly flinched. Already they all called me "the Pastor"; he probably expected something like this. Whenever my coworkers told dirty jokes and saw me coming, they'd say, "Here comes the Pastor. Watch out!"

"Well," he said, "you don't need to worry about it. You don't make those decisions; you just follow orders from headquarters. It's not your responsibility. You don't have to feel guilty."

Even as he spoke, I recalled the German soldiers in World War II saying the same thing: "I'm just following orders. I'm killing these people, but what have I got to do with it? I'm just doing what I'm told."

I left the manager's office without saying any more. But the next day I still felt uneasy, so I returned to him and said, "I just can't do this."

"You know, you're on a track to become a manager," he replied. "You're going to become international—you'll be sent all over the world. And you're going to worry about *this*? You're going to lose everything you've built up here over *this*? Why jeopardize all of that?"

Because I was young and unwise and hadn't planned what to say, I responded, "Well, if to become a manager I have to lie and cheat, I can't do it."

The guy hit the ceiling.

"Are you calling *me* a liar and a cheat?" he demanded.

"No," I said, "I meant that if *I* had to do it . . ."

But I had no way out of it. I knew it was over. I'm amazed he didn't fire me on the spot.

A few days later an American walked up to my counter. Although the man spoke some Spanish, we began talking in English. Eventually I found out he worked with a Christian mission agency that planned to begin working in Argentina.

"If you know anybody who's bilingual," he said, "we're going to publish an evangelistic magazine, translating many of the articles from English. If you know of anybody, let me know."

"I'm your man," I said immediately.

So within four days of first speaking to the manager about my uneasiness, I resigned from the bank. My mom celebrated my decision, even though I left for half the salary. Risky? Sure. But I had no regrets.

My family did go through some tough financial times after I left the bank. Nevertheless, my mom couldn't have been happier. Imagine if I had stayed in that institution, making money for overseas investors. I would have missed out on the privilege of leading souls to heaven.

Falls Back vs. Forges Ahead

Defense might win championships in sports, but I doubt it's the best strategy for life. Constant worry about defending your territory, your resources, your heart, your schedule—it can't help but take a toll, and probably sooner than later.

Every day you see folks walking down the street who seem perfectly normal, in good health, well-dressed . . . but who overflow with insecurities and fears and the weirdest defense mechanisms imaginable. They can't move ahead in life because they're too busy retreating.

I know a middle-aged couple, both professing Christians, with possessions galore. But it's always been "This is mine; this is yours," never "This is ours." They lack even a shadow of intimacy with each other. They cannot communicate with love and tenderness and can hardly remain civil to each other. Each tries to protect his or her "turf."

One views the other as unspiritual; the other sees the first as a total independent. Neither trusts the heart of the other—one thinks the other doesn't know God well enough; the other thinks the first isn't a good team player. Their marriage is nearly an armed confrontation.

The result? Their adult children have sided with one parent, leaving the other isolated, desperate, and paranoid—"the whole world's against me." From my perspective, much of this tragic situation can be traced to security issues, self-protection, and their attempt to find safety through absolute control of material possessions. Both fear the other, want to protect his or her own, and therefore can't move ahead. Their self-defense mechanisms have led to great tensions and a heartbreaking alienation of the family. I find both spouses charming independently. But together? That's another story.

They have no contentment, no happiness, no joy, no pleasure. Because neither will let God provide their security, they protect themselves from each other and wind up miserable. They never surrendered to God, either through each other in their actions or to each other in their words. They opted for invulnerability instead of security, and ended up with something far worse than if both had lost everything. It's hard to see how it could get any worse.

Their marriage convinces me that falling back into a defensive position simply cannot get you moving forward into the future you want.

I love a song by Michael W. Smith. The lyrics of his song give tribute to Cassie Bernall, the Columbine High School student who affirmed her faith in God an instant before a bullet took her life. The lyrics remind all of us that following Jesus does have its tough moments. No, Christians aren't shielded from misfortune. Yes, we may have to pay a certain price—didn't the Master pay with the cross? Didn't the apostle Paul pay with beatings and jail time before the Romans finally executed him? The Christian life isn't a picnic. But following Christ *always* offers a wonderful life.

I wonder—are you dancing for the Lord? Are you alive to Jesus Christ? Are you forging ahead into the Promised Land? Or are you stuck in the desert?

A short while before he died in a plane crash, professional golfer Payne Stewart gave his testimony at First Baptist Church in Orlando. "When I die," Stewart said, "I'm going to a special place—but I want to live a special life here and now."

He did exactly that. He lived only a few months after giving his testimony, and then the Lord took him to heaven—not one second too soon, not one moment too late. Stewart lived with confidence and zest to the very end because he knew that true safety can be found only in Jesus Christ. He refused to fall back into a nervous, defensive posture, but instead forged ahead until the day the Lord took him home.

If there's another kind of safety, I don't want it.

Restrictive Outlook vs. Expansive Outlook

When we try to provide our own security, we can't help but narrow our vision. We start to look inward and play things close to the vest. We don't notice the misery of others, nor do we care, because we're too busy trying to manage our own little world.

When we look to God to provide the security we need, however, our eyes remain free to start scanning the horizon for new opportunities. When we refuse to worry about our safety but entrust that aspect of our lives to the Lord, we release untold energy for more constructive causes.

After my dad died, our family quickly plunged from relative wealth to desperate poverty. We lost it all: property, farms, vehicles, and servants. In three years everything disappeared, leaving us in utter deprivation.

Somehow we rented a house with one bedroom and a living room that we converted into a bedroom. We also turned the garage into a bedroom (although it couldn't keep out the dust). At one point we owed eight months of back rent. Only the mercy of our landlord kept us from getting tossed into the street.

Yet even when we had nothing, I don't recall a sense of gloom in the house. Some days, all we had to eat was a big loaf of French bread, flavored over the fire with garlic. Or maybe we'd get a tomato and split it into eight pieces. On really good days we'd have one steak to divide among the eight of us. Yet at each meal we would get on our knees and pray to the Lord, thanking him for his provision.

You might think that such poverty would close my mom's heart, but it didn't. Not even scarcity could dry up Mom's generous spirit. Her expansive outlook prompted her to continue helping others. When a beggar came to the door, she gave what she could. She continued this pattern until the day she died. After we grew up, we learned there was no use in sending her money; she wouldn't buy herself anything. We gave her a piano once, and she turned around and gave it to my brother.

"It's for you, to sing," we protested.

"I don't need it," she replied. "I can sing without a piano." Mom embodied the message of Psalm 112:5–8:

> Good will come to him who is generous and lends freely,
>   who conducts his affairs with justice.
> Surely he will never be shaken;
>   a righteous man will be remembered forever.
> He will have no fear of bad news;
>   his heart is steadfast, trusting in the LORD.
> His heart is secure, he will have no fear;
>   in the end he will look in triumph on his foes.

The whole time we lived in abject poverty, Mom gave us a strong sense of security. Through prayer and singing and by affirming the promises of God, she kept us from fear and despair. We enjoyed no human security, yet we never felt overly deprived. Mom challenged us to believe that God would provide in the nick of time. She continually quoted Bible promises to us, especially a few basic ones:

- Deuteronomy 31:6, "The LORD your God goes with you; he will never leave you nor forsake you."
- Isaiah 41:10, "So do not fear, for I am with you; do not be dismayed, for I am your God. I will strengthen you and help you; I will uphold you with my righteous right hand."

- Matthew 6:25, 33, "Therefore I tell you, do not worry about your life, what you will eat or drink; or about your body, what you will wear. Is not life more important than food, and the body more important than clothes? . . . But seek first his kingdom and his righteousness, and all these things will be given to you as well."
- John 14:27, "Peace I leave with you; my peace I give you. I do not give to you as the world gives. Do not let your hearts be troubled and do not be afraid."
- John 16:33, "In this world you will have trouble. But take heart! I have overcome the world."
- Romans 8:28, "And we know that in all things God works for the good of those who love him, who have been called according to his purpose."
- Philippians 4:19, "My God will meet all your needs according to his glorious riches in Christ Jesus."

Mom recited these verses to us over and over during the toughest times. She'd tell us repeatedly, "God knows even the minute details of your life; they're all under his control." She also would recount stories of George Mueller (a nineteenth-century evangelist and manager of orphanages), tales in which God provided milk or bread at the last moment. She encouraged us to expect God to provide—and he did, in unusual and unexpected ways. The truths she kept repeating became utterly real to us and I fully believed them. I still do.

I'm absolutely convinced that genuine security boils down to knowing and believing the promises of God. So let me ask you: Are you confident that when the Lord makes a commitment, he never backs down?

Now, Mom wasn't perfect. She certainly was no businesswoman. She never suspected the worst of anybody and usually believed whatever someone told her. It was mainly through her gullibility that we lost everything. It enraged us kids.

Yet none of that reduced our respect for her or her faith.

A number of years after my father died, a letter came to our house from a man who had cheated my mother. "Mrs. Palau," the man wrote, "I lied to you after your husband died. I bought a tractor from you. I told you the motor was no good, the block was cracked, it didn't work. You believed me and I gave you a few dollars for the tractor. My conscience won't let me be at peace. I cheated you and your children. I've got to send you this check because I simply can't go on living this way."

That check arrived at a time when we had run out of cash, and there was no one to help us. To us that letter looked like a marvelous miracle. And it happened because Mom taught us to trust the Lord and the promises of God, even when we had nothing else to go on.

What would happen, I wonder, if today we took the Word of God as seriously as we take the word of our doctor? We walk into his office, report to the front desk, and dutifully follow the directions of some person in white who says, "Fill out this form and wait until you're called." We sit down and eventually get summoned to the examination room, where we wait some more. Finally the doctor comes in and says, "Sit on the table." So we sit on the table. He prods and pokes and listens and looks, and through it all we sit there like good boys and girls. After a while he says, "I know what the problem is." He gets out a pad of paper, with a pen scratches a few illegible lines, and says, "Go to the pharmacy and have this prescription filled."

So we go to the pharmacist. Probably we have never met this person. But she disappears behind a wall and a few minutes later returns with a bunch of red pills, yellow pills, and a bottle of green liquid. "When you get up in the morning," we hear, "take a spoon of this. And before every meal, take two of these pills." And we obey to the letter. We don't ask to see the pharmacist's license. We don't wonder if those pills contain chalk. We just get up in the morning, swallow the spoonful, and down two pills before our oatmeal, toast, and coffee.

So why is it that when the Lord gives us a prescription or makes us a promise in his Word, we often say, "Now, wait a minute. We have to interpret this"? If we treated the doctor and the pharmacist the way we treat the promises of God, we would be dead in weeks.

The only true security lies in Jesus Christ. Only when we believe that he is everything, our all and in all, only then will we discover and enjoy genuine safety. Jesus is the Rock, our strong and immovable protector, and those who look to him for help are radiant with joy (Ps. 34:5). The Bible declares that all the promises of God are answered "Yes" in Jesus Christ (2 Cor. 1:20)—in other words, they're all yours. So anchor your faith to the promises of God and enjoy true security!

Focused on Danger vs. Focused on Opportunity

Those who seek emotional or financial invulnerability—the men and women who desire somehow to become bulletproof—inevitably end up focusing on the dangers of life rather than its opportunities. And for that reason they usually end up with a pile of regrets.

An elderly man approached one of our counselors during a mission in Australia. "I fear that I am going to die and my life will have been insignificant," he confessed. What do you say to such a man? In the same mission, a newsman said to me, "You seem to have it all put together. I don't have it all together, and I don't know that I ever will."

I can't say for sure if either of these two men suffered from a faulty source of security, but my guess is that they both did. When people look to find their true safety in the power and love of Jesus Christ, they discover a new ability to focus on the opportunities ahead rather than the dangers. In this way they avoid coming to the end of their days and saying, "I fear that my life will have been insignificant."

My life was headed toward insignificance until I reached the age of seventeen. I refused to get serious about spiritual things. But that began to change as carnival approached that year.

Carnival happens forty days before Easter. Everybody holds big parties and goes dancing and drinking and gets into all kinds of stuff. Think Mardi Gras, but with a Latin beat. After carnival, everybody becomes "holy." But during carnival, anything goes.

Some friends of mine had invited me to a wild party. But God was at work in my young, rebellious life. *If I continue this way*, I thought, *I'm going to wreck my life.*

The week of carnival I found myself alone at my grandmother's house. And for the first time in almost four years, I started reading a Bible. I put it by my bedside and I prayed, "Lord, get me out of these dances. If you get me out of them, I'll serve you forever. If I go to these dances, I'll wreck my life. Who knows what I'll do, Lord. I could commit some awful sin—but I'm a coward. I don't know how to say to my friends, 'I'm not going to go.' Do something, Lord. Get me out."

I wondered what God would do. I woke up the next morning, the first day of carnival, and felt something odd in my face. I had no pain, but when I went to look in the mirror, I saw my face bloated like a fat balloon. It was almost like I had tennis balls inside my mouth. What happened? I still don't know. Maybe a bug bit me during the night. Maybe in my dreams I punched myself. I don't know what happened, but I looked awful!

And I said to myself, "The Lord has answered my prayer."

How could a young man go to a dance looking like this? He couldn't. So I called up my friends. "I'm not going to the dance," I said.

"Why not?" they asked.

"I'm sick," I replied. "You should see my face."

They all came to the house, and when they saw me they said, "Oh, yeah—you can't come tonight." But carnival is a week long. So they said, "Maybe you can come tomorrow or on the weekend."

But since I believe God had answered my prayer, I said, "Nope, that's it." Oh, I was still a coward; I didn't tell them why I wouldn't go. But when I walked back inside the house, I said, "Lord Jesus, I'm yours forever. I don't want to have anything to do with the world. I'm going to serve you."

I bought myself a new Bible. I decided to move to another city where my mother had tried to start a new life. I started all over, as if I'd been converted for a second time. I began to study my Bible. I got involved in a local church. In a few months I began to speak to audiences of little children. The church used to hold evangelistic street meetings, and the elders would let me say a few words, then a few more. And suddenly it was such fun to serve Jesus Christ. The excitement of those early days seemed like heaven. I had put the world behind me and had begun a fresh, new period in my life. I had discovered that the only safety worth having is in Jesus Christ.

Nobody finds ultimate security by focusing on the possible dangers. They find it only when, by the power of Jesus Christ, they focus on the opportunities God places before them. They choose the safety only Jesus can bring and enjoy a wild adventure in the bargain.

There's no reason you can't do the same thing.

Where Do You Find Security?

Invulnerability is an illusion. No one can make himself or herself bullet-proof, no matter how hard he or she tries. Living in this world entails pain, without exception.

Still, we all need to feel safe. Every one of us longs for a strong sense of security. How will we find it?

Some look for it in bank accounts, multiplied possessions, and financial stability. Have you heard of the American businessman who thought he could provide security for a Mexican fisherman? As the American gazed over the ocean from a pier in a small coastal fishing village in Mexico, a tiny boat with a single fisherman pulled in and docked. The American saw several large yellowfin tuna on board and complimented the Mexican on the quality of his fish.

"How long did it take to catch them?" he asked.

"Only a little while," replied the fisherman.

"Then why didn't you stay out longer and catch more?" the American wondered.

"I have enough to support my family's immediate needs," replied the Mexican.

"But what do you do with the rest of your time?" he demanded.

"I sleep late, fish a little, play with my children, take a siesta with my wife, Maria, and stroll into the village each evening, where I sip wine and play guitar with my amigos. I have a full and busy life, señor."

"I am a Harvard MBA and could help you," the American insisted. "You should spend more time fishing, and with the proceeds buy a bigger boat. With your earnings from the bigger boat you could buy more boats, and eventually you could own a whole fleet. Instead of selling your catch to a middleman, you could sell directly to the processor, eventually opening your own cannery. You would control the product, the processing, and the distribution. Of course, you would need to leave this small village and move to Mexico City, then to Los Angeles, and finally to New York City. From there you could run your growing business."

"But señor," the fisherman asked, "how long will this take?"

"Oh, about fifteen to twenty years," the businessman replied.

"But what then?"

"That's the best part," the American laughed. "When the time is right, you would announce an initial public offering and sell your company stock to the public, becoming very rich. You wouldn't have to worry about anything. Your financial future would be secure."

"Then what?"

"Then you would retire and move to a small coastal fishing village, where you would sleep late, fish a little, play with your grandkids, take a siesta with your wife, and stroll to the village in the evenings, where you could sip wine and play guitar with your amigos."

It doesn't make much sense, does it? Don't waste your time by trying to provide for yourself the security that only the Lord Jesus can deliver. Allow God to do what he does best: "Let the beloved of the LORD rest secure in him, for he shields him all day long, and the one the LORD loves rests between his shoulders" (Deut. 33:12).

How to Be Safe According to the Bible

1. *Recognize that ultimate safety is available only in God.*
   "I will lie down and sleep in peace, for you alone, O LORD, make me dwell in safety" (Ps. 4:8).
2. *Whenever you feel threatened, run to God, not riches.*
   "The name of the LORD is a strong tower; the righteous run to it and are safe. The wealth of the rich is their fortified city; they imagine it an unscalable wall" (Prov. 18:10–11).
3. *Trust in God more than you fear men.*
   "Fear of man will prove to be a snare, but whoever trusts in the LORD is kept safe" (Prov. 29:25).
4. *Ask the Lord for safety.*
   "There, by the Ahava Canal, I proclaimed a fast, so that we might humble ourselves before our God and ask him for a safe journey for us and our children, with all our possessions" (Ezra 8:21).
5. *Realize that habitual sin removes God's hand of protection.*
   "We know that anyone born of God does not continue to sin; the one who was born of God keeps him safe, and the evil one cannot harm him" (1 John 5:18).
6. *Understand that God himself placed you right where you are.*
   "LORD, you have assigned me my portion and my cup; you have made my lot secure" (Ps. 16:5).
7. *Be generous with the resources God has given you.*
   "Good will come to him who is generous and lends freely, who conducts his affairs with justice. Surely he will never be shaken; a righteous man will be remembered forever. He will have no fear of bad news; his heart is steadfast, trusting in the LORD. His heart is secure, he will have no fear, in the end he will look in triumph on his foes" (Ps. 112:5–8).
8. *Take care of your family by providing a safe place for your children.*
   "He who fears the LORD has a secure fortress, and for his children it will be a refuge" (Prov. 14:26).

9. *When trouble does come, place your hope in the promises of God.*
   "In the day of trouble he will keep me safe in his dwelling; he will hide me in the shelter of his tabernacle and set me high upon a rock" (Ps. 27:5).
10. *No matter what happens, take refuge in God.*
   "Keep me safe, O God, for in you I take refuge" (Ps. 16:1).

9

A Sense of Destiny

Activity or Significance?

Do you not know that in a race all the runners run, but only one gets the prize? Run in such a way as to get the prize. Everyone who competes in the games goes into strict training. They do it to get a crown that will not last; but we do it to get a crown that will last forever.

The apostle Paul, in 1 Corinthians 9:24–25

It has to rank as one of the saddest shows I've ever seen.

Two men had developed an unusual friendship. One had climbed the corporate ladder to become an extraordinarily wealthy and powerful executive. The other had never accomplished much of anything, despite a sharp intellect and strong sense of self. He wound up a vagrant. Yet the two could talk about sensitive issues and confront each other with hard truths like no one else. They maintained their odd bond even while screaming their lungs out at each other.

One day, doctors interrupted life-as-usual by telling the executive he didn't have long to live; his diseased heart could fail at any time. The man urgently needed a heart transplant, but wasn't eligible for one. When the vagrant learned the terrible news, he quickly offered to donate his own heart to his friend—effectively sentencing himself to death. A horrified state refused to allow the procedure, so the vagrant filed suit to force officials to allow the operation. His own lawyer tried to convince him to drop the case, but he would not be dissuaded.

"I don't want to get to the end of my life and not have accomplished anything," he angrily explained. "I've done nothing of value! Now I have the opportunity to really accomplish something with my life. So what if I live forty more years and *still* do nothing? But if I give my heart to this man, I will not have lived in vain."

By the end of the show the vagrant had lost his case, leaving the audience with a feeling of deep sadness, both for the dying man and for the living man who wanted to die.

Do you identify even a little with the man who wanted to give up his heart? Do you feel as if your life is unfolding in vain? If so, take heart. You *can* take steps to correct the problem.

Do I Count?

All of us need to feel that our lives count for something, that we exist for some purpose, that our lives have meaning. We all want to enjoy a sense of destiny. And we need to feel significant. That is why so many of us ask ourselves the crucial questions:

Who am I?
Why am I here?
Where am I going?
Why have I enjoyed privileges denied to others?
Who put me on earth and what does he want from me?
What's the purpose for my life?

I firmly believe there *does* exist a purpose for your life. There *is* a divine plan. And you can find the answers to your most significant questions when you meet Jesus Christ.

"But don't all religions give those answers?" some ask.

No, not at all. And anybody who makes such a claim just hasn't been paying attention. I have often been in India among Hindus, in China among Buddhists, in Japan among Shintoists. None of them pretends to tell you who you are, where you came from, or your purpose in life. No world religion, other than Christianity, tries to tell you what happens when you die or claims to give you the assurance of eternal life. When well-meaning individuals tell me, "All religions lead to God," I usually point out that some faiths, like Buddhism, don't even *believe* in one God. When people say, "All roads lead to God," they are being sincere and kind and nice and very American—but they haven't been talking to actual Buddhists or Shintoists or Hindus.

Jesus Christ alone claims to tell you who you really are, why you're here, and where you're going. Each of us wants more than just a nice life, a good family, sound finances, secure retirement, and robust health. Deep inside we all seek spiritual purpose. Because God has "set eternity in the hearts of men" (Eccles. 3:11), we will all wrestle with dissatisfaction and an unsettled spirit until we find and act on our God-given purpose.

Activity or Significance?

Despite all the current hype about spiritual issues, however, our age doesn't seem particularly good at divining purpose or meaning. It seems much better at activity—and the more furious and nonstop, the better.

While all of us need to know that we matter, sometimes we settle for a flurry of busyness. We tell ourselves that if we're always busy, that must mean we're in demand and that we count for something. While inwardly we crave a sense of purpose and destiny, we settle for mere productivity and busyness.

Of course, I see nothing wrong with keeping a full schedule. The apostle Paul told the Corinthians, "We work hard with our own hands" (1 Cor. 4:12), and he encouraged them in turn to "always give yourselves fully to the work of the Lord, because you know that your labor in the Lord is not in vain" (1 Cor. 15:58).

God himself commends fruitful activity, so long as it serves a worthwhile purpose (Exod. 20:9). When the apostle Paul learned that some of his friends were *not* busy, but instead took to idleness, he commanded them to pick up the pace and earn the bread they ate (2 Thess. 3:11).

The problem lies not in activity, but in mistaking it for significance. Just because we're busy doesn't mean that we're fulfilling some grand purpose. The trick is to get busy about the right things.

It would help to consider several ways in which significance differs from mere activity. Why does it pay to seek meaning before busyness? Let me suggest five areas of comparison.

Activity	Significance
• Efficient	• Effective
• Keeps Busy	• Pursues Meaning
• Seeks Worth	• Enjoys Worth
• Tyranny of the Urgent	• Triumph of the Important
• Gains Admirers	• Attracts Colleagues

God wants us to be busy about the right things.

Efficient vs. Effective

Some business executives treat efficiency as if it were the holy grail of industry. They spare no effort to refine their operations into the most efficient enterprise possible. Yet many of them still fail. Why?

Because "efficient" doesn't necessarily mean "effective." One can efficiently produce a commodity that long ago lost its effectiveness. No doubt with today's technology, someone could efficiently manufacture exquisitely crafted 8-track tapes. But why?

Bill Murray played a wacky television weatherman in the film comedy *Groundhog Day*. People jumped when he spoke and he got things done with breathless economy. His talent and efficiency made him influential and busy—but yielded a life without meaning. In the movie, some unseen power forces him to relive a single day countless times until he finally "gets it right." Only then does he connect with people, find meaning, and continue on with life.

A few years back I met someone who inadvertently opted for efficiency over effectiveness. Someone invited me to give a brief Bible study for a small group of businessmen who met every Tuesday for lunch. Of the six regulars, three followed Jesus Christ and three were searching.

I told a story about an English princess who said to me, "Mr. Palau, I've always wanted to talk to an evangelist like you. I have to ask you a few questions. The first one is this: Do you have the assurance of eternal life? And if you do, how did you come about it? If one wanted to have the assurance of eternal life, what would one have to do? Could you help me?"

"Oh, your Royal Highness," I told her, "that's all I do! I can help you find eternal life." So I explained how she could invite Jesus into her life.

As I told the story, I saw tears trickling down the cheeks of one especially wealthy businessman. He tried to cover it up, but I noticed. And I thought, *Ahh . . . this guy has a tender spot. Something is going on inside.* When the lunch concluded, I walked over to him and said, "Jimmy, I noticed you were crying when I told the story of the princess."

"Yes," he admitted, a bit startled, "you caught me."

"Why were you crying?" I asked.

In great frustration he blurted out, "Why is it that I go to church in one of the mainline denominations, I've attended church since I was a kid, but I still feel as if my life lacks purpose? I've never had the assurance of eternal life—and here I am, sixty-five! Why am I missing out?"

I gave a few brief answers, but soon he had to leave for his office at the insurance firm he owned. As we parted company, Jimmy turned to me and said, "Insurance, Luis, insurance . . . but no assurance."

How's that for an invitation to an evangelist?

"Jimmy," I said, "let's get together for lunch."

So a few days later we met at a club downtown. As soon as we sat down, swarms of well-wishers came by the table to say, "Hi, Jimmy!" "How you doing, Jimmy?" "How's your wife, Jimmy?" Money can win you a lot of friends, but not necessarily a purpose in life.

When his cloud of admirers finally left us alone, Jimmy asked, "Why did you invite me to lunch?"

He didn't know it, but I had learned he told one of the other guys, "I'll bet Luis wants to hit me up for money. That's why he wants to have lunch." But I had bigger things in mind.

"Jimmy," I replied, "the other day you told me that you didn't have the assurance of eternal life. Before lunch is over, I want you to go home with that assurance."

As his eyes turned red, he said, "I've got to tell you why I said that, Luis. I had a brother—we were partners in business—and he committed suicide just a year and a half ago. He didn't leave a note; he didn't leave a letter. He had not committed immorality, he was a good husband, he was successful in business, he had no debts. I cannot explain why my brother took his life."

He paused, then continued. "I have five kids, and all of them are unbelievers—basically, they say they're atheists. And I cannot figure it out. I've gone to church all my life. I go to communion. I took them with me when they were kids. But after they were confirmed, they refused to come to church and none of them follow Jesus Christ today." He confessed that he'd failed his kids, failed his wife, failed as a spiritual person. And then he began to weep quietly at the table.

"Jimmy," I said, "don't go blaming yourself. Let's not talk about your kids. Let's think about that later."

"But look, I'm a good man," he insisted. "Don't keep telling me I'm a sinner. I know you evangelists! You are always saying we are all sinners."

"I didn't say that," I replied, "*you* said it."

He nodded his head and through tears admitted, "Inside I'm crying. I'm crying all the time."

"Look, cry no more," I replied. "The most important thing right now is that you personally open your heart to Jesus Christ."

"My church is only three blocks away," he answered. "Why don't we go over there to pray?"

"Jimmy," I replied, "I want you to pray right here, over lunch."

"Right *here*? At the lunch table?" he asked nervously. "But everybody in the club is watching me."

"So don't close your eyes," I said. "They will never know we are praying. Keep your eyes open."

And right there in that restaurant, this powerful businessman with the efficient insurance operation invited Jesus Christ into his life. For sixty-five years he had lived without a sense of purpose. He felt guilty because his kids had rebelled, confused because his brother took his life. All that began to change when he asked the Lord to come into his heart.

Jimmy continues to meet with other Christian businessmen who pray and study the Bible together. A short letter I sent him that quotes a Bible verse assuring him of eternal life hangs in a frame on his office wall. "This way," he explained, "people will ask me about it and I can tell them about my experience."

After a lifetime of business success but personal disappointment, Jimmy has exchanged corporate efficiency for life effectiveness.

Keeps Busy vs. Pursues Meaning

A scene from the science fiction movie *Starman* illustrates for me much of modern culture. In the film, an alien stranded on planet Earth takes on the appearance of a recently deceased man. The fellow's widow befriends the alien and helps him reach a rendezvous point where his pals can pick him up. Along the way the pair endures a series of harrowing encounters. In one scene, the starman has to drive a car, even though he's never taken the wheel before. He has watched his friend drive, however, so he thinks he knows what to do. As they approach a busy intersection, the signal light turns yellow. He guns the car through the crossing, nearly causing a catastrophic accident. His terrified companion lambastes him for almost getting them killed and asks if he really understands the rules of the road. Starman says he does: "Red means stop. Green means go. Yellow means go very fast."

What a picture of our society! We "go very fast" because we don't understand the purpose or the significance of life. We mistake activity for meaning and thereby endanger our very lives.

A few years ago I visited the British Broadcasting Corporation in London to do an interview. As I walked in, someone said to me, "By the way, there's a man who wants to see you. Peter France. Do you remember him?"

Yes, I remembered him. Peter did a program on our Mission to London in 1983. At the time he didn't believe in Jesus Christ, but was searching. He filmed the program primarily because he wanted to catch us in some embarrassing comment or incident.

During one interview he told me that while studying at Oxford he had served as chairman of the Humanist Society. After graduation he moved to Hong Kong to work for her Majesty's government.

"One day I got the Humanist Society magazine from Oxford and saw a photo of this generation's student Executive Committee," he said. "I was feeling very restless with my spiritual life, not believing in God, not having a purpose in life. I looked at the faces one by one, and they all seemed so empty and so lonely. And I said to myself, 'That's exactly how I've felt the last twenty years.' From then on I began to say, 'We're a bunch of empty people pretending that we know what we're talking about.'"

He told me he had begun to read Catholic theologians. He'd even picked up the Bible. In the middle of our interview he asked, "What if I die without Jesus Christ, Luis? I've always said I'm an atheist. What about it?"

"Well, there's hell to pay, Peter," I replied.

So that's what he called the program, *Hell to Pay*. The BBC showed it on New Year's Eve several years in a row.

Our last interview for the program took place in a London cab. As we were making our good-byes, he said, "Luis, let me ask you this. What if when you die it turns out that everything you believe wasn't so?"

"I'll give you the Billy Graham answer and then I'll give you the little old lady's answer," I said.

"No, no," he replied, "give me the little old lady's answer."

"A communist at Red Square was preaching against Christianity," I explained. "A little old lady stood in the crowd, listening. Suddenly she challenged the communist and they began to argue. The communist finally asked the woman, 'What if when you die I'm right and you're wrong?' 'Well,' the little old lady replied, 'when I die, if you're right and I'm wrong, we're both in the same boat. But if I'm right and you're wrong, you are in bad shape.'"

It sounds like a simplistic answer, but Peter France responded, "Oh my gosh, I never thought of it like that." The story got him thinking seriously about Jesus Christ. I didn't see him again until fifteen years later when I walked into the BBC offices. By then he sported a beard and I hardly recognized him.

"Do you remember me?" he asked.

"Yes," I said, "you're Peter France."

"Do you know what I did for you?"

"Yes, you did a movie some years ago. I've been praying for you."

"You don't remember me, do you?"

"I do, too. I've quoted you all over the world, about your emptiness and the lonely faces of the club in Oxford."

"You remembered!"

"Have you come to the Lord?"

"I *have* come to the Lord. Now I am making a series to be shown on BBC this Easter."

After years of searching, Peter France at last saw the huge difference between keeping busy and finding purpose. He'd kept extremely active as chairman of the Oxford Humanist Club, as a representative of the British government, and as a gifted television producer for the BBC. He had activity galore; what he didn't have was meaning. He found significance when he found Jesus Christ.

Jesus gives meaning to life in many ways. I think one of the most awesome thoughts in all of the Bible is a verse in the book of Jeremiah. God says to the prophet, "Before I formed you in the womb I knew you, before you were born I set you apart" (Jer. 1:5).

I must have been eighteen or nineteen years old the first time I read this verse. I remember marveling, *This is amazing!*

Before my father and mother got together to do what fathers and mothers do when they want a baby, God knew all about Luis Palau. And he knew all about you, too. Even if you're the result of a one-night stand. Even if your mother gave you away. Even if you were brought up in an orphanage. Even if you've never met your mother or father. Don't let any of that hound you. Even then you can say, "Lord, although I wish I'd known my dad and mom, nevertheless, you made me. I'm alive and I am here because you wanted me to be born. And God, you say in the Bible that you have a purpose for every one of us, including me."

Before egg and sperm ever came together in your mother's womb, God already knew the color of your eyes. He knew the name your parents were going to give you (whether you like your name or not). God knew what kind of flappy ears you were going to have, what sort of nose you would get, where you were going to be born (Ps. 139:14–16). It's awesome to realize that God knows every last thing about you!

God has a purpose and a plan for your life, whether you were born into a church-attending family or not. Whether you're Catholic or Protestant, Jewish or Mormon, Muslim or Seventh Day Adventist, atheist or agnostic. None of that makes any difference. Jesus gives meaning to life because he tells us, "I knew you fully, even before you became an embryo in your mother's womb. And I have a purpose for you to fulfill, tailored to your unique personality, background, and characteristics."

Jesus also gives meaning to life by opening our eyes intellectually. That's why the Bible is so important. It's through the Bible that God teaches us about the purpose and meaning of life.

> The law of the LORD is perfect,
>   reviving the soul.
> The statutes of the LORD are trustworthy,
>   making wise the simple.
> The precepts of the LORD are right,
>   giving joy to the heart.
> The commands of the LORD are radiant,
>   giving light to the eyes.
> The fear of the LORD is pure,
>   enduring forever.
> The ordinances of the LORD are sure
>   and altogether righteous.
> They are more precious than gold,
>   than much pure gold;
> they are sweeter than honey,
>   than honey from the comb.
> By them is your servant warned;
>   in keeping them there is great reward.
>
> Psalm 19:7–11

You can trust the Bible 100 percent, because it is God's revelation to us of everything he wants us to know about his character, his work in the world, and our relationship to him. Its teachings are well-rounded, not lopsided, as even the best of human authors are. Scripture enlightens our minds and gives us understanding about life's meaning. Read it daily.

I recommend that you use two identical editions for your Bible reading. Use one for reading only; use the other for writing your notes and observations in the margin of the text you've just read. If you're just getting started as a Bible reader, the *Starting Point Study Bible* (Zondervan) will be of great help.

Perhaps you already belong to a church, yet you say, "Luis, I don't have a sense of direction. I don't have any meaning for my life. I don't understand any of this."

It's not religion you need; it's Jesus Christ. Jesus offers you meaning and purpose, just as he offered it to Peter France. Don't settle for mere activity, not even activity in some church or religion. The only way to enjoy lasting significance is by settling down with Jesus Christ.

Seeks Worth vs. Enjoys Worth

A young Episcopalian layman in Oregon called me this year and said, "On my forehead I've always imagined one word: Loser." He sounded intelligent and well-educated, yet he thought of himself as a joke. I felt so sad for him; he had never grasped and embraced the tremendous worth that Jesus Christ gives to all followers.

I think millions of men and women struggle with this issue. So how do they respond? They pack their schedules with activity, hoping to gain a feeling of worth by amassing a staggering list of accomplishments. Their whole lives they chase after some elusive sign or evidence of their value as persons—and they wind up exhausted and despairing.

The good news of the gospel declares that we do not have to create our worth; we need only appreciate, grasp, and live out the worth God already has given us in Jesus Christ.

What makes us glorious people? Let me suggest several biblical answers.

- *We were made in the image of God* (Gen. 1:27; James 3:9). Unlike birds or horses or even angels, the Bible says we are created in God's own image!

- *We have the capacity to create life* (Gen. 1:28). I think this is one of the most amazing gifts of God. You and I can produce a life! Such power gives dignity to your sexuality.
- *We have the capacity to rule over other creatures* (Gen. 1:28). God made us managers over his world, not emperors over our own. Yet he still put us in charge.
- *We have the capacity to pray and get answers to prayer* (Phil. 4:6). In the mystery of God, you can move the hand that made the world.
- *We have the capacity to love* (1 John 3:11). Awesome!
- *We have the capacity to make and keep promises* (Ps. 15:4).
- *We have the capacity to make choices* (Josh. 24:15).
- *We have the capacity for fellowship with God* (2 Cor. 13:14).

The Bible says we were made a little lower than the angels (Ps. 8:5). It says Jesus Christ has made us kings and queens and priests (Rev. 1:6 KJV). We have the ability to spend time in worship of almighty God. You can sit under a tree and look up to heaven and talk to God and say, "Lord, I love you." Worship doesn't require a church with an altar and a crucifix above it, with the Virgin Mary on the right and Saint Peter on the left. We worship whenever we simply enter the very presence of God and bask in his holiness and love. This is not an illusion, but a biblical revelation.

The Bible says we were created to be indwelt by almighty God (1 Cor. 6:19). What a glorious concept! Some run around these days, claiming, "I am God." No, they're not. But I think I know what they're trying to say. They mean, "I want God, I was made for God, I need to know God." And that's exactly what happens when the Spirit of God, through Jesus Christ, makes your body into a temple for God.

The cross of Jesus Christ reveals the greatness and meaning and significance God intends for your life. You are so valuable to God that he gladly died for you in your place. You are *that* valuable. God would like to enjoy your company for all eternity!

"Father," Jesus prayed, "I want those you have given me to be with me where I am, and to see my glory, the glory you have given me because you loved me before the creation of the world" (John 17:24). He wants us in heaven! And he wants it so badly, he said, in effect, "Here's my body. I'm coming to do your will, O God. Through my death, let these people come to heaven."

We were created for glory. We were created for grandeur and for success and for magnificence. Knowing that we are created by God gives us a sense of dignity and purpose. We were created to be respected. And loved. And honored. And applauded. We eat it up, because we were made for this.

Men and women can lack educational credentials and social fineries and economic resources, but through knowledge of their worth in Jesus Christ, they move through life with dignity, bearing, and self-acceptance. I've seen tens of thousands of people throughout the world without education, without money. They live on a survival diet. And yet they amaze me by their obvious sense of dignity, confidence, and authority.

If Christians would only understand and embrace five or six basic images that God uses repeatedly to describe them, they would never again have to suffer a problem with self-esteem. The Scripture declares that every believer is:

- A child of God (John 1:12–13)
- An heir of God and fellow heir with Jesus Christ (Rom. 8:17)
- A temple of the Holy Spirit (1 Cor. 6:19)
- Adopted into God's family (Eph. 1:5)
- Part of the body of Jesus Christ, connected to Jesus, the head (1 Cor. 12:12–27)
- Seated in the heavenly places with Jesus Christ (Eph. 2:6)

We do not need to desperately seek out personal worth, laboring urgently to somehow achieve it. God beckons us to acknowledge and live out the worth he has already made abundantly available to us.

Tyranny of the Urgent vs. Triumph of the Important

What rules your schedule—the urgent or the important? The two are often not the same. The urgent clamors for your attention, demands your time, insists on your presence, calls loudly for your energy . . . yet may not hold a vital place in the true scheme of things. The important, on the other hand, genuinely requires your attention, time, presence, and energy, even though it may not scream for any of them.

Consider a silly example from home life. What kind of urgent things might demand your attention, even though they can't claim supreme importance? Maybe a shaggy lawn . . . a noisy washing machine . . . a stained carpet . . . a new deck. Every one of them might yell for your time. But are any of them vitally *important*, on par with your kids . . . your spouse . . . your parents . . . your God?

While the noisy voices in your life may well deserve a place on your schedule, they don't necessarily belong at the top of the list, no matter how loudly they shriek. To find true satisfaction in life, we must learn not only how to distinguish the urgent from the important, but to choose the latter over the former.

And how do we determine the identity of the "important things"? Those determinations usually come easier for a Christian than for many others because Christians have the guidance of the Word of God and the indwelling Holy Spirit. In my opinion, everything a Christian does should be geared toward fulfilling the Great Commission (Matt. 28:18–20). When your primary goal is to introduce men and women to Jesus Christ, you bring an eternal dimension to your life. You engage in activities that will stand the test of eternity. Material things can be fun and should be enjoyed as gifts of God, but they shall pass.

If you're a Christian, everything you do—whether you're a lawyer, a doctor, a teacher, a factory worker, a stay-at-home mom, a secretary, an administrative assistant, a sales clerk—everything takes on meaning if your chief goal is to help fulfill the Great Commission. Then everything that happens makes sense; everything has purpose and meaning. You have lots of money? Good. Not enough money? No problem. Success in politics? Fabulous. You're a well-known lawyer? Great! Use your leverage to extend the kingdom.

If extending the kingdom of God is your goal, everything makes sense, everything has purpose, and you don't have to despair. Life becomes tremendously exciting. As I look back now in old age, I think my mom and dad exemplified this kind of purposeful living. My dad's real goal was to plant churches and introduce people to Jesus Christ. His construction business served as a means to an end.

God has called us, not only to go to heaven when we die, not only to enjoy life, but also to partner with him in a tremendous worldwide reclamation project. Together, as a global team, we reach out to all nations of the world, proclaiming the good news of Jesus Christ. Such a massive endeavor gives purpose and meaning to life. It gives financial success a new significance. It gives education a purpose. It gives personal connections tremendous meaning. Our friends, our abilities, our finances—all of them work together toward accomplishing one massive project: reaching, if possible, every person on the face of the earth, generation after generation, until the return of Jesus Christ.

My son's father-in-law, Robert Levy, is a great example of a guy who's busy and phenomenally successful, but whose life revolves around Jesus Christ and the Great Commission. I've been with him in his home, in his office, on the road, and at our campaigns. He lives the gospel message. Truth be told, he reminds me of my dad; perhaps that's why I have such a special affection for him.

Robert is utterly unashamed of Jesus Christ. He doesn't make an effort to be godly and faithful to Christ; he just *is* without even realizing it. He talks about Jesus Christ as quickly as he talks about chickens (his business) or computers or banking. I don't think he even considers if someone might not like the topic; he doesn't appear to think in those terms. He's so in love with the Lord, so sold on Jesus Christ, that it doesn't even occur to him to feel cautious.

Yet Robert has developed friends in the highest places all over the world. He's on a first-name basis with leading authorities in business, politics, and international finance. He personally introduces men and women to Jesus Christ and frequently leads Bible studies. He asks for my schedule and prays for me every morning. I'll bet if I were to pick up the phone right now, he'd know where I'm going to be next Thursday. He's a tremendous example to me of someone who has chosen the important over the urgent—and God has blessed him for it.

Gains Admirers vs. Attracts Colleagues

I know many men whose nonstop activity gains them hordes of admirers. Observers see their frenetic schedules and astonishing output and can't help but feel impressed. And yet that's as far as it goes. Fans may applaud, cheer, and maybe even give these men an achievement award, but the men remain pretty much on their own.

When a divine purpose directs your activity, however, you soon discover that potential colleagues start showing up at your door. God sends associates and partners and coworkers to help you complete the assignments he gives. If you're in sync with God's heart, you don't see these men and women as competitors, but colleagues.

I met a man a while ago whom I'd take with me anywhere. Bob Mortimer has joined me on stage to tell audiences how God can use anybody. He usually grabs everyone's attention right away. You see, Bob isn't your average speaker. He's missing both legs and his left arm, yet he jokes about handicaps.

He carries a golf cap and from his wheelchair says to anyone who will listen, "You know, there really are no handicaps in this world." Then he pulls out his golf cap, puts it on, and continues. "Handicaps are up in our head. You see, I have a handy cap right here; it's a cap, and it's handy. This is the only handy cap I know. With Jesus Christ, even though you may lack three of your limbs, you're not really handicapped."

His wife—an attractive, wonderful woman—invited Bob to church. That's where he met Jesus Christ. They now have three beautiful children together. Bob may be missing three limbs, but he's still fully Bob, soul and spirit. Only his body appears two-thirds gone. He's a contented, happy man who laughs at his disability. He proves that wholeness can be ours through Jesus Christ. We don't need much body to know and serve God! I admire Bob, but I'm thrilled to be counted as one of his colleagues.

Actually, I consider myself immensely blessed to count on colleagues all over the world. A few years ago our team visited Bolivia. I had heard of a powerful woman with a great reputation for godliness and had asked her to come to the La Paz crusade. She agreed. When I asked her to pray for us, she said, "Get on your knees." We immediately fell to our knees, she laid hands on us, and then prayed up a storm. She might have been shoeless and illiterate, but that didn't stop her from being a powerful woman of God.

In the West many individuals try to create their own dignity through dress and appearance and makeup and name-dropping, but it can't compare with the nobility and authority that come from walking close to God. True dignity issues from knowing that you come from the hand of God, were rescued at the greatest price, and have a purpose filled with eternal meaning. All over the world, I find admirable men and women who exude the greatest dignity. Yet gratifying as that is, I find it even more satisfying that I call these noble men and women *colleagues*.

Great, but Fallen

You and I were made for greatness, for glory, for love. God fearfully and wonderfully made us in our mother's womb.

Yet if that's true—and it is, according to the Bible—then what has gone wrong? Why don't we feel great or glorious or lovable? If we were made to be awesome, why do we often behave so un-awesomely? If we were made for greatness, why do we so frequently grovel in the mud? Why do we mess up our lives when God means those lives to be fantastic?

In his book *People of the Lie,* M. Scott Peck shows how educated, decent, and good people hurt their own children by the way they talk to them, by their behavior, by the foolish decisions they make. Then when their hurtful behavior comes to light, they try to cover up and think their kids are not going to know.

They know.

Time and again we ask ourselves, "Why did I do it? Why did I fall? Why did I fail? Why did I lose my cool?" The answer is, we suffer from a spiritual sickness. We're diseased. We have a fatal flaw that only God can correct. Humankind is great, but fallen. Sin has marred God's beautiful work of art. That's why we can't cure ourselves, as much as we might want to. We have something wrong with our hearts that requires a character transplant.

I wonder how God feels when we stupidly turn down all the astonishing possibilities he offers us. He offers us life, purpose, meaning, significance, and we say, "Out of my way, God. I'd rather roll in the mud, lose my self-control, and make an idiot of myself."

None of us want to see ourselves as losers who deserve all the bad we get, who feel miserable and deserve to be miserable. "Yes," we may say, "I went to bed with my neighbor because my husband was beating up on me. But I didn't really mean it. I'm not a bad person. I did it in a moment of weakness. But I'm not a bad person."

It's true that all of us have sinned and fallen short of the glory of God (Rom. 3:23), but that doesn't mean we're as rotten as we could possibly get. Most people I know are not wicked, perverse, or downright wretched. But all of us *are* weak; all of us *are* sinful. And to enjoy the greatness, glory, love, and purpose that God wants for us, we all need Jesus Christ to do for us what we cannot do ourselves.

We are great, but fallen. And Jesus Christ offers us the only solution for our terrible problem.

Mr. Secretary Finds Meaning

I believe many in this generation are searching for purpose. They're saying, "I feel I was made for greatness and I'm trying to find my way to God." I like to say to them, "May I show you the answer I've found? Test it out for yourself; give it a shot."

Why not do things God's way and find out if he's right? I've found millions around the world in every culture for whom his way *works*. So why don't you give God a chance? God himself encourages us to discover for ourselves the truth of his Word. "Test me," he says, "and see if I will not throw open the floodgates of heaven and pour out so much blessing that you will not have room enough for it" (Mal. 3:10).

James A. Baker III, the former U.S. secretary of state, did just that about a decade ago. In the waning days of the first Bush presidency, he told four thousand top officials from all over the world about his discovery. "I have to tell you about my journey of faith," he declared to the august crowd, which included President George H. W. Bush, Colin Powell, and more than forty heads of state.

He described how his first wife died of cancer, leaving him with four children. Her death prompted him to start asking hard questions: *Where did my wife go? Will I see her again? Will we recognize each other? What will our relationship be like? Will we be together? What is going to happen?*

For a long time the Bakers had attended church, taken communion, and done all the things churchgoers do. But Baker never thought seriously about eternal issues until his wife passed away.

Eventually he met Susan, the woman who would become his second wife. Her former husband had been an alcoholic and their marriage ended ugly. After marrying Baker, she started attending a Bible Study Fellowship group. By investigating God's Word, she found both Jesus Christ and the answers to many of her questions. She tried to introduce her new husband to Christ, but he just couldn't "get it." He kept telling his wife, "But I am unworthy. I cannot earn the love of God." And Susan kept repeating, "Jim, no one can earn the love of God. It's a gift!"

As he flew all over the world, heading from crisis to crisis and meeting to meeting as secretary of state, Baker continued to ponder those big questions: *What about eternal life? Where am I going if this plane crashes?*

Finally he met with some U.S. senators who really know and love Jesus Christ. "Guys," he said, "I can't take it anymore. How did you come to peace with God? What have you done?"

These believers explained that to know God we must take a step of faith, open our hearts to Jesus Christ, let him come into our lives, forgive us our sins, and give us eternal life. "Yes, you will go to heaven," they said. "And yes, you will know your first wife." They answered his most pressing questions. At that point he dropped to his knees in one of the Senate side rooms and surrendered his life to Jesus Christ.

Later, in a room full of dignitaries from around the world, James Baker declared, "I want to tell all of you here that my life has meaning since I became a follower of Jesus Christ."

How did this powerful man find meaning in life? Not by jetting around the world and talking to heads of state. Not by defusing world conflicts. Not by representing the United States of America at the highest levels of international diplomacy. In other words, not by spending himself in frenzied activity, no matter how politically significant.

James A. Baker III found purpose in his life and significance in his activities through his personal relationship with Jesus Christ. He took God up on his offer to "test me," and he discovered the truth of the greatest advertising claim in history.

And you can find the same thing.

How to Find Significance According to the Bible

1. *Remember that you were created with astonishing worth.*
   "What is man that you are mindful of him, the son of man that you care for him? You made him a little lower than the heavenly beings and crowned him with glory and honor" (Ps. 8:4–5).

2. *Realize that God chooses to dwell not in temples of stone, but within his own children.*
   "Do you not know that your body is a temple of the Holy Spirit, who is in you, whom you have received from God?" (1 Cor. 6:19).

3. *Remember that God specially chooses every one of his children.*
   "For we know, brothers loved by God, that he has chosen you, because our gospel came to you not simply with words, but also with power, with the Holy Spirit and with deep conviction" (1 Thess. 1:4–5).

4. *Consider every redeemed soul a present from the Father to the Son.*
   [Jesus said,] "This is the will of him who sent me, that I shall lose none of all that he has given me, but raise them up at the last day" (John 6:39).

5. *Never forget that all believers have been given a fabulous identity.*
   "But you are a chosen people, a royal priesthood, a holy nation, a people belonging to God, that you may declare the praises of him who called you out of darkness into his wonderful light" (1 Peter 2:9).

6. *Make sure you're involved in meaningful, lasting work.*
   "'Do not work for food that spoils, but for food that endures to eternal life, which the Son of Man will give you. On him God the Father has placed his seal of approval.' Then they asked him, 'What must we do to do the works God requires?' Jesus answered, 'The work of God is this: to believe in the one he has sent'" (John 6:27–29).

7. *Acknowledge that God invites you to partner with him in doing great things around the world.*
   "[God] has committed to us the message of reconciliation. We are therefore Christ's ambassadors, as though God were making his appeal through us" (2 Cor. 5:19–20).

8. *Choose eternal rewards over short-term returns that quickly fade.*
   "Do you not know that in a race all the runners run, but only one gets the prize? Run in such a way as to get the prize. Everyone who competes in the games goes into strict training. They do it to get a crown that will not last; but we do it to get a crown that will last forever" (1 Cor. 9:24–25).

9. *Maximize your effectiveness by continually evaluating your schedule.*
   "Be very careful, then, how you live—not as unwise but as wise, making the most of every opportunity" (Eph. 5:15–16).

10. *Don't allow the mistakes of your past to hamstring your future.*
    "One thing I do: Forgetting what is behind and straining toward what is ahead, I press on toward the goal to win the prize for which God has called me heavenward in Christ Jesus" (Phil. 3:13–14).

10

An Anchor for the Soul

Positive Thinking or Hope?

> Those who hope in the LORD
>   will renew their strength.
> They will soar on wings like eagles;
>   they will run and not grow weary,
>   they will walk and not be faint.
>
>   The prophet Isaiah,
>   in Isaiah 40:31

Norman Cousins, the late author of *Head First: The Biology of Hope and the Healing Power of the Human Spirit*, used to say that human beings can live for a few weeks without food, a few days without water, a few minutes without air, but not one second without hope. I think he was right.

When hope eludes us, we soon lose our way and either give up, run down, or check out. A man I met a few years ago, a successful Hong Kong businessman named Wilson, knows well not only the misery of living without hope, but also the exhilaration of finding it.

Wilson was born in Vietnam to Chinese parents, the eldest of nine children. When the war began, his dad sent him to Hong Kong with instructions to get a good college education. "I don't want you fighting in the war," he said. "Marry a good Chinese girl and take care of the family. If we get killed, you take care of your brothers and sisters."

Wilson moved to Hong Kong and earned a degree in engineering; then he became an architect. After making some money, he married a Chinese woman, a nonpracticing Buddhist like him. Within a few years, he had two daughters—and an affair on the side.

One day he discovered a business partner had cheated him out of ten million American dollars. Furious with rage, Wilson determined to kill the man. *It's a question of how, that's all,* he thought. *If he's going to cheat me out of a fortune, then I'm going to finish him off. He's gone.*

While Wilson tried to figure out how best to eliminate his business partner, his wife found out about his sex partner. Things suddenly got a lot stickier. What to do now? Wilson wanted his lover, not his wife. *If I kill this guy,* he reasoned, *maybe they'll catch me and I'll go to jail. Then what will happen to my girls? Neither can I kill my wife to stay with my lover. Kill the lover? I can't.*

Desperate and without hope, Wilson finally concluded, *I'll kill myself. That will finish it off. The kids will have plenty of money, and it will all be over.*

While he contemplated how to shoot himself, a city bus rumbled by. Wilson absentmindedly read the advertisement posted on the vehicle's side: "The Hope of Man." He snapped to attention, read the sign again, and thought, *Boy, do I need hope!* Moments later another bus passed, festooned with the same advertisement promoting our first Hong Kong crusade: "The Hope of Man."

That was all it took. Wilson decided to attend.

On a humid Saturday night Wilson walked to the stadium alone, sat down alone, and heard the gospel for the first time. By night's end he had asked Jesus Christ into his heart, but he chose not to speak with a counselor. As he exited the stadium, someone gave him what we call the "green book," a slim volume containing some follow-up material. A few moments of reading made him think, *What a decision I've made. I'm really forgiven! Maybe I'm going to change.*

But still he knew almost nothing about the Christian life.

The next Monday, Wilson and another engineer were negotiating a deal. When they finished, his colleague turned to him and said, "You know, Wilson, I'd like to have coffee with you to talk about another subject."

"Okay," Wilson replied.

At their coffee get-together the man said, "I've done business with you before, but this time I want to talk to you about somebody named Jesus."

Wilson stared at his friend, stunned.

"You're the first person who ever talked to me about Jesus," he exclaimed. "Last Saturday night I went to the stadium and decided to follow Jesus. Now you want to talk to me about him. I don't really know anything about him; I just decided to follow him. Tell me what he's like."

For the next hour this seasoned Christian explained the gospel thoroughly. The following Sunday he took Wilson to a good church in Hong Kong. Wilson, however, told neither his wife nor his lover about any of this; he didn't want either of them to know. He enjoyed the service and returned the following week, soon making it a habit. But when one Sunday the pastor preached a sermon against adultery, Wilson blanched. *It's one thing to follow Jesus and go to heaven*, he thought, *but quite another to give up my lover.* So after just a few weeks of attending church, Wilson stopped going.

It was then his wife hit him with a big surprise.

"Why don't you go to church anymore on Sundays?" she asked.

"How . . . how do you know?" Wilson stammered.

"Oh, I know," she replied. "In fact, I'd like to go with you."

After a long pause—and more than a few misgivings—Wilson agreed to her request. Still, he doubted the wisdom of his decision. Why would he want to go to church with his wife, the woman he wanted to toss aside? Nevertheless, he kept his word.

He discovered the pastor had begun preaching a series on the Ten Commandments—and in three weeks the spotlight would fall on the seventh commandment: "Thou shalt not commit adultery."

Wilson began to sweat.

Not knowing what else to do, he asked for an interview with the pastor. In an avalanche of words he poured out his tormented heart. "I decided to follow Jesus," he confessed, "and I'm serious about it—but I have this lover. What do I do?"

The pastor saw Wilson's genuine heart and replied forthrightly. "If you really want to follow Jesus," he said, "this is what you must do: give up your lover. Look, you have lots of cash, so give her some. Give her a big check and say, 'Sorry, babe, it's over.'"

Wilson hated the pastor's advice. He loved his girlfriend, not his wife!

Weeks went by, then months. Wilson struggled with what he ought to do and what he wanted to do. Some conversions are like that; it takes years to clean up the mess created by a lifetime apart from Jesus Christ.

After a long battle, Wilson finally made up his mind. He handed his lover a huge check and said, "It's over. Good-bye." And that was it.

A few days later his wife heard the pastor preach about baptism. "I want to be baptized," she declared.

"Okay," Wilson replied, "I want to be baptized, too." But still he felt no love for the mother of his children.

What happened next, he told me through tears.

"I was sitting on the front row of the church while the women were being baptized," he recalled. "My wife came down, the pastor immersed her, and when she came up out of the water . . . I looked at her and said out loud, 'You know, she's actually prettier than I remembered.' And I fell in love with her all over again."

Now many things started falling into place for Wilson and his heal- ing family. He called his dad in Vietnam and led him to the Lord, right on the telephone. Soon afterward he visited his native country and led his mother to Jesus Christ (she and Wilson's father had separated). All but two of his brothers and sisters eventually placed their faith in Jesus Christ. What was left but to stage a family party?

"My dad and mom got together again," he told me, again through tears, "and they were sitting there, holding hands—in front of us all!"

Understand that many traditional Chinese couples simply don't show physical affection in public. Never. But here sat his dad and mom, holding hands in front of the whole family. Hope had invaded their hearts, as well.

I heard this story for the first time in 1997. We met because he served as the treasurer for our second Hong Kong campaign—just a decade after he found hope through an advertisement on a passing bus. What a change! From a murderous, suicidal adulterer, to a king living with spiritual authority, glory, honor, and dignity.

That's the kind of robust hope Jesus Christ can bring to anyone. Including you.

A Little Short of Hope?

All of us need hope, even more than we need food or water or air. A hopeless existence just doesn't seem worth living. All of us instinctively know this, so we spend our days scouring for hope.

Sometimes, however, we settle for something a little short of hope. In a legitimate desire to feel good about where we're headed, we mistake positive thinking for genuine hope.

Positive thinking is good, just not good enough. While it beats the tar out of negative thinking, nobody can hang a future on it. You can repeat sunny maxims, look for the bright side, search for silver linings, and pump yourself up all you want, but if that sums up your battle plans, you'll be staring into oblivion the moment the black clouds roll in and refuse to roll out. And positive thinking can't do much for you when it's time to face that ultimate black cloud, death. The Grim Reaper doesn't smile no matter how many times you repeat the phrase, "I'm good enough. I'm smart enough. And doggone it, people like me!"

The problem with positive thinking is that thinking positively wields too little power over the greatest forces that confront us. While positive thinking can put us in the right frame of mind to tackle our problems, it can't ultimately do much about the problems themselves. If I'm sitting in the cab of a runaway truck hurtling down a mountainside, thinking positively may allow me to avoid panic and devise a last-moment escape—but if I round the bend and find the road washed out, positive thinking won't keep me from plunging headlong to the bottom of the mountain.

It's good to think positively, but such thinking can take us only so far. To go the rest of the way, we need hope—solid, biblical hope. So how does hope differ from positive thinking? How is it better? Let's consider five ways that hope outshines positive thinking, and see how to go beyond positive thinking to reach genuine hope, both now and for eternity.

Positive Thinking	Hope
• Improves Outlook	• Guarantees Outcome
• Good at Spin	• Good at Regrouping
• Lessens Apprehension	• Builds Courage
• Looks for Imminent Change	• Counts on Permanent Change
• Crosses Its Fingers	• Bows Its Head

Improves Outlook vs. Guarantees Outcome

Positive thinking can do wonders for an individual's outlook. When Thomas Edison tried and failed one thousand times to find a suitable filament for his new electric lightbulb, a reporter thought he must have felt terribly discouraged over his failure. "Failure?" Edison asked. "We haven't failed. At least now we know 1,000 things that won't work." And years later when the great inventor spent five years and his entire fortune of four million dollars in a futile attempt to develop a magnetic ore-separating process for low-grade iron deposits, he declared, "Well, it's all gone, but we had a good time spending it!" Henry Ford summed up the power of positive thinking when he said, "Whether you think you can or think you can't, you're right."

But while I'd much rather spend time with a person who thinks positively than with someone who complains all the time, I'm blessed most of all by those who radiate a living hope. Positive thinking may have the power to change one's outlook, but genuine hope has the power to guarantee one's destiny.

The Bible does not picture hope as mere wishful thinking, along the lines of, "Boy, I really wish it would happen, but who knows whether it ever could?" Rather, it sees hope as an expectation of future blessings that remains as yet invisible.[1] Positive thinking puts on rose-colored glasses and says, "I hope it doesn't rain this afternoon," when it knows the forecast calls for thundershowers and sprinkles already have begun to fall. Hope looks expectantly into the growing darkness and says, "I'm confident we'll be okay," even when the crops have grown waterlogged and bankruptcy lurks around the corner.

The real difference between the two comes down to source. Positive thinking flows from the human will, from the choice to believe that everything will turn out all right in the end (whether it actually does or not). Biblical hope takes its stand on the unchanging character of God, that he means what he says, and that he will certainly keep all his promises (whether it looks that way or not). In other words, positive thinking depends on us, while hope depends on God.

That is why the apostle Paul could look back on the personal journeys of his Ephesian friends and remind them that, before they came to Jesus Christ, they had been "without hope and without God in the world" (Eph. 2:12). Paul's friends might have been able to think positively even without God, but they could never enjoy true hope. The biblical equation is simple: No God, no hope.

Christians can be sustained, even in tough times, by the liveliest hope on the planet. Because the purposes of God center in Jesus Christ, those who are "in Christ" can remain confident that whatever happens to them occurs only under the watchful, loving eyes of the Almighty. Because God has promised to take care of them and see them safely to their heavenly home, and because he already has demonstrated his faithfulness by raising Jesus Christ from the dead, Christians can live in the certain hope that all really will be well. And that remains true even when some of us get sick with cancer, die in train wrecks, or perish in house fires.

Even now history rushes to its terminal point. The climax of history centers in God's Son, Jesus Christ—not only in his death on the cross for our sins, not only in his present role as our living Lord, but especially in his bodily return to earth. For good reason God calls the second coming of Jesus Christ—the most frequently prophesied event in the whole Bible—"the blessed hope" (Titus 2:13).

Despite what you may hear, believers do not wait for Armageddon, though Armageddon will happen. We're not waiting for the Great Tribulation, though the Great Tribulation will come. We're not looking for the antichrist, though "the beast" will make his appearance. We *are* looking for the return of God's Son from heaven. Yes, there will be wars and rumors of wars, famines, earthquakes, pollution, doomed peace conferences—that is all true. But we don't focus on any of that. We wait for "the blessed hope" when Jesus returns to earth to rule the world in peace and righteousness.

This is Hope with a capital "H"! Chapter four of 1 Thessalonians describes how God's Son will arrive with the trumpet blast of God, the archangel will shout, and the resurrected bodies of those who have died in Jesus Christ will rise from their graves. The spirits of those who died in Jesus will return with him, and their bodies, souls, and spirits will reunite. Believers alive at that time will be transformed "in the twinkling of an eye" (1 Cor. 15:52) instantly remade into men and women fit for heaven. The Bible says we shall all meet with the Lord in the air, "and so we will be with the Lord forever" (v. 17).

Why does God give us this unusual information? Why make such an otherworldly promise? The Bible tells us these things so that when our loved ones die, we will not "grieve like the rest of men, who have no hope" (v. 13). With such a marvelous future, we can live in hope, come cancer or catastrophe. So the Bible says, "Encourage each other with these words" (v. 18).

My dad died from bronchial pneumonia when he was thirty-four. My mom died from cancer at age eighty-three. My grandma died when she was sixty-three. One of my closest friends died in a motorcycle accident when he was nineteen. All of them died knowing Jesus Christ—so when Jesus returns in the clouds, they'll all come with him.

And when my turn comes, the gravediggers will bury my corpse in Oregon if I die there, but I won't be there. My body will wait for the second coming of Jesus Christ when we shall all be raised from the dead, and Jesus will return with all the countless millions who have died believing in him—multitudes beyond our imagination. Among them will come all the babies who died as newborns, as well as all the little ones who died on abortion tables. Even now all of them are rejoicing in heaven, waiting for the command to return to earth with Jesus. That's my firm hope, based not on human willpower, but on the promise and character of God.

Do you remember when the space shuttle *Challenger* exploded on January 28, 1986, just seventy-three seconds after takeoff? I'll never forget the stunned faces of those on the ground at Cape Canaveral, including the parents of teacher/astronaut Christa McAuliffe. The next day *USA Today* printed a photograph of a horrified Nancy Reagan as she watched the disaster unfold. "Oh my God, no!" screamed the headline, repeating the First Lady's own words.

In the midst of that tragedy, the relatives of one doomed astronaut received a special consolation. Mission specialist Ron McNair believed in the Lord Jesus Christ, and just before he boarded the shuttle he told his family, "Jesus and I will be going up together." He had no idea that he would soon go farther than outer space. As a shocked nation watched, Ron kept on going right up to heaven.

In a eulogy to the deceased astronauts, President Ronald Reagan said, "We know in our hearts that you now make your home beyond the stars, safe in God's promise of eternal life." For Ron McNair, at least, the former president got it exactly right. At this very moment Ron lives beyond the stars, in a place we call heaven. And one day we'll be with him again.

I look forward to the moment when, as the book of Revelation says, we, the servants of Jesus Christ, "will see his face" (22:4). What a beautiful face it must be! I feel eager to see him as he really is, to experience what Isaiah the prophet meant when he promised that "your eyes will see the king in his beauty" (Isa. 33:17). What a thrill to see Jesus when he returns, to fall at his feet in worship. Then we will be able to say, "So this is the way you look, Lord Jesus." What an exciting day!

Meanwhile, the Lord wants to keep us in suspense. He wants us to love him with overflowing happiness powered by inexhaustible hope. As Peter said, even though we don't now see him, we believe in him, and we are "filled with an inexpressible and glorious joy" (1 Peter 1:8).

Positive thinking may be great for improving one's outlook, but to guarantee what is to come, you need solid, biblical hope. And in a very real sense, for those who choose such hope, heaven begins right now. In his marvelous little book, *The Great Divorce*, C. S. Lewis suggests that the moment we leave this world, we will discover that our experience of heaven or hell actually began while we were living on earth. What comes in the hereafter will amount only to an affirmation, a continuation, and an intensification of what we choose here. So choose well!

Good at Spin vs. Good at Regrouping

Everybody's talking about "spin" these days, about how to put the best face possible on (what are often) some pretty ugly mugs. Positive thinkers generally make excellent spin doctors. Where you see a dilapidated house, he envisions an incredible investment opportunity. Where you notice a stain, she detects the chance to try out a new spot remover. Where you smell a skunk, they whiff a fabulous example of natural adaptation.

Now, I'm all for putting on the best face possible. Why unveil the Mummy when you could introduce Prince Charming? "Spin" can help us see the good in something, and I see nothing bad about that.

The chief weakness of "spin" is that it functions well only up to a certain point. Happy faces and smiling masks just can't hide the devastation etched deep into the features of some weary travelers. They don't need "spin," they need to regroup—and that's where hope does such a fantastic job.

Solid, biblical hope not only prepares us for eternity, but also helps us to function in the here and now. When the living hope pouring out of the heart of God energizes your soul, no problem or difficulty can "tap out" your inner resources. While "spin" does well at covering up embarrassing blemishes, it's not much good at providing emergency medical relief. If "spin" is a makeup artist, then hope is a reconstructive surgeon. "Spin" slaps on a new coat of paint, while hope remodels the house. Hope looks full into the angry face of adversity and keeps on moving ahead, while "spin" either tucks tail and runs or simply refuses to acknowledge hardship.

Hope doesn't promise a life free from difficulty; it simply provides a sure way through the difficulty. "We do not want you to be uninformed, brothers, about the hardships we suffered in the province of Asia," wrote the apostle Paul to some friends. "We were under great pressure, far beyond our ability to endure, so that we despaired even of life" (2 Cor. 1:8). Paul freely admitted that his hardships not only exceeded his coping abilities, but that the overwhelming pressure nearly choked the life out of him. And yet he persevered. How? Paul answers,

> This happened that we might not rely on ourselves but on God, who raises the dead. He has delivered us from such a deadly peril, and he will deliver us. On him we have set our hope that he will continue to deliver us.
>
> 2 Corinthians. 1:9–10

No force in the universe comes near to matching the ability of godly hope to help us regroup in the face of severe challenges. Several years ago my wife, Pat, proved to me the awesome power of hope when she faced a frightening medical challenge.

I had been in Scotland for five weeks. The last few days of our meetings, Pat flew in to join me. We had planned to take time off just to relax and enjoy each other's company.

With about three days left in the campaign, she gathered herself and said, "Now, I hate to tell you this, but touch here; I think I've got a lump." Sure enough, I felt a lump about the diameter of my little finger. The blood rushed from my face.

"Oh, Babe," I said, "we'd better get back home and go straight to the doctor."

That's exactly what we did. I prayed that the lump would turn out to be benign; it revealed itself as malignant. The specialists scheduled Pat for surgery the very next Sunday, then told her to expect two years of chemotherapy after that. The awful report shook us to the core. Especially me.

When we returned home from the doctor, I rushed to the basement and began to weep—not out of despair, but at the thought of all the things I hadn't done with Pat, all the places I hadn't taken her, all the ways I had fallen short as a husband. As I fled downstairs, crying and grieving, from upstairs I heard the piano playing. I listened as my wife, in a clear, soft voice, began singing some of her favorite hymns: "Under His Wings" and "The Church's One Foundation Is Jesus Christ Our Lord."

And I thought, *Lord, what a time to sing!* It seemed totally inappropriate.

But as the lyrics of those old songs continued to drift down to the basement, carried along by Pat's confident but gentle voice, I began to change my mind. Her singing no longer seemed so out of place.

What a marvelous thing, I thought, that a Christian can hear terrible news and still go to the piano and sing the old, affirming hymns she's known since college. To declare her love for the Lord, that her hope rests in him alone—how amazing!

Real hope is not blind hope. Real hope can afford to be objective, to look reality in the face. Consider the story of Abraham in the Old Testament. By the time God promised this man and his wife, Sarah, that they would give birth to a son, the elderly couple had long since qualified for Medicare. Now, Abraham was no fool. He knew that, humanly speaking, such a thing could not happen. The Bible says that "he faced the fact that his body was as good as dead—since he was about a hundred years old—and that Sarah's womb was also dead" (Rom. 4:19). Nevertheless, "against all hope, Abraham in hope believed and so became the father of many nations" (v. 18).

Why does the Bible say, "Against all hope"? Because, from a purely human perspective, Abraham and Sarah had no hope of conceiving a child. They had passed the age of childbearing years. Yet despite that enormous obstacle, the Bible says "Abraham in hope believed." Abraham knew the character of God and that the Lord's word could be trusted completely. This old man wasn't some wild kook screaming, "I believe! I believe! I'm going to jump into outer space!" No, he placed his hope squarely in the character and power of God, "being fully persuaded that God had power to do what he had promised" (v. 21).

Over breakfast coffee, Abraham may have looked at his wife and said, "Sarah, there is no hope for you. And look at me; I am a corrugated old man. There is no way we can have a baby. But God has said we're going to have one, and we're going to have one." Talk about outrageous hope!

Had Abraham written up his story for a weekly magazine, had he appeared on *Oprah* to tell it, he would have been laughed straight off the set. How could such an old man and ancient woman have a child? Abraham would have explained, "The only reason I can hope such a thing is because I believe the living God."

I think my wife learned to exercise this kind of outrageous hope from her mother. One afternoon I asked Pat, "When you think of heaven, what's the first thing that comes to mind?"

"That my mother will walk," she said.

At forty-eight years of age, my mother-in-law took a polio sugar cube vaccine—and promptly contracted the disease. She's been confined to a wheelchair ever since. Yet for almost forty years, the hope of God has put a step in her spirit, even if her body can't follow suit. Hope allowed her to regroup after a massive setback, and it continues to keep her rollin'.

I saw a similar dynamic at work in my own mother. About ten years ago doctors discovered a massive tumor growing on her liver. They looked at the X-rays, shook their heads, and said, "No surgery. No chemotherapy. No other medicine, just pain killer."

Yet Mom remained at peace with the Lord and in good spirits with everyone else. She knew that a glorious future awaited her in heaven. As she neared the end, I remember thinking, *One of these days I'm going to have to fly to Orange County in California. A casket will lie in front of us, and we'll bury it in a crypt in Southern California. It's all ready; it's all prepared. But we are not going to bury my mom. We're going to bury her body, her temporary home. By the time I get there, my mother will be with Jesus.*

At her funeral on December 27, 1993, someone read from John 14, the very passage that had comforted me at ten years of age when my father died: "Do not let your hearts be troubled," Jesus said. "Trust in God; trust also in me. In my Father's house are many rooms; if it were not so, I would have told you. I am going there to prepare a place for you. And if I go and prepare a place for you, I will come back and take you to be with me that you also may be where I am" (vv. 1–3).

That afternoon I told the mourners that I had spoken with my mom about two days before she died. She could hardly talk, but she managed to get out about six phrases. How wonderful to hear from the lips of your own mother that she loves the Lord Jesus Christ, has the assurance of eternal life, and harbors no doubts about the reality of heaven or the presence of the Lord Jesus Christ! She knew that at the moment she stopped breathing, she would receive a warm welcome to her heavenly home. And she expressed the hope that on the day of resurrection, her body would be resurrected from the grave and she would exult in the ultimate manifestation of eternal life.

The reason we have hope, the reason we avoid desperation, the reason we don't beat our breasts—no matter what comes—is that God has given us "hope as an anchor for the soul, firm and secure" (Heb. 6:19).

And that, friends, is a long way from "spin."

Lessens Apprehension vs. Builds Courage

Positive thinking really can reduce some of our fears. Suppose you're camping in the Umpqua National Forest near Crater Lake in southern Oregon. You've enjoyed a fabulous day of hiking and sightseeing, and now it's time to retire for the evening. A full moon and myriad brilliant stars light up the clear western sky, and you snuggle into your sleeping bag content, dreaming of the next day's adventure.

Suddenly you hear a snuffling among the fir trees just to the south of you. A huge shadow falls across the walls of your paper-thin tent, and it looks as if *something* is slowly moving toward you. You grope about for a flashlight, trying to keep silent—at that moment you wish you had not read the most recent edition of the *Outdoorsman*, which described in gory detail one man's harrowing escape from a ravenous, eight-hundred-pound bear.

At such a moment, positive thinking can do quite a lot to relieve your fear. You might remind yourself that bears generally steer clear of human campsites, unless someone leaves out the groceries (and you remember that you safely stowed yours in a cooler in the car trunk). Or you might tell yourself that the species *ursus* generally fears the species *homo sapiens* more than the other way around. Or you might recall that the park ranger told you earlier that he might be snooping about in your area late that evening. Any of these positive-thinking suggestions might calm your nerves.

On the other hand, "Late Night Snack" might be tattooed across your forehead.

In that case, you don't need positive thinking; you need courage. (A loaded Remington wouldn't hurt, either.) Hope has a way of producing courage that mere positive thinking can't duplicate.

Hope builds courage in human hearts, not by denying reality, but through banking on absolute certainty. When you place your hope in the trustworthy promises of God, nothing can ultimately shake you—not even impending death. When the apostle Paul reminded his friends about the certainty of heaven, he closed his remarks by saying, "But thanks be to God! He gives us the victory through our Lord Jesus Christ. Therefore, my dear brothers, stand firm. Let nothing move you" (1 Cor. 15:57–58).

Nothing *can* ultimately move us when we remember that heaven, our future home, is an actual place, a location just as real as New York, London, Paris, or Bangkok. The Word of God says, "Now we know that if the earthly tent we live in is destroyed, we have a building from God, an eternal house in heaven, not built by human hands" (2 Cor. 5:1).

The Bible pictures heaven as a real and stable home. It paints heaven as a city, a house, a mansion, a permanent place. Somewhere up there—the Bible always portrays it as "up there"—exists a place called heaven. For the Christian, death means leaving an earthly house and moving to a heavenly house.

One day a man's daughter married and moved just across the bay. Often the father would look out in the direction of her new home. When somebody asked him, "Why?" he replied, "I just want to look and see where my girl is living."

Heaven is the place all believers will one day call "home." Jesus referred to heaven as "my Father's house" and promised that he was going there to prepare a place for us. It's going to be beautiful. "No eye has seen, no ear has heard, no mind has conceived what God has prepared for those who love him," the Bible declares in 1 Corinthians 2:9. Though we do not understand all the details, ever since Jesus Christ left this earth, he has been busily preparing a place for you and me.

On the cross, Jesus Christ purchased the reality of heaven. That is why he took our sins and rose from the dead, to give us the absolute assurance that we will rise from the dead, that our bodies will be lifted up from the grave, and that we shall always be with the Lord. Children can understand this as well as adults; in fact, I think little ones can sometimes understand it better.

My friend Joe has a son named Peter. When Peter was about seven years old, his family moved from Michigan to Florida. Peter did not much care for the move, since it meant leaving behind Mr. Whittle, a trusted family friend. Peter hated the idea of living two thousand miles away from his elderly friend.

One morning at breakfast the family received a phone call saying that Mr. Whittle was dying of cancer. As soon as Peter heard the news, he rose from the table and ran to his room. Joe thought his son must be really broken up and said to the others, "Leave him alone."

Before the rest of the family had finished eating, however, Peter returned with a piece of paper—and a request. "Dad," he asked, "would you send this letter to Mr. Whittle before he dies?"

Joe wondered what his young son might want to say and replied, "All right, Peter, I'll do that for you. But can I read it before you send it?"

"Oh, sure," Peter replied.

Moments later big tears flowed from my friend's eyes as he read the carefully scrawled note: "Dear Mr. Whittle, I hear that you are going to heaven. Isn't that great? Your friend, Peter."

How many of us would have used the word "great" to describe Mr. Whittle's news? More likely we would have said, "How awful! He's going to die of cancer." But Peter looked at things differently. He knew that Mr. Whittle had committed his life to Jesus Christ and he knew his friend was on his way to heaven.

All of us can enjoy the same kind of assurance. We, too, can know that heaven is our true home and that one day we will move there to live forever with Jesus. F. B. Meyer, a famous social worker and preacher from England, displayed just such a confidence. A few hours before he died, he wrote a postcard to a friend in which he said, "Dear brother, I have raced you to heaven and I'm getting there before you. I'll see you there. Love, F. B. Meyer." Three hours later he left to be with the Lord.

That is the way I want to go, and it is the way every Christian can go: with the absolute assurance of heaven. God offers all of us the assurance of a home in heaven. He wants all of us to join him at his house—even four-star Soviet generals.

Just before the fall of the Soviet Union, a Russian four-star general attended a peace conference in the West. A businessman friend of mine and his wife sat down with this man, and in conversation the wife quoted a Bible verse.

Immediately the general collapsed into a chair, tears in his eyes. A KGB agent assigned to the general found himself maneuvered by my friend to the other end of the living room, while my friend's wife continued her conversation with the general.

"General, why are you crying?" she asked.

"When you quoted that Bible verse," he explained, "it reminded me of my mother. When I was a little boy, my mother always used to quote that verse."

And then this woman, with all the courage of a heaven-bound Christian, got nose-to-nose with the professional soldier and asked, "General, do you know God?"

"No, I don't," confessed the Russian, "but I have always wanted to know him, especially since my mother died."

"General," she declared, "you can meet God within twenty minutes, right here."

When he replied, "I'd like to," this brave woman opened her Bible and explained how he could open his heart to Jesus Christ. Less than twenty minutes later, that man bowed his head and asked Jesus to give him eternal life. A year later I met my friend in Europe and asked him how the general was doing. I wondered if this convert had continued to pursue his relationship with God upon his return to Russia.

My friend didn't hesitate. "Man, he is growing in the things of God!" he exclaimed. "Not only that, but he's got a Bible study with eight or ten Russian military officers. They have a Bible study and prayer time every week, right in Moscow."

Skeptics may laugh when they hear stories like these, but let them laugh. Some say, "Oh, you Christians. You always promise pie in the sky in the sweet by-and-by." You know my answer to that? "You'd better believe it. I've got myself a pie in the sky in the sweet by-and-by. I'm nibbling on it now, and it tastes mighty good."

Don't worry about those who make fun. I don't care what they say. The citizens of heaven are my friends, and the more of my friends who go there, the more I want to go myself.

That's the hope of the believer. It's a glorious hope, a real hope. Never doubt that the Lord meant what he said: "I am going there to prepare a place for you."

Looks for Imminent Change vs. Counts on Permanent Change

Positive thinking works best when the good times it envisions lie just around the corner. It's generally much easier to maintain a positive outlook when we believe our fortunes look ready to skyrocket. It's much harder to keep an optimistic attitude when our immediate prospects look dim. When all we have going for us is a rootless conviction that the sun will come out tomorrow, a year of overcast skies can effectively douse our enthusiasm.

On the other hand, while biblical hope never abandons the possibility that tomorrow really will bring a better day, it places its eggs in the basket of eternity. While it, too, looks for good things to come sooner rather than later, it bases its hope not on human willpower but on the love of God. As the prophet Jeremiah told his people after a withering invasion devastated his nation,

> It is good for a man to bear the yoke
> while he is young.
> Let him sit alone in silence,
> for the LORD has laid it on him.
> Let him bury his face in the dust—
> there may yet be hope. . . .

> For men are not cast off
> > by the Lord forever.
> Though he brings grief, he will show compassion,
> > so great is his unfailing love.

Lamentations 3:27–32

The Bible rings with story upon story of how God delights in intervening in history for the benefit of his people. He loves to bring good out of evil and blessing out of catastrophe. He instructs us to "call upon me in the day of trouble; I will deliver you, and you will honor me" (Ps. 50:15).

Yet even when God chooses (for reasons known only to him) to keep us in some difficulty, he never removes our ultimate hope. Another ancient prophet, Habakkuk, showed in what basket he had placed his eggs:

> Though the fig tree does not bud
> > and there are no grapes on the vines,
> > though the olive crop fails
> > and the fields produce no food,
> > though there are no sheep in the pen
> > and no cattle in the stalls,
> yet I will rejoice in the LORD,
> > I will be joyful in God my Savior.
> The Sovereign LORD is my strength;
> > he makes my feet like the feet of a deer,
> > he enables me to go on the heights.

Habakkuk 3:17–19

You cannot express such a strong hope without first adopting an eternal focus, something we instinctively long for. We sense that God has "set eternity in the hearts of men" (Eccles. 3:11). We know we are not made only for seventy or so years on earth. We rightfully believe he wants the best for us, both now on earth and one day in heaven.

During a campaign in London, an Englishman joined me on the platform the evening I was to talk about heaven. Charles Cortell broke down when I told him, "I'm going to speak about heaven and eternity tonight." After drying his tears, Charles told me that his only child had died in a household accident when she was only two years old. One day his little sweetheart jammed her chubby fingers into an electrical socket, and by the time Charles could race to her side, she was dead.

"Luis," Charles said, "to me, heaven is the most beautiful place anywhere. I can't wait to get there. My sweet little girl is up there."

Although this extraordinarily talented man ministers to some of the most powerful politicians in England, he told me, "The main thing is heaven. I hardly care about anything else. I don't care about money. I just can't wait to see my little girl."

Eternity has captured his heart.

My own father died singing and clapping because he knew he was about to exchange his temporary home for an eternal one. My mother told me that Dad sat up in bed, clapped his hands, and as his head fell back on the pillow, he pointed up to heaven and declared, "I'm going to be with Jesus, which is far better." A few moments later he was gone.

We seal our eternal destiny the moment we receive Jesus Christ into our hearts. The Bible teaches that heaven is the happy, eternal home prepared for the children of God, a place where God will wipe away every tear from our eyes. Death shall be no more, abolished forever, along with moaning and crying and pain. Just think of it: no cancer, no AIDS, no household accidents. No more sin, no more temptation, no more criticism, no more backbiting, no more gossip, no more domestic abuse. All of that, gone, banished for eternity.

The Bible describes heaven as a marvelous place, filled with delightful surprises. Everything the poets ever dreamed of, everything the politicians ever promised, God will freely and abundantly give us in heaven. The paradise that musicians sing about, poets write about, and everyone fantasizes about is offered to us in the gospel of Jesus Christ. No one will ever be able to stop the pure and overflowing pleasure of God's children. Unending music and singing and praises to God will fill the air of heaven.

A dying Christian friend once invited me to join her son and two little granddaughters for prayer. When I arrived at her hospital room, she said, "Oh, Luis, I'm so glad you came, because I've been waiting for you. Just before going to be with the Lord, I wanted you to pray with me one more time."

I took her hand and we prayed. When we finished, she turned to one of her granddaughters and said, "Susie, Grandma is going to heaven today."

The little girl began to cry. "I don't want you to go, Grandma!" she wailed. "I want you to stay." "But the Lord is calling me home," replied this dear lady, softly. "I will go there before you, Susie, and then when you come one day, I'll be waiting for you at the gates of heaven, with my arms wide open, to welcome you home."

While eternal life begins down here the moment we receive Jesus Christ, we will enjoy it in all its dimensions when we get to heaven. The Bible declares heaven is our fantastic eternal home, better by far than any dream.

This is God's plan. This is God's desire—and every one of us can be ready for eternity when we die.

Crosses Its Fingers vs. Bows Its Head

Have you ever considered the vast variety of ways we try to gain a leg up on life? We cross our fingers. We knock on wood. We break wishbones. We throw salt over our shoulder. We wish upon a falling star. We pluck four-leaf clovers. We make a wish when blowing out birthday candles.

What is all of this but an attempt to think positively? Whether you call it superstition or seducing fate, at bottom all such practices are designed to boost our confidence that things really will turn out well for us.

How much better to entrust our future to the God who directs the course of the world and all things in it! How much more reassuring to pray to a personal God who loves us, who desires our best, who has the power to do "whatever pleases him" (Ps. 115:3). Crossing one's fingers may give a little comfort, but bowing one's head in prayer can bring great confidence:

> Do not be anxious about anything, but in everything, by prayer and petition, with thanksgiving, present your requests to God. And the peace of God, which transcends all understanding, will guard your hearts and your minds in Christ Jesus.
>
> Philippians 4:6–7

Of course, there's praying, and then there's *praying*. As a young man I used to attend a weekly all-night prayer meeting with friends. But typically I prayed with a negative attitude toward life.

Sometimes I worried about my bad habit, but I didn't know how to break the cycle. I would wake up in the morning and spend time reading the Bible, but my prayers always sounded like a wailing and a cry, rather than joy and exuberance in the Holy Spirit. I would start out something like this: "Oh God, here comes another day. Lord, there are bound to be temptations. Please help me, Lord. I don't want to dishonor you. Don't let me fail you, Lord. I'm so weak. My passions are so strong. Lord, give me power. Don't let me stumble. Lord, I am so incapable. When opportunities come, please help me. Otherwise, I'm doomed to fail."

Like I said, a wailing and a cry.

Then at about twenty-six years of age, my wife and I participated in a seven-month missionary internship program. One day the instructor asked, "How do you start your day with the Lord? Do you get up and say, 'Oh, Lord, here we go again! That alarm always seems to ring too early. It's Monday and I have to go to work again. Lord, please help me. Lord, strengthen me. Lord, don't let me lose my cool. Lord, help me make it to the 5 o'clock news.' Do you start with a wailing and a pleading prayer? Or do you start with a note of praise and glory to God?"

His words struck home. I began to notice that positive believers such as the apostle Paul always began with a note of optimism and expectation: "But thanks be to God, who always leads us in triumphal procession in Christ," he wrote in 2 Corinthians 2:14, "and through us spreads everywhere the fragrance of the knowledge of him."

Such an attitude stands light-years from mere positive thinking. Christian optimism is based not on human willpower, but on the promises of God and on the person of Jesus Christ. The resurrected Christ lives within us. He is alive! He's almighty! He has conquered death, sin, and the devil! And therefore we can wake up in the morning with a positive outlook, no matter the circumstances.

My mentor, Ray Stedman, once said that 2 Corinthians 2:14 reveals "an unquenchable optimism." When you understand your rights and privileges in Jesus Christ, when you intelligently enter the spiritual Promised Land (that is, the Spirit-filled life), then you possess an unquenchable optimism.

Do you feel like a failure? Maybe you envy the kind of victories others seem to enjoy. If that describes you, then learn Paul's secret. An authentic Christian, no matter how small or large his or her field of work, can enjoy an unquenchable optimism, day by day. Like Paul, he or she looks to Jesus Christ and refuses to dwell on circumstances.

To be confident and effective, prayer needs to be instructed by Scripture. The more my prayer flows from my immersion in the Word of God, the Bible, the more confidence I have in my requests. My confidence is based on the promises of God himself.

These days I get up in the morning and say, "Lord Jesus, it's a new day. I'm healthy, or at least partially so. I thank you, Lord, that I have another twenty-four hours to serve you. You are with me. You never leave me. You never forsake me. You promise to give me the words I need. You will give me discernment and wisdom. Although I will make mistakes, you can use even them to glorify yourself. What a great God you are!"

We can choose to rejoice because God dwells within us. Nothing can quench our optimism. Not sickness. Not financial reversals. Not even a plane crash.

A few years ago I met a woman who survived the horrendous plane crash on the island of Tenerife, the worst aviation accident in history. Two Boeing 747 jetliners collided on the runway and went up in a monstrous ball of flame. Only 61 people of the 644 on board the two planes survived. This woman told me that as she saw her plane break up and burst into flame, she cried, "Jesus, I'll see you in a few minutes!"

Despite wearing her seat belt, an explosion threw her clear of the plane. She remembers sliding down the wing of the three-story-high 747, her legs burning. For some reason she held tightly to her purse. (What a silly thing, on her way to heaven with her purse!) She passed out with the thought, *I'm going to heaven!*

About an hour later, she woke up, stiff and sore and lying in the grass. "Oh no!" she exclaimed. "I'm still in Tenerife!" But what impressed me most was her prayer when the plane exploded: "Jesus, I'll see you in a few minutes!"

No one and nothing can snatch a believer out of the hands of Jesus. So why *shouldn't* we go through life with an optimistic attitude, choosing to pray rather than to cross our fingers and hope for the best?

One of our team members, Jim Williams, had a college roommate and friend named Dave Kraft. Dave was a brilliant young man with an upbeat dad who pastored a Baptist church. When Dave graduated, he became a minister, married a fine young woman, and later left the pastorate to run a youth summer camp.

When Dave was about twenty-eight, the doctors diagnosed him with a cancer they could do nothing about. Slowly his body began falling apart. Specialists from the best hospitals in the country tried everything they could think of, but nothing worked. Naturally Dave's church friends prayed for him, but eventually it became obvious the Lord wasn't going to heal him. Finally Dave transferred to a hospital close to his father. Dr. Kraft witnessed the quick deterioration of his son, until all sorts of tubes and machines had to be plugged into Dave just to keep him alive. I arrived in town to preach at Dr. Kraft's church when Dave looked in especially bad shape.

The Saturday before I was to speak, Dr. Kraft and I met to discuss the next day's services. Understandably, he didn't seem too concerned about what hymns to sing or what announcements to give.

"You know what, Luis?" he said. "My son is just about to go. And I feel so eager that he goes to be with the Lord. I just can't stand to see my boy suffer so much. I wish you'd pray."

So we bowed our heads, and he prayed first: "Lord, would you take David home today? I can't stand to see him suffer." I agreed with his prayer and we parted company.

The next morning when I arrived at the church to preach, Dr. Kraft seemed relaxed. He spoke to me about the service, but I didn't ask about his son. After we had both taken our places on the platform, a deacon approached me and whispered in my ear, "Luis, be very careful about what you say, because Dave Kraft died last night. We don't want to shake up the pastor."

After pondering the news for a moment, I rose from my chair while the congregation sang. I knelt beside my friend, put my arm around him, and said, "Dr. Kraft, I just heard that your son died last night. I just want to encourage you," and then quoted a Bible verse.

He smiled and answered, "Luis, you don't have to encourage me. Let me tell you what happened." And while the church continued singing, Dr. Kraft told me the whole story.

"Last night I went to the hospital with my brother, and we both chatted with Dave for a few minutes," he said. "We prayed there until Dave said to his uncle, 'Would you leave the room? I want to talk to my dad alone.' Then he turned to me and said, 'Dad, come over here. I want you to put your arms around me.' So I went over by the bed and knelt down beside Dave to put my arms all around him. It wasn't easy, since all kinds of tubes and equipment surrounded him.

"After a few moments he said, 'Dad, I want to sit up.' I helped him to sit up and he told me, 'Dad, I know that tonight I'm going to be with the Lord. I want to thank you, because you have been such a terrific father. I want you to tell mother that I love her, that you two have been such a great example to me. You showed me the way to the Lord, and I want to thank you before I go to be with him. Dad, I want you to pray with me because I won't see you for a few years, and I want to talk with the Lord together with you.'"

Dr. Kraft choked up, but in a few moments continued his story. "Dave," he told his son, "before I pray, I want to tell *you* something. You lucky guy, you are going to see the Lord before I do. Just think, David—tonight you are going to see Moses, Joseph, David, Saint Paul, and all the great saints of the Bible. You lucky guy. I should have gone before you, but you are getting there before me."

Even then Dr. Kraft hadn't quite finished his story. "David," he reassured his dying son, "best of all, you are going to see the Lord Jesus. Promise me one thing. When you see the Lord Jesus, would you tell him that your father loves him very much?"

Father and son then prayed together and Dr. Kraft left the room after saying, "Dave, I'll see you in heaven."

About 4 o'clock that morning, hospital officials called to say, "Dr. Kraft, your son just died."

Do you know what astonished me most about this whole episode? As this grieving father poured out his moving story, he seemed perfectly relaxed. "Luis," he said, "now I am at peace because I know that Dave is with the Lord. I wish I were there now."

I wonder—do you have that kind of assurance? Are you certain about where you are going? If not, why not pray right now and open your heart to Jesus Christ as your Savior and Lord? Don't cross your fingers in the vain hope that somehow you might make it to heaven on your own. Ask Jesus to come into your life, to forgive your sins, to make you a child of God, and to provide you with a permanent address at his Father's house.

The Most Positive Thought of All

There's no thought quite so positive as the assurance of a permanent home in heaven. One day a little boy, the son of an atheist, visited his friend's church. When he returned home he said to his father, "Daddy, today I was invited to go to heaven, and I accepted."

Every day such invitations get accepted everywhere around the globe. One day while visiting a family in the north of Scotland, I asked the lady of the house, "How many children do you have?"

"Four," she replied, "three here in Scotland and one already in heaven."

How long will *you* live on earth? Twenty years? Forty? Seventy? And then where will you go? Where will you be a thousand years from this moment? For sure, none of us will be here. We are all going to be somewhere else, and there are only two possibilities. So where will you be?

All normal people care about eternity. One night at our crusade in Hong Kong, one of the most famous professors in the People's Republic of China sat in the audience. Though he officially claimed to be an atheist, he admitted he felt impressed by what the Bible says about the future. He told one of my friends how it moved him to see thousands of people committing their lives to Jesus that evening.

As an honest man or woman, you should care very much about where you go when you die. If you are a father or mother, God has given you boys or girls. Have you prepared them for eternity? And you—are you prepared? All other questions take a backseat to this one.

Freedom is important. Food is important. Family is important. Finances are important. Having fun is important. But the question of all questions is this: *Where will you go when you die?* Do you approach the future armed only with positive thinking? Or does mighty hope fill your soul?

The most dramatic event of your life will be your flight to eternity. Make your destination heaven.

How to Find Hope According to the Bible

1. *Adopt a positive, proactive attitude.*
   "Be strong and take heart, all you who hope in the LORD" (Ps. 31:24).

2. *Focus on God's constant love for you.*
   "May your unfailing love rest upon us, O LORD, even as we put our hope in you" (Ps. 33:22).

3. *Discover how hope is both active (seeking) and submissive (waiting).*
   "The LORD is good to those whose hope is in him, to the one who seeks him; it is good to wait quietly for the salvation of the LORD" (Lam. 3:25–26).

4. *Immerse yourself in God's Word.*
   "For everything that was written in the past was written to teach us, so that through endurance and the encouragement of the Scriptures we might have hope" (Rom. 15:4).

5. *Don't be shy about asking God to intervene on your behalf.*
   "The widow who is really in need and left all alone puts her hope in God and continues night and day to pray and to ask God for help" (1 Tim. 5:5).

6. *Watch for God's footprints in your life.*
   "But as for me, I watch in hope for the LORD, wait for God my Savior; my God will hear me" (Micah 7:7).

7. *Remember that hope is a choice, especially when you're discouraged.*
   "Why are you downcast, O my soul? Why so disturbed within me? Put your hope in God, for I will yet praise him, my Savior and my God" (Ps. 42:11).

8. *Look at suffering as a means to strengthen your hope.*
   "We rejoice in the hope of the glory of God. Not only so, but we also rejoice in our sufferings, because we know that suffering produces perseverance; perseverance, character; and character, hope. And hope does not disappoint us, because God has poured out his love

into our hearts by the Holy Spirit, whom he has given us" (Rom. 5:2–5).

9. *Reflect often on the certainty of Christ's return.*

   "Set your hope fully on the grace to be given you when Jesus Christ is revealed" (1 Peter 1:13).

10. *Recognize that God is the source of all genuine hope.*

    "Know that I am the LORD; those who hope in me will not be disappointed" (Isa. 49:23).

Epilogue

Choose the Best

Gods "best" is not like anyone else's "best." It really does stand at the top of the list.

I've been all over the world and I've had the opportunity to sample a lot of "the best" this world has to offer. I've eaten great food. Seen great sights. Heard great speakers. Stayed in great places. Watched great performances. Enjoyed great events.

But no matter how "great" these things were, they always left a little to be desired. Maybe the steak tasted fabulous, but the room seemed too dark. Or the speaker was phenomenal, but he went on a little too long (I should talk!). Or the room was amazing, but I ran out of toilet paper. Some little thing didn't seem quite right, and despite how much I enjoyed the main event, this defect kept the experience from being all it might have been. In other words, this world's "best" depends a lot on circumstances.

But you know what? God's best doesn't.

When God promises us his best, he doesn't always mean that he'll make all our circumstances turn out just the way we think we'd like them. Instead he means that he'll be with us completely in whatever circumstances we find ourselves—and that's why his "best" beats anything else out there by a long, long way.

Sarah Edwards reminded me of that, several years ago.

I met Sarah one night in England just before we began a crusade event. Some members of our team came to me and said, "Luis, you're going to be surprised. Tonight we're having a girl give her testimony. She's twenty-one; her name is Sarah Edwards."

I looked around and saw that Sarah already had seated herself on the platform. She looked attractive and well dressed, but nothing in her appearance gave me a clue as to why she'd be speaking that night. So I approached her and said, "Sarah, I hear you're going to say something tonight?"

"Yes, sir," she replied.

"What are you going to talk about?" I asked.

"You'll find out," she said.

"Why are you here?" I wondered out loud.

"You'll find out," she repeated. She paused, smiled, then gave me one clue about her testimony. "Mr. Palau," she continued, "in the front row are my dad and mom. My dad is an atheist; he hates God, all his life he's insulted God—and now it'll be even worse because of what I'm going to say tonight."

Her statement got me really intrigued. *What is Sarah going to talk about tonight?* In a few minutes, Sarah got up and moved to the podium. She seemed to walk a little wobbly, but nothing too noticeable. She grabbed the podium and began to tell us what happened.

Her father had always been an enemy of God, always blaspheming God, cursing Jesus, and laughing at the Bible. He was an educated man but a mess. At fourteen years of age, Sarah attended a camp. She listened to the gospel of Jesus and gave her heart to Christ. A few years later, when she turned eighteen, her parents sent her to Liverpool University, not far from her home.

About six months into college, she began to feel something strange in her legs. She went to see the university doctor, and after some tests, the doctor said, "Sarah, this is unbelievable. You have a form of cancer that we cannot treat. We're going to have to attack your disease fast before it keeps creeping up and you lose your life while you're still in college."

So they amputated the legs of this beautiful, attractive, charming girl. When she was only eighteen and a half, surgeons cut off her legs just above the knee. You can imagine what happened with her unbelieving father! He began to curse God even more. But by then, Sarah already had Christ in her heart.

The night Sarah told her story, I closely watched her dad as she described how she'd opened her heart to Christ at age fourteen.

"I know that one day when I get to heaven," she said, "God is going to give me a new pair of legs and no one will ever cut them off again. And I know something else. Because I have Jesus, I realize this life is not forever; when I go to heaven, I will *really* love life. Perhaps no guy will ever want to marry me here because I don't have these two legs. But if no man ever marries me, I don't mind that much, because Jesus is really my real friend. He is our friend."

By now her old dad was crying. I jumped up as soon as Sarah finished her testimony, and I gave an invitation. And that man who had cursed God was the first man to rise to his feet when I said, "If you want to follow Jesus, come and follow Jesus, like Sarah." He grabbed his wife, Sarah's mother, and they both came forward and gave their lives to Jesus Christ.

How's that for "best"?

To enjoy the world's best, you want your two legs. But to enjoy God's best, it doesn't matter a whole lot whether you have them or not—you have *him*, and that makes all the difference.

Sarah knew God's best that night when her parents chose to place their faith in the God she loved so much. She might have stood on the platform a little wobbly, but I can guarantee you she felt an overwhelming joy that no one with two strong legs but no relationship with God could ever experience. God's "best" really *is* best!

You know, the Lord wants the best for you. He wants to teach you what is best for you and to direct you in the way you should go. Are you listening for his voice? Are you ready to go where he directs you to go and do what he asks you to do?

Remember, that's the only way you'll ever enjoy the best of the best. No matter your circumstances, *you* can have God's best.

And you can have it starting today.

Notes

Foreword

1. Excerpted from Anne Graham Lotz, *My Heart's Cry* (Nashville: W Publishing Group, 2002), xiii.

Introduction

1. 1 Corinthians 12:31 NIV; second translation, NLT.

Chapter 1: A Festival in Your Heart

1. Ambrose Bierce in *The Portable Curmudgeon*, ed. Jon Winokur (New York: New American Library, 1987), 133.

2. William Shakespeare, *As You Like It*, 5.2.43–45.

3. Dr. Joyce Brothers, "You Can Lead a More Joyful Life," *Parade*, October 15, 2000, 6.

4. Nancy Haught, "MIND-SET/Satisfaction: Tough Life Experiences Led Columnist-Novelist Anna Quindlen to Be Awake to the World and Not Miss Happiness," the *Sunday Oregonian*, October 22, 2000, L11.

5. Ibid.

6. Brothers, "You Can Lead," 7. The popular psychologist also suggests ten simple ways "for making every day a great day": 1. Think that good things will happen. 2. Express gratitude to a loved one. 3. Put your gripes away in a box. 4. Be patient with an annoying person. 5. Do something special for yourself. 6. Reach out to someone who needs comfort. 7. Focus deeply on each moment. 8. Learn from a mistake. 9. Look closely at a flower or tree you haven't noticed before. 10. Smile.

7. Hannah Whitall Smith, *The God of All Comfort* (Chicago: Moody Publishers, 1956), 7.

8. John Piper, *Desiring God* (Sisters, OR: Multnomah Books, 1996), 34.

9. Romans 8:9.

10. Haught, "MIND-SET," L11.

11. See Luis Palau, *Say Yes: How to Renew Your Spiritual Passion* (Grand Rapids: Discovery House Publishers, 1995) for a full meaning of "an overflowing cup" and "the fullness of the Holy Spirit." Or request an excerpt by writing to me at palau@palau.org.

12. Brothers, "You Can Lead," 7.

13. Haught, "MIND-SET," L11.

14. Brothers, "You Can Lead," 6.

15. Merrill C. Tenney, general ed., *The Zondervan Pictorial Encyclopedia of the Bible,* vol. 3 (Grand Rapids: Zondervan, 1975, 1976), 714.

16. C. S. Lewis, *The Screwtape Letters* (New York: Bantam Books, 1982), 75.

17. Write to me at palau@palau.org to request a copy of my article, "Planting Your Roots Deeply into the Local Church."

18. Carolyn Kizer quoted in Robert Byrne, comp., *1,911 Best Things Anybody Ever Said*, Section III, reading 245 (New York: Fawcett Columbine, 1988), 320.

Chapter 2: An Oasis of Delight

1. "What's New," www.compuserve.com, February 5, 2001.

2. Ibid.

3. Many people have asked me over the years, "How can I find 'the right one'?" There are no easy formulas to know which man or woman is "the right one" for you, but let me ask some questions.

(1) *Is she or he a Christian?*

The Bible says a believer should never be joined together with an unbeliever (1 Cor. 7:39; 2 Cor. 6:15). If you are a believer and your girlfriend is not a Christian, forget it. Finish it tonight. If the fellow you like is not a Christian, you have to drop him. Why? God says so. Reason says so. Experience says so. Too many Christians face marital problems because they disobey the Lord and marry an unbeliever. If you are interested in someone who isn't a Christian, you can pray for him or her, ask God to bring him or her to Christ—but don't start dating until you are sure he or she belongs to God.

(2) *Am I proud of him or her?*

If you're embarrassed about your girlfriend and all you want to do is kiss her in the dark, that isn't true love. If you're embarrassed to introduce your boyfriend to your friends or family, something is wrong. Ask yourself, "Am I ashamed or embarrassed of him or her?"

When a man or woman is ashamed of his or her "significant other," the best thing to do is to forget it. It can't be real love. In a healthy couple, the husband praises his wife (Prov. 31:28). True love praises the beloved. It doesn't consider him or her inferior.

(3) *Am I jealous or suspicious of him or her without good reason?*

It's a bad sign when you don't want your girlfriend to talk to any other guy or your boyfriend to talk to any other girl. Jealousy is usually an indication that what you have isn't real love. Now, if you see someone kissing your girlfriend, that's not jealousy; that's fact.

One day at a crusade a single young man singing in the choir came to me and said, "Mr. Palau, Mr. Palau! My girlfriend is over there with another guy."

"Thank the Lord, man," I replied.

"What do you mean, 'Thank the Lord'?" he asked. "Somebody else is with her!"

"Aren't you glad you found out *before* you got married that she didn't love you?"

"Oh yeah," he replied sullenly. "Well, thank you." And he left to sing in the choir.

In his case it wasn't jealousy, but fact. Jealousy is a sick attitude of the heart that's always suspicious and always wondering and never content or at rest. Love isn't like that.

(4) *Do I respect her or him?*

The Bible says love does not act improperly (1 Cor. 13:6–7). Love is pure. So when your friend insists on too much touchy, touchy, and squeezy, squeezy, watch out. Do you take liberties in handling him or her? Be leery of a man who insists he loves his girl so much that he can't keep his hands off her, because it probably isn't real love at all. When the passion is gone, so is the so-called love.

And ladies, if your boyfriend mistreats you when you're dating, be sure that he'll beat you up when you're married. Some women tell me, "Yes, my boyfriend sometimes gets a little rough and slaps me around, but when we get married I'll change him." He'll change, all right; he'll change from slapping you to using a stick on you.

If a man acts improperly toward you as a single, you can bet he'll get worse once you're married. And don't say, "I like to fight with my boyfriend; it feels so good when we make up." It just isn't so.

(5) *When I pray about marriage, do I have peace in my heart or confusion?*

Never even think about marrying someone without first praying about it for many hours. Get on your knees every week and spend significant time with God. Read the Bible; think about it; make notes in a notebook. Seek the mind of God. If you marry flippantly, you'll suffer.

The Bible promises that the peace of God will guard your heart and your mind in Christ Jesus (Phil. 4:7). If, when you pray about this fellow or this girl, you don't have peace in your heart—stop. Don't go forward. Wait. When the Lord doesn't give you peace, it's a sign something is wrong. If this is the woman or the fellow for you, you will enjoy peace in your heart. You will have a quietness about it.

Also look for counsel from Christian couples who obviously love each other, who really get along. Ask for their advice. Don't make this decision on your own.

(6) *Are we suited for each other?*

The Bible says you need a partner suitable for you (Gen. 2:18). Do you fit each other? Often an outgoing person marries a quiet person, while a hard-nosed person marries a pliable person. Opposites really do attract.

You need to ask yourself, "Is this God's woman for me? Is this God's man for me? Are we going to get along at every level?" Not just, "Do I like her eyes and all the kissing stuff?" Not only, "Do I like his body, his looks, his car?" Those things are important, but very secondary. Make sure you emphasize the crucial.

4. Write to me at palau@palau.org to request a copy of Luis Palau, *What Is a Real Christian?*

5. I recommend Marriage Savers® (www.marriagesavers.org) as a resource for building a stronger marriage.

Chapter 3: A Friend Who Sticks Closer Than a Brother

1. Julie Schmit, "Deep Secrets Told among Passengers on Airlines," *USA Today*, June 1, 1993, B1.

Chapter 4: A Fresh Start

1. See "The Last Campaign," *Life*, February 1991.

Chapter 5: A Priceless Gift That Costs Us Nothing

1. Jay Leno quoted in Robert Byrne, comp., *1,911 Best Things Anybody Ever Said*, 393.

2. Associated Press, "Missionary Whose Wife, Daughter Perished in Peru Lays Trust in God," *Holland Sentinel online*, July 5, 2001, http://www.hollandsentinel.com/stories/070501/new_0705010033.shtml.

3. The Rev. Paul Williams, "Peace: Will It Ever Happen to Me?" St. James Churches, 2001, http://www.saintjames.org.uk/sermons/peace.htm.

4. "Jesus, I am Resting, Resting," lyrics by Jean S. Pigott, 1876.

Chapter 6: A Winner at the Game of Life

1. John Piper, *Desiring God,* 10th Anniversary Expanded Edition (Sisters, OR: Multnomah Books, 1996), 162.

2. David G. Meyers, quoted in Dr. Joyce Brothers, "You Can Lead a More Joyful Life," *Parade*, October 15, 2000, 6.

3. See 2 Corinthians 8:13–15.

4. "Finding a Faith—and a Wife," *The Door*, December 1992, 2.

5. Mark Twain in *The Portable Curmudgeon*, ed. Jon Winokur (New York: New American Library, 1987), 97.

6. Marlo Thomas quoted in Robert Byrne, comp., *1,911 Best Things Anybody Ever Said*, 171.

Chapter 7: A Lifelong Source of Thrills

1. "Favorite Summer" segment, National Public Radio, August 1, 2001, http://www.npr.org/features/feature.php?wfId=1126757.

2. Microsoft *Encarta Encyclopedia 2000*.

3. Microsoft *Encarta Encyclopedia 2000*, article on "Extreme Sports."

4. *The Random House College Dictionary,* rev. ed., s.v. "Adventure," (New York: Random House, 1988), 20.

Chapter 8: A Shield All Day Long

1. Robert M. Yoder, "How Hamilcar Wilts Prepared for Everything and Got It," in *Your Own Book of Funny Stories* (New York: Pocket Books, Special Scholastic Book Services Edition, 1950), 134–36.

Chapter 10: An Anchor for the Soul

1. "Hope," *The New Bible Dictionary*, 2nd ed., ed. J. D. Douglas, et. al. (Wheaton: Tyndale, 1962), 489.

T hank you for reading this book!
Every reader's experience with a particular book is different.
So I hope I hear from you about what you found helpful, insightful, or
thought-provoking. I also invite you to send me your specific questions
or concerns—or tell me if you disagree with something I've said. That's
okay too!

Here's how to reach me:

Luis Palau
P.O. Box 1173
Portland, OR 97207, USA
telephone (503) 614-1500
fax (503) 614-1599
palau@palau.org
www.palau.org

Free Online Offers

You'll find free excerpts from my other books at www.palau.org.

While you're online, please take a minute to sign our www.palau.org guest book and read what other readers have to say about *High Definition Life*. Then please feel free to add your own comments on our "Readers Say" page. You'll also find online discounts if you want to obtain another copy of this book for a relative or friend.

Also be sure to check out the online version of our daily "Reaching Your World with Luis Palau" two-minute radio program. You'll find a link right off our www.palau.org home page. There you can sign up to receive our free weekly "Healthy Habits for Spiritual Growth" devotional e-zine.

All of these resources are designed to encourage and inspire your faith.

God richly bless you in every area of your life as you seek his best!

Luis Palau is an internationally known evangelist and speaker and the author of numerous books, including *God Is Relevant, Where Is God When Bad Things Happen?* and *It's a God Thing*. Well-known for his successful festival evangelism ministry, he now sponsors and speaks at six major festivals in the United States and abroad every year. Palau's ministry is based in Portland, Oregon, but his evangelistic outreach is global.

Steve Halliday is president of Crown Media, Ltd., a literary company that specializes in book editing and collaboration. He and his wife, Lisa, live in Portland, Oregon.